THE BOOK

THE BOOK

A HUMBLE QUEST INTO THE HEBREW SCRIPTURES

JOSEPH HESKEL KOUKOU
EDITED AND ILLUSTRATED
BY SANDRA KOUKOU

authorHOUSE®

AuthorHouse™
1663 Liberty Drive
Bloomington, IN 47403
www.authorhouse.com
Phone: 1-800-839-8640

Published by AuthorHouse   04/27/2015

ISBN: 978-1-4969-0224-5 (sc)
ISBN: 978-1-4969-0203-0 (hc)
ISBN: 978-1-4969-0223-8 (e)

Library of Congress Control Number: 2014906454

Print information available on the last page.

This book is printed on acid-free paper.

Scripture quotations marked KJV are from the Holy Bible, King James Version
(Authorized Version). First published in 1611. Quoted from the KJV Classic
Reference Bible, Copyright © 1983 by The Zondervan Corporation.

To purchase a printed hardcover or paperback book of this title write to: www.authorhouse.com.

ADVANCE PRAISE FOR

THE BOOK: A HUMBLE QUEST
INTO THE HEBREW SCRIPTURES

An interesting and well written *tour de force* showing unifying themes in the Hebrew Bible, and how these themes were an inspiration to the Jews of Iraq and Iran, and to the founders of the modern state of Israel. As the Rabbi of the Ashkenaz section of Montreal's Spanish & Portuguese Synagogue, I would encourage my congregants to read this book, and to thereby be inspired by the courage of Ms. Koukou and of her father.

To Ms. Sandra Koukou, *hizqi u-verukha*, for doing such a marvelous job in editing and illustrating your father's work.

Rabbi Emanuel (Menahem) White, PhD

The Biblical scholar Rashi commented on verse 12 of Psalm 62: *"God hath spoken, twice I have heard this;"* beyond the direct meaning, each verse can have more than one interpretation. It is characteristic of the Bible that it can be read at different levels of understanding. The work of Joseph Koukou reflects the profound impact of the Book of Books on his prisoner status, on the courage of his convictions, his worldview and his understanding of current events. He found refuge, consolation and hope by clinging to the Bible. His work demonstrates that the message of the Bible can both resonate with and seduce the soul: *"For thy law is my delight"* (Psalms 119-77).

Dr. David Bensoussan

ADVANCE PRAISE FOR *THE BOOK*

JOSEPH HESKEL KOUKOU

Né à Bassora, Joseph Heskel Koukou avait dix ans quand sa famille s'était installée en Iran. Homme d'affaires, il était impliqué dans la vie de sa communauté juive et de ses rapports fraternels avec l'ensemble des groupes, indépendamment de leur religion, de leur culture et de leur appartenance ethnique.

Quand Khomeini a pris le pouvoir et établi le régime islamique, il fut arrêté comme juif et a passé plus de quatre ans derrière les barreaux. Il a relu et médité le Tanakh, la Bible juive. Dans son ouvrage autobiographique, il fait le récit de son incarcération et rend compte de la vie des juifs sous le régime des mullahs. Le livre est également un précieux document sur l'histoire des Juifs ainsi que sur celle du Proche Orient. Joseph Heskel Koukou nous transmet ses profondes réflexions sur sa lecture du Livre et sur les événements qu'il a vécus.

Un magnifique ouvrage.

Naïm Kattan, *Adieu Babylone : Mémoirs d'un Juif d'Iraq*
Chevalier de l'Ordre du Canada, Chevalier de l'Ordre national du Québec, Chevalier des Arts et Lettres de France, et Chevalier de la Légion d'honneur

Above: Original French text by the Canadian author; English translation on the back cover

Note: In the latter years of life, Joseph changed his surname to Koukov.

ADVANCE PRAISE FOR *THE BOOK*

Rien ne semblait prédestiner l'homme d'affaires Joseph Koukou à s'immerger dans l'étude des Écritures Bibliques. Emprisonné à tort, durant presque cinq ans, dans l'inexpugnable prison iranienne d'Evin d'où l'on ne sort rarement en vie, il découvre en lui cette foi qui soulève les montagnes et qui lui permet d'étudier et de décrypter la Bible Juive. Une nourriture spirituelle qu'il fait partager à d'autres prisonniers entrevoyant alors une lumière dans le couloir de leur désespoir. Mais pour se voir attribuer un tel don de compassion, il fallait que cet homme soit habité par une rare spiritualité au point de déstabiliser juges et bourreaux par son seul regard, sa voix sereine, son sang froid, aux pires moments d'une menace imminente d'exécution. Joseph Koukou, Orphée charmant les cerberes de l'enfer? Tout simplement une âme et un coeur inébranlables ouverts sur sa foi envers le destin de l'Humanité.

Le chapitre 3 donne froid dans le dos : nous plongeons dans la terreur sourde des rouages politico-religieux du régime iranien, et dans laquelle Sandra—la fille du prisonnier—se faufile sans peur, avec pour seules armes la détermination et l'amour d'une jeune fille de 23 ans pour son père.

Raphaël Levy, *L'Homme qui voulait changer le monde (transl. The Man Who Wanted to Change the World)*

Above: Original French text by the Canadian author; English translation on the back cover.

ADVANCE PRAISE FOR *THE BOOK*

This book, *"A Humble Quest Into The Hebrew Scriptures"* by Joseph Heskel Koukou, is unique in its intent and message. The inspiration to write this book came to Mr. Koukou when he was in a prison in Iran, not knowing what to expect from the Iranian authorities that put him in jail. Any person in this situation becomes desperate and his desperation led him to be closer and closer to spirituality. As such, he tried to look at events, past and present, using the Hebrew Bible as his main guide. The Bible, known also as *"The Book of Books,"* was printed millions of times and in many languages. The Bible is an enigma by itself. It was read and studied by many generations and the more it is studied the more discoveries are found. Mr. Koukou admits that he is not a Biblical scholar, but that stands to his credit. He is not influenced by others' opinions, so his interpretations become a soul searching and original in every chapter of his book.

His analysis and findings rekindle faith in the heart of any reader who wants to benefit from those ideas. His analysis provides, among other things, an interesting explanation about diversity. Diversity, he wrote, is a part of the Divine wisdom. Its purpose is to create incentives for improvements and for progress. In fact, however, it serves as a base for animosity, jealousy and hatred.

The book is written in a very lucid language and is divided into several short chapters. Many readers may find this approach very practical for understanding the message of this book.

Sami Sourani, Reader in Jewish History and Contributor to *Iraq's Last Jews,* by Tamar Morad, Denis and Robert Shasha, eds.

ADVANCE PRAISE FOR *THE BOOK*

An amazing story from a great man, Joseph Koukou, and a devoted, intelligent daughter, Sandra.

Joseph Koukou, through his belief in God, succeeded in maintaining his calm and an inspired state of mind during his four-and-a-half years in prison in Iran. He helped others through their suffering and used his time wisely in studying the Bible and other faiths, which helped him face his hard time.

His brave and intelligent daughter, Sandra, together with her determined mother, Evelyn Koukou, left no stone unturned to secure her father's life.

It is an inspiring book, written by brave and intellectual people who have faith in God and themselves. The references to the Bible are intertwined with Jewish and Babylonian history, which makes the reading experience full of interest and can be educational to the reader of any generation.

Gladys Peress Mooallem
Born in Baghdad, Iraq and left in 1951
with the exodus of the Iraqi Jews
Women's Learning Group Coordinator
Spanish & Portuguese Synagogue, Montreal
womenlearning.weebly.com

*I am grateful to many,
not least to my youngest daughter,
Sandra, whose staunch devotion led to
my release from the prisons
of Ayatollah Khomeini. She edited and
illustrated this book from cover to
cover, faithfully working to safeguard
a memory from falling under
the gavel of time.*

*To my wife, Evelyn, daughters,
Maureen and Cynthia, and son,
Abraham, who stayed the course and
stood behind me until I was able to
join them, alive again as a husband
and father, a free man.*

Im Eshkachech Yerushalayim

If I forget thee, O Jerusalem,
let my right hand lose its cunning;
let my tongue cleave to the roof of my mouth,
if I do not set Jerusalem above my greatest joy.

Song lyrics based on Psalm 137: 5 and 6

The empty headed have declared that
the curses are more numerous than
than the blessings, but they have not
spoken the truth. The blessings are uttered
in broad general terms, while the curses
are stated in more detail, to awe and
frighten the hearers.

Ibn Ezra (1089 – 1164)
In reference to a passage from Leviticus:
I am the Lord your God, which brought
you forth out of the land of Egypt, that
ye should not be their bondmen;
and I have broken the bands of your yoke,
and made you go upright. (Leviticus 26:13)

Do not grow old
no matter how long you may live.
Never cease to stand like children
before the great mystery into which
we were born.

Albert Einstein (1879 – 1955)

CONTENTS

Foreword | *xvi*

Acknowledgements | *xxi*

Introduction | *1*

Letter From The Editor | *9*

PART ONE — MY FAMILY'S EXODUS | *13*

1. Trust in God | *15*
2. Moment of Truth | *24*
3. Rendezvous with Destiny | *29*
4. Journey to the Other Side of Hell | *52*

PART TWO — SEEKING CLUES FROM BIBLICAL HISTORY | *61*

5. In Search of Essence | *63*
6. A Rare Visit | *65*
7. God's Intent Unfolds | *68*
8. Major Elements of the Hebrew Scriptures | *71*
9. Fear of God | *75*
10. What Can We Learn from the Kingdom of Israel in Biblical Times? | *77*
11. The Prophets | *92*
12. The Jewish Nation in Exile | *111*
13. What Can the Bible Bring to Light in Relation to Modern History? | *121*

PART THREE — RETURN TO THE SOURCE | *129*

14. What's in a Blessing? | *131*

15. Israel: Return to the Source | *136*

16. Arab Nationalism: the Turning Point | *148*

17. What's in a Name? | *153*

18. World War II and Beyond | *161*

PART FOUR — REFLECTIONS | *179*

19. The Link Between Action and Destiny | *181*

20. In Quest of God | *185*

21. Self-Help and Personal Destiny | *190*

22. The Power of Prayer | *197*

23. The Big Three: Interfaith Relations | *202*

24. Nature's Silent Messages | *209*

25. Communism Versus Religion | *213*

26. The Role of Religious Leaders | *216*

EPILOGUE | *227*

Tribute from a Fellow Prison Inmate at Evin | *242*

Bibliography | *245*

About the Book | *251*

About the Author | *253*

Index | *255*

PHOTOGRAPHS

Exterior wall inscription, a tribute to the donators of Ettefagh,
the Iraqi Jewish Synagogue of Teheran | 12

A page [No. 8 - Volume I of 4] from the author's
handwritten manuscript, circa 1982 | 60

My Father | 124

My Mother | 125

My Family | 126

Wedding Day | 127

A page [No. 59 - Volume IV of 4] from the author's
handwritten manuscript, circa 1982 | 128

Four pages from the author's father's handwritten manuscript written in the
Iraqi Hebrew alphabet (known as Hetzi Kulmous) *and in the*
Iraqi Jewish language (Judeo-Arabic dialect). | 178

§

Author photograph by Henry Dallal

ILLUSTRATIONS

Theodor Herzl | *141*

Chaim Weizmann | *144*

David Ben Gurion | *171*

Albert Einstein | *189*

Pope Benedict XVI | *205*

§

Cover: Oil on canvas by Sandra Koukou, inspired by Michele Molinari's photograph entitled: *"Morning Light on Moses' Mountain…"* [www.Art.com]

FOREWORD

THIS BOOK WAS WRITTEN LOOKING BACK on my life in my hometown of Teheran, which culminated in my incarceration in the prisons of Ayatollah Khomeini. It was in the Evin facility, where I studied, read, and reread the Hebrew Scriptures (Tanakh in Hebrew), that I made it my business to decipher the historical significance of the Tanakh in a biblical context. In hindsight I also realize that my story is about miracles. One of them is simply the fact that I came out of that prison alive. I have learned that faith is not solely an aspect of religious upbringing, but truly can move mountains, as it did for me. As a result, I undertook to share the intrinsic message of the Hebrew Bible not only with the younger generation, my children, and grandchildren, but with people of all faiths and denominations.

It is my hope that this study of the Scriptures will be like a friend or companion to those who find that they need, or could use the help of, an interpreter of a book of such monumental proportions, one whose bottom line can get lost in translation. I hope that after reading this book all the way to the end, they may come away from their journey as awe inspired as I was—even before the prison doors opened to send me back into the world as a free man.

My book is based upon the premise that revelation, prophecy, and the biblical events written down in the Scriptures are part of an authentic whole. It also hinges upon the concept that, although throughout world history, many religious leaders have encouraged even the good to do evil in the name of religion, in a globalized world, the time has finally come for religious leaders of all faiths to see that they have no choice but to find a way to coexist in peace.

In this work, all English translations of biblical text are quoted from the King James Version of the Hebrew Bible, as I find it to be closest to the Tanakh's original Hebrew text.

The word *TaNaKh* can be broken down into three components:

T stands for *Torah*, the 5 books of Moses.

N stands for *Nebi'im*, the 21 books of the Jewish Prophets.

K stands for *Ketubim*, the 13 books of Jewish history and literature.

I have found that the Tanakh in general—and the five Books of Moses in particular—is written with a literary speak that can capture a child's imagination while holding its appeal to human conscience at the adult level. It achieves both results through symbolism and storytelling. The rewards for adolescent readers are gained insight from trials and errors portrayed through life stories. As a full-grown adult, one's former understanding transforms into even deeper insight. At some point, the avid reader may detect a design at work, and an underlying theme may eventually emerge for the reader who delves deeply. The body of work known as the Hebrew Bible, or Tanakh, of the Judeo Christian Bible, will from this point forward be referred to as The Book.

I used to visit the Tate Gallery[1] in London to look around and discover the old and the newer paintings, sculptures, and other art objects. In a hall for contemporary paintings, I noticed a tableau. The artist had covered the entire surface with smears of multi-coloured paint and called it *The Village*. My only thought was: *How can such work find its way to such a reputed museum?* Looking around, I spotted a teacher around whom were gathered a number of students. I asked the teacher if he could help me understand *The Village*.

---

[1]   Now known as the Tate Britain.

"Look!" he said. "This is a village built on the slope of a hill. You see that row of mud huts on top and several of them almost parallel to one another farther down? This is the centre of the village where they do their Monday market, and this is the entrance of the village where they shut the gate at night to keep the wild beasts from entering. There is more to describe, but sorry, my students are waiting!" I was thrilled to see how much I was able to find on that canvas from all that the blessed man had explained. The work that I had taken as a joke had suddenly become a masterpiece!

So it appears with the Bible. As a common thread emerges from start to finish, the reader's reward for time spent with the Tanakh is a better understanding of its universal message related through poetry and prose. Once that thread becomes apparent to the reader, it is difficult to remain indifferent to the Scripture's colossal underlying theme, and the reader may begin to feel as though he or she is partaking in the events!

The Ten Commandments in the first five Books of Moses serve as the building blocks on which constitutional and judiciary systems the world over base themselves. The Tanakh in its entirety is integral to the Christian Bible, and as such, it is estimated that over 7.5 billion copies of the Hebrew Scriptures have been printed since the invention of the printing press, the majority of them being the King James Version.[2] Translations have been made in many languages and dialects. It is therefore not only important for Jews to familiarize themselves with The Book; it is incumbent for adherents of other faiths to explore its message, since their leaders often resort to the Hebrew Scriptures to support and authenticate many of their own teachings.

> And so they bequeathed to posterity a double gift: a moral law within a unique vision of history, and a body of splendid and passionate writing, revered and studied

---

[2]   Stevens, David, 2011. *Some Amazing Facts About the King James Version.* [online] Available at: <http://biblicalinsights.net/?p=661/URL>. [Accessed 30 June 2011].

across the centuries by more people than have ever come under the spell of any other literature.[3]

Christian priests and clergymen regularly quote from the Hebrew Scriptures to validate many themes they deliver in their sermons. And, if Jesus declared, *"For verily I say unto you, till heaven and Earth pass, one jot or one title shall in no wise pass from the law, till all be fulfilled"* (*Matthew 5:18*), it seems fair to say that Christian believers draw much from an understanding of the Hebrew Bible in tandem with the four Gospels of the New Testament. Likewise, in the Koran, several issues relate to events originating in the Torah, to Abraham and Moses, and *Bani Essraeel* (the Children of Israel) and still others. The Book can be used as a reference to clarify issues relating to Moslem teachings as well. In fact, the Koran recognizes the Jews as People of the Book, *Ahlal-Kitāb*. The deeply pious and sincere Omar Abd al-Azziz, eighth Umayyad Caliph, was the first to formally codify the rules for *ahl aldhimma*, a status reserved for all non-Muslims, which, at the core considered the Jewish and Christian minority communities as People of The Book.[4]

Millions of believers keep a copy of The Book in their library or at their bedside as a spiritual anchor or support, or as a kind of protection against evil, while many crave to understand its core message, and where they stand in relation to it. Scores of books attempt to explain various aspects of the Torah and its purpose; a majority of readers remain perplexed and at a loss to understand its message. They often put The Book aside in disappointment.

For example, one area of difficulty for readers of Jewish theology is with the Zohar, a book authored by Rabbi Shimon Bar Yochai, a second century tannaitic sage said to be active after the destruction of the Second Temple in 70 C.E. The mission of this renowned twelfth-century scholar and teacher, who worked together with his students and friends, was to shed light on God's word as revealed by the Scriptures through special teachings known as Kabbalah. Due to the densely esoteric nature of the

---

[3]   Abba Eban, *Heritage: Civilization and the Jews*, 29.

[4]   Martin Gilbert, *In Ishmael's House: A History of Jews in Muslims Lands*, 31.

Zohar, the most highly skilled scholars easily become entangled in its complexities and often find themselves at a loss to decipher its underlying message.

Despite a common perception about the Torah's complexities, the Prophet Moses himself said it with much simplicity, steering his people inward: "*For this Commandment which I Command thee this day, it is not hidden from thee, neither is it far off … but the word is very nigh unto thee, in thy mouth, and in thy heart, that thy mayest do it*" (*Deuteronomy 30:11–14*).

The intent of my book is to get as close as possible to the meaning of Moses' declaration and to demonstrate how easily it can be put into practice. I am no certified scholar, neither did I attend Yeshiva theological schooling; it was Nature herself back in my early teens that made the greatest impression upon me. Nature's silent language itself validated Moses' tenet for me, such that I see the same message he proclaimed in the Book of Deuteronomy in the mountains, the blue sky, the Sun, the Moon, the countless shining stars, and a host of phenomena in the Universe. My inspiration also comes from Persian poetry, particularly as exemplified in a verse that one of my former schoolteachers once quoted from Persia's Shakespeare, Sa'di Shirazi (1184-1283):

A man reaches a point where all he can see is God. It numbs the mind then, just to imagine, what heights man can verily attain.

ACKNOWLEDGEMENTS

MY GOAL IN WRITING THIS BOOK is to develop a discussion of the Hebrew Scriptures in a way that may inspire readers, whether knowledgeable or not about the subject, to either rediscover its wisdom or to take the plunge if they haven't chosen to do so already. My deepest thanks go to my fellow congregants with whom I continuously looked forward to sharing Sabbath Morning Prayer services. Their gift of conviviality and warmth are to me as links in an unbroken chain of cherished memories. My thanks go to them as they do toward our dear Rabbi Nir Shalom of our beloved Babylonian Jewish Centre of Great Neck, New York, who made each new Sabbath morning one more reason to look forward to the one that lay ahead.

My deepest thanks also go to my good friend Isaac Ainachi, who along with Rabbi Shalom, facilitated a meeting with Rabbi Shimon H. Alouf of Congregation Ahaba ve Ahva of Ocean Parkway in Brooklyn, New York. I am grateful to Rabbi Alouf for his encouragement. His wisdom and grace inspired me to complete the work on this book.

Rabbi Yedidia Ezrahian, a powerful contributor to the popular monthly *Shofar Magazine*, which publishes articles on topics that range from Jewish theology to events of current interest, has received me on several occasions at his home where we discussed various aspects of my book. Rabbi Ezrahian's articles are widely read and appreciated, and his views are heavily solicited by members of the Jewish community. I am humbled by the insight I gained as a result of our exchanges.

I also wish to thank my good friend, Moez Youssian, who encouraged me to keep writing, and offered help throughout the writing process.

My heartfelt thanks go to my daughter-in-law, Nicole Setty Koukou, for taking the time to annotate and pinpoint wherever the reading was problematic. I am grateful for her feedback as a reader and have incorporated all of her suggestions, as they are truly excellent improvements upon the unpublished manuscript.

I thank my wife, Evelyn, and daughters Maureen, Cynthia, and Sandra, and my son, Abe, along with their families for their unfailing love throughout the worst times and the best.

Last but not least, I wish to thank my daughter, Sandra, who helped bring about the events that saved me from annihilation at the hands of the Islamic regime of Iran. She has dedicated long hours of precious time away from her family, her work, and her own book, to edit my book. I am grateful, too, for her bringing to mind various events not previously incorporated in my writing and for the artistic skill and passion that grace the cover illustration and drawings on the pages that follow.

Joseph H. Koukou
May 2012

INTRODUCTION

*The superior man acquaints himself with
many sayings of antiquity and many
deeds of the past in order to strengthen
his character thereby....In the words and
deeds of the past there lies hidden a
treasure that men may use to strengthen
and elevate their own characters. The
way to study the past is not to confine
oneself to mere knowledge of history but,
through application of this knowledge, to
give actuality to the past.*[5]

WHAT IS ENERGY? EVERYTHING, YOU MAY SAY. Albert Einstein
may certainly have agreed.

Since the human mind is a powerhouse of potentially positive or
negative energy, thoughts can be harnessed into positive or negative
pursuits. An equally vast universe exists within each person alongside
the one without, inhabited by stars and their galaxies—it is the deeper
most inner self in every human soul that is our common humanity. We
may for an instance attempt to apply Einstein's equation from his work
in quantum physics linking energy to mass—his famous formula of
relativity expressed by the equation $E = m c^2$— toward Human Energy!
And, we may then try replacing Einstein's symbol "E" for Energy to
represent, instead, *Effectiveness in being of service toward the greater good.*

Seen in this light, we can then balance the equation on the other
side, replacing the "m" for the mass of an object by "t" for *thought*, then
multiplying that object by a good dose of intensity using the symbol

---

[5]   Richard Wilhelm, trans., *The I Ching or Book of Changes*, 69.

"*f* ²" for *feeling squared*—representing that force that ignites thoughts and translates them into action. We then have the following equation for personal effectiveness in serving the greater good: $E = t f^2$. And if thoughts are things, as it has been reiterated by many of our luminaries, then it may be fair to say that they carry a weight of their own, a physical mass! This concept may sound very similar to what has been widely embraced in recent years as the Law of Attraction.

Contemporary thinking often leaves the Hebrew Bible by the wayside, unawares that the concept generally known as the Law of Attraction is basic to the Hebrew Scriptures. It lies at its core, perhaps most evident in the Golden Rule. My father's inspiration to write this book was Moses' very own prescription for self-help: "*For this Commandment which I Command thee this day, it is not hidden from thee, neither is it far off … but the word is very nigh unto thee, in thy mouth, and in thy heart, that thy mayest do it*" (*Deuteronomy 30:11–14*).

For many odd reasons, fewer and fewer of our youth and contemporaries take solace in biblical wisdom, and instead prefer the infinitude of the virtual world over the infinitude of the world within. We in the West seem to have made of ourselves the generation that picks its fruit too often from a screen. True, that screen opens out to many useful vistas, but it can exist alongside the one in which we live and breathe at the present moment, without displacing it. We tend to consult the world depicted on a screen more than the one which communicates itself through the gift of our senses. Has the natural world—*and its history!*—lost its lustre?

Many young people, persuaded that stories from the Bible are primitive and passé, seem desensitized to the deeper messages rooted in such stories as—to give one example—the Garden of Eden. Can the Garden of Eden, be recognized as Life itself, the Self, lived in the present, wholly sensitive to its mysteries, the vast potential for good? Can the poison apple, be a metaphor for the Ego, that opposing force that dissuades, that sways one's attention, away from the mysteries of the Garden, to thoughts about things that are supposedly difficult to acquire, or are missing?

Since a tender age when I was old enough to know I was alive, I saw my father as a man who seemed forever connected to that place from which everything is possible: the here and now. This is the very place to which Moses alluded in the above passage, depicted verily as residing at the tip of our lips and in the depths of our hearts, entirely achievable, if only we choose to look beyond the surface and delve within. For that too is a gift: the gift of choice. That virtual world to which we now have access can be a blessing, like the Garden of Eden, or a rotten fruit—depending on whether we are balanced in our approach. Likewise, banishment from the Garden of Eden can symbolize a graduation from one strata of existence to another, from a self centred consciousness to one that is interdependent upon important others, and ultimately, a consciousness that abides in harmony between constantly evolving internal and external worlds. What a boring read would have been the Bible, you might say, if humankind's evolution was written in a form other than through metaphor and storytelling!

During my first pregnancy, I read the Bible from cover to cover, all the while searching for a name for my unborn child. I found it in the Book of Ruth in Na'Omi. While it took me the whole of three months to read that work which my father referred to as *The Book* from cover to cover, I gained profound insight into the kaleidoscope of my own humanity. Had the scribes needed a password to lock up the whole of the Hebrew Bible, it may simply have read something like this: *"golden_rule."* Instead of giving us the nuggets on a silver platter by telling what happened, they chose to show their universal message through symbol and metaphor, and gave us the option to engage in spiritual gymnastics through storytelling.

In his work on *The Book*, my father puts the flashlight on parts of Scripture that, to me, confirm Nietzsche's following affirmation: "The errors of great men are venerable because they are more fruitful than the truths of little men."[6] Since we live in a world peopled by many who seek the same things we do, God has outlined a blueprint, and given it a voice through the word of the prophets. He has also given us choice. Just as we can learn from the errors of the great, we can spend a lifetime committing our own with no regard for any possible blind spot or hindsight. The

---

[6]   Walter Kaufman, ed. and trans. *The Portable Nietzsche*, 30.

Hebrew Bible makes the great figures of history appear before us life-size; my father believed that therein lay the genius of Judaism!

How else did the author's compatriots, the Jews, hold on for so long despite the odds that tried for close to four millennia to sweep their faith away? What role did the prophets play that resonates among us moderns today? What resulted when prophecy was traded for idolatry? Is today's excessive materialism a modern form of idol worship? What can history teach us about the propensity to repeat itself when unheeded? Are modern eyes too sophisticated to view it—history—as a continuum with an organic energy of its own, as bold and alive as the air we breathe and the blood that runs through our veins? Why is it that we read in some modern authors that we are witnessing the end of history?

Edward Edinger (1922-1998) explained the archetypal image in hexagram 26 of what the Chinese call the *I Ching*, showing how it represents "The Taming Power of the Great." Dr. Edinger, a Jungian psychologist, described this concept to signify a strengthening of character, and likens it to the "taming of wild animals through a process of human culture—which is a civilizing, domesticating process that tames raw human energies by pitting them against historical and cultural facts. This has the effect of reminding the individual that he or she is not the first and only person to come into existence. And the net result of the acculturating process is a taming of the instincts."[7]

Dr. Edinger, who passed away before his book was published, *The Ego and Self: The Old Testament Prophets: From Isaiah to Malachi*, typically wrote with a deep and piercing humanity nurtured by a deep love and concern. His editor, J. Gary Sparks, commented on Edinger's work in the book's Foreword by describing our time as one of "me, me and more me," a pattern which he believes we use as a defence "against the increasingly crushing brutality of a world that is at best callous and amoral."[8] Edinger's theme centred on self mastery through the taming of the ego by listening

---

[7]   Edward F. Edinger. *Ego and Self: The Old Testament Prophets: From Isaiah to Malachi*, 69.

[8]   Ibid, 1.

to the voice within to connect with the universal Self. The metaphor he used in his work for the voice of the Self within every human being was none other than the voice of the Jewish prophets.

My father held no doctorate besides his own humble meanderings through many successes and failures over the 88 years of living. Having listened to the melodious prayers he sang holding his prayer book on Saturday mornings, and having witnessed how effortlessly he managed to impact the lives of many, both close of kin and beyond, it seemed that his insight into matters of the soul found its source in the Scripture he knew so well and loved so dearly. He talked only to uplift, and he walked the talk by using his knowledge as a wellspring for action.

Verily, few in our circle of family and friends can fathom that Joseph Koukou is no longer of this world. However, the love he inspired testifies to the veracity of a line from Thomas Campbell's poem, *Hallowed Ground*: "To live in hearts we leave behind / is not to die."[9] My father is alive and well, even after his departure some years before his book will be put to print.

His intense exploration of Scripture, despite being locked within the bowels of a cruel regime, extends a drawbridge to help uncover, for some—and recover, for others—the beauty and depth of the Scripture. In doing so, he succeeded with top marks to ignite my own interest to dust off the cover of my copy and rediscover its hidden treasures. I can only speak from a highly personal perspective in having found immeasurable joy, not to mention respite from routine, as a result of regular participation in Shabbat services followed by a group discussion of the relevant Torah portion, *parasha*, of the week. Verily, on Shabbat, what naturally permeates the spirit is the realization that cell phones aren't alone in their need to recharge.

I also got to know more of my father's endless reservoir of loving kindness and strength of character throughout our work together between two cities separated by a seven hour drive and linked by telephone, over

---

[9]   Thomas Campbell. *The Poetical Works of Thomas Campbell: "Hallowed Ground,"* Stanza 6, 163.

the course of three years. I listened from afar, as his words delivered with remarkable precision, a sense of where he wanted to go with his ideas, and marvelled at the absolute mastery with which he covered the material. I admired his firm grasp on what he set out to convey. It was that single-minded determination that inspired me to sign up for the journey, bringing me to a place alongside him to edit and illustrate his book, bewitched as I was by the ever present gleam in his eyes and conviction whenever he spoke about the "majesty of all this" during our walks on sunny days in his neighbourhood. His head would turn upwards and his hand would salute the vast blueness of the firmament....

Outside the walls of Evin Prison overlooking places in the vicinity of my childhood home, perched on the foot of the white peaked Alborz Mountains, stretches a countryside scene of our extended family's bicycle expeditions, of our sunny mornings spent on horseback amid cherry blossoms, of singing brooks and the sound of sheep grazing on the first green blades of spring, when Iran still belonged to poetry and the Persians. At his funeral, our family and friends got a closer glimpse onto the texture of my father's soul from a eulogy by a former inmate's story about what happened on the other side of those walls. It was the story of a young Jewish businessman who was sentenced to death by the revolutionary court after being labelled a Zionist spy. Upon returning to Iran for a temporary visit, the guardians of the Islamic revolution snatched him from his room at the Hilton Hotel on the outskirts of Teheran close to the mountainside suburbs where we lived. It was headquarter for many foreign reporters and journalists at that time shortly after the fall of the Persian monarchy.

As the coffin stood solemnly in front of the crowd that came to bid him a final farewell, a long time photographer friend's eulogy brought to life the story of how my father held the youth by one arm and asked the friend, Firouz Farokhzad, to grab him by the other, as they walked with the young man along the path leading to the executioner, speaking softly in his ear: "Allow your faith to guide you and hold your head high, for Jews walk their faith only in such posture."[10]

---

[10]   Mr. Farokhzad's *"Tribute from a Fellow Prison Inmate at Evin"* appears after the Epilogue.

Looking back on the times we were graced by my father's presence, it delights me to reflect on my role as a collaborator, having had no clue at the onset as to what he would have been pointing the flashlight toward, in the last segment of life. I knew it had something to do with the brilliant way he survived life in prison. I knew too that his gentility and capacity to care, and to uplift so many, was rooted in his conviction that everything finds its source in God's love.

And while he was no Nietzsche, my father was an adept at connecting the dots after a careful read of the entire Hebrew Scriptures. I do know this for sure, that he selected from the Tanakh those passages he considered key to unlock a consistent theme. For me, they manage to bring to life what Nietzsche himself nudged us to be wary of—that moment when he warned that humankind would choose to kill God, instead of lean toward Him: "I disturbed this sleepiness when I taught: what is good and evil *no one knows yet,* unless it be he who creates. He, however, creates man's goal and gives the earth its meaning and its future. That anything at all is good and evil—that is his creation."[11]

Dad and I became each other's sounding boards throughout what turned out for me, to be a journey into his soul, and hence into the deep recesses of my own! When at one point he suggested that we take a pause from keyboard and screen to reflect over the phone, he uttered a humble recognition that he had learned so much about his daughter, in a way that he never would have been able to before. How could I have answered any differently? While fine tuning his ideas on the screen, we had given each other a lot to take away, as each embarked on a new path.

Now, having completed this work together, I am grateful for having stumbled upon my own very intimate personal discovery as a result of our open-ended journey through this humble quest into the wisdom of the Hebrew Scriptures. I find my own demons laid to rest, since my father's carefully chosen biblical quotes have enabled me to take away the acceptance that God's creation *is* at once pregnant with good *and* with evil, and that the best I can do is lay down the fight against the latter, and instead grasp the higher road, as it was intended. And, why? Turning

---

[11] Walter Kaufman, ed. and transl. *The Portable Nietzsche*, 308.

towards the landscape within, I come away knowing that in the here and now lays an opportunity to choose … aspire … overcome … and finally: to shine—since the object of this whole exercise of living is verily to *"…Let there be light…" (Genesis 1:3).*

Editing my father's book was like taking a journey on the cusp of a rainbow. I was a passenger enjoying a ride to higher ground, compelled to search—as he did—for gold. From the reams of poetry and prose he lovingly absorbed in prison, he carefully unrolled each bolt of fabric and showed me how with an eye for discernment, one may find along the numerous colours, textures and patterns, a single unifying thread. He wrote about his life experience and the way in which he saw it manifestly linked to the book that gave him so much, as he sought to convey the notion that *we may just* be missing out in a huge way—should we choose to leave its pages unturned.

Sandra Koukou
04 July 2014

LETTER FROM THE EDITOR

NO ONE IS EVER PREPARED FOR SUCH A LOSS, as I painfully learned when my father died in his beloved small town of Great Neck, Long Island, New York, on 11 August 2012.

Joseph Koukou, of blessed memory, was born in Basra, Iraq, on the 6th of June, 1924, and passed away before his book was ready for print.

As a refugee who was forever grateful to have been granted political asylum in the United States, he felt compelled during his latter years to share something of what, for him, was none other than a "love affair with God," as one niece, Thelma Dallal Kattan, had aptly named it. I don't think anyone had come up with a better way to describe the kindness and gentility that sculpted his playful spirit. Some called him a classy man. Others recalled how he had uplifted them. My eulogy described his soul as having a vocabulary of its own. This notion was greeted with nostalgia by all the congregants who had befriended him during the years they spent alongside one another on Sabbath mornings. Their eyes stitched themselves onto every gesture, their ears to every word for solace, as I offered a line by a poet from a book about grieving handed to me by that niece, my cousin Thelma, the day before: "To live in hearts we leave behind / is not to die."[12]

Contrary to the mentality prevalent in Eastern societies in Iran during the fifties, Youssef, as his friends called him, never differentiated between a son and daughter. "My children are flowers in a garden," he often mused. "Each has its own unique perfume!" Similarly, I can count on two hands the number of people he uplifted, even one whose heart didn't want to go on. Well, that relative did live for longer than a quarter century after my father sat at his bedside and convinced him that life is truly a thing of immeasurable beauty.

---

[12] Thomas Campbell. *The Poetical Works of Thomas Campbell: "Hallowed Ground,"* Stanza 6, 163.

As we gathered around his bed that Saturday that marked the end of his life, I pondered over our work together over the last three years, with countless hours funnelled over the phone piecing together this labour of love. My niece, Sharon Arazi, had begged him to hold off until I arrived from my home in Canada, and our brother, Abe, from his home in Colorado. As he lay there in pain just before accepting the morphine, he told her about a dream he just had in which his father, who is well described in the pages that follow, passed him by, gave him his back, and turned to walk away. From all that I had learnt from his dear eldest son, Youssef, throughout our work on this book, my grandfather seemed to be saying, "Follow me—your time has come; it's not so bad up here."

A sportsman who skied, climbed mountains, and rode horses, even one of his own back in Iran; he had been as strong in life, as he was in dying. I was unready to let him go before allowing his ear to capture a distant voice that rang on my sister, Maureen's, cell phone, which I gently placed against Dad's ear. It was his nephew Henry Dallal from England, the sportsman and now famous photographer who at better times shared the love of the outdoors and of horses with the uncle and mentor who inspired him so. I had listened to my cousin's tears a few months earlier, in the wee hours of one morning while editing my father's most recent writing, over a phone call between me in Canada and Henry on a sunny beach in Oman. He was on an assignment to complete a coffee-table book and had just learned that Uncle Yussef had been admitted to a nursing and rehabilitation centre. "Henry, what did you tell him?" I asked gently pulling the phone away following what seemed like forever. Resolutely the voice came back to my ears.

"I wished him the same courage and strength he inspired in me at the time of my own father's approach toward the inevitable."

And then, as my hand and my Aunt Violet's succumbed to his gentle, loving touch, my father lifted his arm wrapped around ours, up and down, up and down—fighting the effects of the morphine. He did this for three-and-a-half hours with my hand cradled in his, and then on to four without stopping a single moment. Up and down, up and down…. It seemed as though his strength in dying cued me to go ahead and deliver his labour of love to the publisher, since he had reached the finish line with the very last touches from where he lay earlier at the nursing centre, from the bed in which he spent his last two months with us. That was where I told him that the biggest miracle was this: that Joseph had managed to live until the ripe old age of eighty-eight years without medication. Suddenly, a childlike smile popped out of oblivion and landed on his gentle features!

While painstakingly threading through every last paragraph, we got to know each other far better than was possible under any other circumstances. His voice now resonates in my dreams with the same authenticity—and humility—of a man compelled to share his "love affair with God" with anyone who cares to listen. Even as he is gone, those he called flowers are now turning toward the sun ... the wealth of loving kindness he left behind. I am one of those flowers. I turned toward the sun one day by the water's edge near my home in Lachine, Quebec, Canada. I asked him to send "another sign" besides the crystal-clear words he had given me in Persian as I woke up from a dream one day in late August 2012 shortly after he passed away. I asked him to send me just one more sign, because I was unemployed—and because he had always been my rock.

The next day I was called for an interview and got the job. My first day at work was 11 September 2012, the day after we held prayers at his gravesite, the traditional thirtieth day after the passing of the deceased according to Jewish tradition.

That was when I knew for certain that, beyond a certain *point in our awareness*, the bottom line abides solely within reach of the Master Orchestrator. I am reminded by the true story of our rabbi, who started out as a geneticist, and realized that science can only explain the phenomena up to a certain point. I am forever grateful for my father's gift, and for offering me his hand several hours as he lay in transit to a place from where he watches over his flowers, while a brilliant Long Island sun illuminates an epitaph that reads: *He lived his life as though everything were a miracle.*

Sandra Koukou
21 July 2014

11

Plaque on the exterior wall of the Iraqi Jewish Synagogue of Teheran co-founded by the author's father, Heskel Abraham Koukou. The first line from right to left of the list of donators bears his name in Persian.[13]

[13]   Ettefagh Synagogue, Summer 2009. Exterior Wall Inscription Honouring Donators. [online] Available at: http://www.7dorim.com/Tasavir/kenisa_etefag.asp. [Accessed 01 July 2012].

PART I

MY FAMILY'S EXODUS

1

TRUST IN GOD

IT WAS BUSINESS AS USUAL ON A SUN-DRENCHED Teherani day in the fall of 1979 when two well-dressed men entered my office unannounced. They asked me to go with them for "some questioning." I asked who they were and what their purpose was. They said they were representatives of the Islamic Revolution and that I was soon to learn about the nature of their inquiry.

My blindfold belied only the fact that I was heading from one remote location to another. The journey's end was a square meter of space where the only consolation from the cold and damp was a peephole intended for the guards in the corridor outside. I remained in the belief that "they will find nothing to justify keeping me here" until I began to recall that, a couple of weeks back, they had arrested a man by the name of Habib Elghanian, a prominent Jewish philanthropist and businessman who met his fate by the bullet within only twenty-four hours of his arrest. Fear rippled through my body, and my soul shuddered with images that conjured what may possibly be happening to my family.

Shrunk in helplessness, I started to contemplate Creation and its purpose ... shifting my focus to the Creator, and to my conviction that, no matter how small and negligible I was, everything was happening according to His will.

With an elevated spirit unlike anything I had experienced before, I knelt down and raised my hands upward. As if unbidden, out came the words, "Whatever You desire ... may it be Your will." As I spoke, aching to get closer and feel His presence, I reached out and inscribed the letters of God's name on the wall with my fingers. In the tightness of that space, thoughts raced back and forth about my family. I scratched my head to make sense of my new surroundings, and then resigned myself to accept the knowledge that they were now in a world entirely beyond my

15

protection and abided under His care. It was in such spiritedness that I paid time in Khomeini's prison of Evin, much like a servant who trusted his Master and awaited the outcome.

A month passed before they took me to a mullah for "questioning."

"What are you here for?"

I said that I didn't know. He asked, "How is that possible?"

"A month ago I was asked to come for some questioning, and here I am." Then he asked about my occupation.

When I told him I was a factory owner, a smile crossed his face, and he promptly responded with, "Yours will be a court case." This meant confiscation. Then I was dismissed and sent back to my cell.

The months that passed with no trial in sight seemed endless, but I was finally led into a more comfortable cell. Fifteen inmates shared the space and slept on the floor. The majority were supporters of the former shah and came from a variety of backgrounds. Among them were doctors, professors, generals, ministers, archaeologists, pilots, and even mullahs who supported the shah. Some were members of his secret police, the Savak. I seized upon the positive wherever possible, seeing it as a rare opportunity to learn about the lives of people who came from so many different walks of life, sharing knowledge and oftentimes amusingly colourful stories.

While the sense of unrelenting routine made boredom ever present, I sought a way to curb the tedium and initiated a program of daily lectures by each professional. Before we knew it, things had become so interesting that each looked forward to knowing who the next speaker would be on the list.

We had some Jewish inmates too. Among them was Hakham Baroukh, chief rabbi of Teheran, who had been detained for undisclosed reasons and placed in our ward. As hard as it was to believe, we wore the prayer shawl known as the *talit* and prayed in the prison mosque on

Sabbaths. Some Moslem inmates used to ask us to pray for them. "Your prayers will be heard," they told us.

During my long confinement, I had ample opportunity to go through our Scriptures, as well as the sacred writings of other faiths. It was thus that I found numerous interconnections between them and followed their historical evolution over time. The task became so fascinating that I sometimes forgot about my whereabouts. In this way I kept an even keel and withstood the numerous discomforts of prison life.

We were told about the scarcity of hot water for showers, washing dishes, and doing the laundry. We were allowed five minutes a week in the shower—three at a time. When one went under the showerhead, the other two applied soap, and vice versa. At the end of the five minutes, the facility was cleared for the next three in line. This program was designed to intimidate those in the upper echelons who served within the system during the time of the shah. There was otherwise abundant fuel to run hot water round the clock through the pipes.

One day I randomly walked into the shower room to see if I could find some not-so-cold water to bathe in. It was mid winter and I noticed an inmate in his eighties taking a cold shower. He happened to be Mohsen Foroughi, the former fine arts minister and the son of Mohammad Ali Foroughi, who served as prime minister under the former shah's father, Reza Shah. From under the shower he peered at the expression on my face, and said: "This is how you defy them and keep your civilized ways."

That was enough for me to find my way out of a major dilemma. Soon after, I added jogging to my daily exercise routine and went under the cold shower, hot and sweating, watching vapour rise above my shoulders. The comfort and peace of body and mind after that experience was exhilarating. After that transformation, I actually enjoyed breakfast like never before, and was able to sit down to my reading and writing with a clear mind.

One of our cellmates was a young Jewish boy who had been caught distributing communist pamphlets on the street. He was firmly entrenched in his communist ideals and was of an atheistic frame of mind. All attempts made by my fellow prisoners and me served only to woo him further away from God and biblical wisdom. Even Hakham Baroukh, the well-known leader of Iran's Jewry, was unable to inspire him about the richness of his heritage, since his thoughts were on another plane.

One day we heard his name spoken on the loud speaker and understood that he was being called to report to the office. We all knew what such calls were about. They ranged from answering simple questions to going before the firing squad. As the young boy prepared to be led into the prison office, I asked him if he had any clue what it was going to be about. To my surprise, he muttered, "God knows." At that moment, I didn't know if I wanted to laugh or cry for the poor lad, but was glad to know at least that he knew God and sought His protection. It was also good to find out that all that suspense was only about a pair of pyjamas that had come in a package from his home!

Khomeini's jail brought me in contact with still others who invited me to explore their beliefs. For example, a former Jew and convert to Bahaism explained the virtues of his religion, and then patiently awaited my views. I said, "Bahaism's advocacy for peace and coexistence is praiseworthy. However, I can't see myself moving away from my own heritage, because we still have a mandate to fulfil returning to Jerusalem; it was given to our ancestors through the Scriptures to go back and rebuild the Temple in the city of David."

To add colour to the ambiance of prison life, we had bad guys too. They were thieves, murderers, bank robbers, and others. At one time, I came across a pickpocket and asked him if he could pick my pocket without my becoming aware. He promptly showed me my banknote, saying, "You mean this?"

Another inmate was a thief who specialized in unlocking doors and entering homes to steal jewellery and precious objects. He was admired by the other thieves for his expertise in the trade, and they called him "The Master."

That "Master" happened to be one of our roommates. He once told of one of his adventures, in which a friend called him from Mashad to join his birthday party. Mashad, a city in northeast Iran, is known as the burial place of Imam Reza, a Shiite saint believed to possess powers to grant the wishes of pilgrim visitors to his tomb. Devoted Shiite Moslems visit his mausoleum in throngs at least once in their lifetime.

On the day of the party, the "Master" sat behind the wheel and drove to Mashad. Before reaching his friend's house, he noticed a wealthy couple coming out of their home to drive away. He followed them to their destination and made sure they were staying for a while. He then returned to their home, clicked open their lock, went inside, and helped himself to all that was available in the refrigerator. After that, he picked up their valuables and thanked Imam Reza for his generosity. Then he went on to join his friend's birthday party. As a prisoner, he was often seen staring for long periods of time at his hands. When asked why, he replied that he had been warned that the next arrest for burglary was reason to have his fingers cut off in accordance with Sharia law.

Prison life had its share of amusing moments. One day while reading the story of Job in the Scriptures and fully immersed in the man's perception of the divine in relation to human destiny as he kept company and listened to several controversial opinions from his three visiting friends, an inmate from another cell in our ward known for his craft of thievery came visiting to ask the "Master" how to crack open a certain lock. After sharing a simple technique ("You can do like so and it unlocks in a wink!"), the fellow thanked the Master and then returned to his cell. I went back to Job.

I asked a mullah prisoner if there was anything in the Koran about Job. He said, "Job is highly revered in the Koran as a legend for his towering patience." He wanted to know if we had more on Job's life in our book.

I told him that Job's significance is that, in spite of the calamities he suffered and the enormity of his pain and affliction after leading a life of service to others, he abstained from complaining or uttering bitterness toward his Creator; instead, he strove to deal with his affliction. Even when his wife criticized him and suggested that it was better to

19

blaspheme against God and die than to endure such pain, he asked an interesting question: "Shall we accept the good from God and reject the bad?" Job also had three friends who came to offer him comfort. Instead, they nudged him with comments suggesting that his misfortunes may have been the consequence of sinful acts from the past. They paid little attention to his pain and preferred to keep themselves safe from a similar fate. They persisted in telling Job he may have committed some sins to have ended up so miserably.

Job met with his ultimate destiny when God finally showed His presence by appearing in a whirlwind visit. God asked Job the ultimate question: was he willing to discredit God's judgment?

"Then Job answered the Lord and said, I know that thou canst do everything and that no thought can be withholden from thee" (*Job 42:1–2*).

Then God spoke to Eliphaz, one of the three friends of Job, and said:

> My wrath is kindled against thee, and against thy two friends: for ye have not spoken of me the thing that is right, as my servant Job hath. Therefore, take unto you now seven bullocks and seven rams, and go to my servant Job, and offer up for yourselves a burnt offering; and my servant Job will pray for you: for him I will accept: lest I deal with you after your folly, in that ye have not spoken of me the thing which is right, like my servant Job. (*Job 42:7–8*)

Eventually, God returned Job to resplendence in good health and with wealth that surpassed the splendour of his former holdings.

The mullah was impressed with Job's story in The Book and told me, "Now that you are so interested in theology, it is time that you become Moslem to further advance your knowledge."

I told him, "At this stage in life it's too late for me to change course; on the other hand, you may wish to know more about your own faith and the connection between our two religions—Judaism and Islam. If you read the Torah in its original Hebrew text, you will find that most of the words in the Koran resonate with their Hebrew roots. *Islam*, the word representing peace, comes from the Hebrew word *shalom*. Other words are: *Koran* (to read) from *kara*; *Mohammad* (comely) from *Nihmad*; *Elahena* (our God) rooted in *Elohenu*; *Maqdas* (holy place) from *Mighdash*; and *Shams* (Sun) from *Shemesh*. There are similar connections for almost all other Biblical references.

I went on to tell the mullah that much of the positive counsel in the Koran already exists in the Torah. Islam, with a billion followers, is a reality and owes its endurance to the will of God. In our case as Jews, it is an order from God that we remain true to our faith.

That conversation reminded me of another one I had in better times before the revolution, when there was more freedom of speech. I had consulted with my lawyer at his office for some business advice. It was during the time of the Haj when observant Moslems visited Mecca. As I listened to a discussion between my lawyer and some of his friends about their recent pilgrimage to Mecca, my lawyer turned toward me to extol the virtues of pilgrimage to that holy city as a highly civilized tradition. I saw that he was intent to find any interest I may have had to adopt his religion.

I said, "Jews, too, very often go as pilgrims to Jerusalem and pray at the Wailing Wall, after which they are allowed to use the title *haji* as a prefix to their names. Back to his home from his pilgrimage, the good guy continues his way of life—the bad guy hardly changes any of his old habits and crooked ways."

I asked him if he recalled the Six-Day War, as long as the topic was brought up about espousing a civilized attitude toward life. This was a war between seven Arab countries and Israel. After a crushing victory, no Arab woman was molested and no Arab home was looted. My lawyer quickly changed the subject.

I also had my own share of fear and anxiety as I served time in Khomeini's custody. One day the microphone sounded my name along with that of another cellmate to report to the office. The entire ward sank into a deafening silence. Suddenly, a spasm of fear raced through my veins, as my thoughts picked up on a signal that spelled trouble.

As we both stepped out of our cell, a tall, stocky prison master received us in the hallway, looking suspiciously at my fellow inmate, a former army general of the shah. He was told of a recent report that showed him to have blasphemed Islamic prayer among the occupants in our cell and that I was said to have laughed along upon hearing the general's anecdote. The stocky prison master made it clear to the general that, as a Moslem, he was better off knowing what kind of punishment was reserved for such behaviour.

When the general denied the entire allegation, the chief warden called all the other cellmates into the scene and warned them to utter truth to the incident; otherwise, each and every one of them was to end up serving in solitary confinement until further notice. Not a soul uttered a word, so we were told collectively to turn facing the wall. The chief warden summoned a reporter, who soon entered the scene. We were unable to see the man as we stood with our backs toward him, but knew full well that his job was to document the identity of each one of us before execution. The big guy referred to our position facing the wall and remarked that it was a perfect occasion to mow us all down with the machine gun that he was sporting under his arm. And so, with my forehead against the wall, I ventured to ask the haji if I could say a few words. To my surprise, the request was accepted.

"Haji Dawood, I am a Jew, and I respect all religions. If I hear a Moslem say anything against his faith, I lose any respect I have for him. Such a thing as presented to you did not happen at our place…"

A dead silence prevailed and lasted a few moments, after which the *haji* dismissed us. "You can all go back to your cell." Moments of dead silence lasted a while as some of my companions tarried in frozen disbelief, whereupon the big guy repeated the order of dismissal, and it was back to our cell where the walls had ears, and where I was commended for my defence and handling of the situation.

I told my shell-shocked cellmates that what I had told the big guy was the truth; it was only lucky that he believed me.

My cellmates promptly reminded me that it wasn't the whole truth, so we made it our business to rehash the original scenario. The general had been reading a travel diary written by an Iranian who suddenly at the call of nature was unable to find the restroom in Baghdad's airport. His knowledge of Arabic was severely limited, most of it typically having come from prayers learnt by heart. So, he managed to muster from memory a line from a daily prayer ritual, habitually recited in the language of the Koran in which the believer asks God to lead him in the straight path. With this helpful linguistic tip in mind, he approached an airport police officer and said in proper Arabic, "Lead me to the restroom."

One may have attributed my good fortune in escaping danger at various points during incarceration to sheer luck. But I owed my luck to a trust in God, for I was truly grateful that He didn't allow me to recall this last anecdote at that crucial moment. Numerous anecdotes found their way into our cell discussions at any given time; had I reacted differently, my behaviour may have cost us all our lives.

2

MOMENT OF TRUTH

I FINALLY RECEIVED MY SUBPOENA TO APPEAR IN COURT. The document listed scores of phoney accusations. I was informed that the judge would be a certain high-profile top cleric, known to have sent his own son before the firing squad for allegedly holding Communist beliefs. This mullah, the judge who presided over my case, was duly appointed from among the six top clerics who possessed the authority to veto any decree issued by the Islamic Tribunal.

The Islamic Revolution was on a mission to knock down all of the deposed shah's supporters, and to eliminate any chance of his return to power; its main focus was to effectively disown the wealthy class that in some way did not support the Islamic regime. No lawyer was allowed to the defence of individuals in court. Ayatollah Khomeini had become for them God's divine representative on Earth, and the verdicts issued by his judges, the mullahs, were considered irreversible.

It was heartbreaking news to hear of what befell a general in the police force sentenced to life in prison, when his wife pleaded with the court that her husband did not deserve such a harsh punishment. They asked her if she wanted a retrial, and she agreed. The following week, a second court hearing was held for her husband, and this time around the general was sentenced to death. The sentence was carried out immediately, and from that point onward, no one dared to request an appeal from the Islamic court.

On the day of my court appearance, I saw my Moslem partner and our project manager, his cousin, who were seated next to me. It had been two years since we had last met, when we were taken into custody on our last day from our factory's administration offices on the upper level. It felt awkward to sit side by side after so long, unable to communicate in any way. They sat to my right. I had no idea what expressions they wore on their faces, since it was strictly forbidden to make eye contact or exchange conversation.

When the hearing began, I was asked why we had not paid our taxes fairly. I answered that we had hired a certified public accountant, and that we had paid according to his calculations. I added, however, that there was a strict order from Imam Khomeini not to pay taxes to the shah's regime. The prosecutor's eyes turned sarcastically toward the judge.

"It is interesting to find a Jew heeding the Imam's orders!"

The three of us were accused on many false charges, but I sensed that I was the main target, as the heaviest accusations landed on me. I knew that had a lot to do with the fact that I was the Jew. Then, it was time for witnesses to take the stand. One worker came up to report that, since the last time I had set foot in the factory, a phone call was received from Israel. According to the illiterate worker, the caller left a message: "Please tell Mr. Koukou I am inquiring as to the reason we did not receive the money he promised to send." My heart skipped a beat, not from fear but from ridicule, and as I glanced toward the judge, I saw him struggling to suppress a smile that threatened to creep across his entire face.

Among the other accusations, one particularly outraged me. The prosecutor said that our project manager had attempted to push a certain worker into the factory oven with the intent to burn him alive! As such, the factory owners were considered co-conspirators, thus accessories to the crime.

At that point the judge asked witnesses to take the stand, and three of our workers swore upon the Koran that they had personally witnessed the incident. This entire lie mongering made sense only if one considered that, in those days, workers were given to believe that part of the revenue of companies hiring them was promised to be distributed amongst them. It was a new type of profit sharing that, as it turned out, never saw the light of day.

Soon, a young woman seated amongst the people in the courthouse asked to be called as witness to the stand. She seemed determined and forthright. To everyone's surprise, she testified that for five years she had been employed as our project manager's secretary, and that the story of the worker and the oven was totally unfounded. I was saddened by her testimony, knowing in all certainty that she was going to pay dearly for her truthfulness and courage. In a loud voice I said: "Thank God that the first brave witness has finally emerged from our unit." My predilection was well founded, since it wasn't long after our trial that the secretary lost her job.

By that time the judge's rage came to a peak. "Only one who believed the shah to have been a beneficial element to Iran would welcome a supporter in this hearing."

"Your honour," I replied, "I heard you are a highly knowledgeable personality, and a strong believer."

"Such talk will not help you!"

I replied, "Your religious conviction helps me, because I believe that if I am truly guilty and your punishment is less than what I deserve, up there in Heaven, your action will be complemented. But, if I am innocent, you would know."

As he responded, there was compassion in his tone. He addressed me as "Mr. Koukou" and then declared, "This is the court of the Prophet Ali, and if you are not guilty you will not be harmed."

"Ever since I was old enough to know who I am, I heard about the judgment of the Prophet Ali and looked up to it with respect, and am now finding myself standing before it at a pinnacle moment in my life."

This marked a turning point in my court case. From that point on, a bit of compassion was noticeable in this unrelenting judge, who began to gradually loosen the noose that the prosecutor's questioning had tightened around my pounding heart. Undoubtedly, I had been able to touch the turbaned judge's religious conviction at the core. I was amazed at the calm and resolve that came to my rescue in that crowded court house, where our skilled workers of many years whom I had helped—just as a father does toward a child in need—had blasphemed us, suffering neither qualm nor conscience. My other desire was to remind the judge that, aside from politics, he needed to err on the side of caution, as he sat on a seat of authority as an influential and powerful Ayatollah. I wondered whether my warning appealed to an inherent sense of principle as a judge, or to some kind of residual humanity, or whether it served to feed his vanity. It was an open question that continues to linger in my thoughts. To be sure, this was no Solomon, and there was no guarantee that I was going to come out of Daniel's lions' den alive and well.

The prosecutor would have had me sentenced to death, while the judge—who'd had his own son shot—ordered my name removed from the execution list.

In the ensuing months, the only certainty around the results of my court case was utter uncertainty. As a matter of fact, the weeks of interminable mental torture turned into months, and two years passed before I was given any idea of a verdict on the horizon. I met with my wife and two of my daughters and two of my grandchildren from behind a glass window once every fortnight. Our visitations lasted only fifteen minutes. My wife assured me that the family's combined efforts spared no opportunity to obtain my release. We were, of course, quite aware that all our conversations were monitored, so we were unable to get into any specifics during our brief meetings behind glass. I contented myself with the fruit and vegetable basket my wife brought with her each visitation to Evin.

It took over two years for the judge's sentence to be passed on to me only verbally, but even as I was told the number of years I was to serve, nobody ever told me what crime I had been convicted of. That crime remains a ghost to me and my family until this day. In the eyes of a mullocracy that took Iran back to the Middle Ages, we were plain and simple capitalists, and therefore evil in their sight. Their crime in our eyes was that they wanted at any cost to confiscate the fruit of a lifetime and a labour of love.

It was only after my release that I learned of my wife's endless calls to the prison authorities regarding the status of our file. It developed into a weekly pattern that went on in similar vein for a period of two years. At the end of each phone call, the answer from the other side of the line was categorically: *"Hafteyeh ayandeh, Khahar,* call back next week, Sister."

During the months of incarceration after my rendezvous with fate in the Islamic court of my benevolent judge, I busied myself with study of the Scripture. I was often called upon to do the work of offering cheer to any fellow prisoner who could use some moral support. Meanwhile, it often happened that one of our cellmates was taken away while the rest of us slept. But we were soon abruptly wide awake to the sound of the executioner's gunfire outside and presently found one among us missing from his usual place in our cell.

Outside my temporary home in prison, another storyline took its course parallel to ours. I learned of its many twists and turns from my youngest daughter, Sandra, who, years later, filled in the missing pieces of the saga whereby she risked her life to save mine. In the following chapter she recalls the labyrinth from which a peephole of opportunity was seized to open my path to freedom.

3

RENDEZVOUS WITH DESTINY

ON ONE OF OUR USUAL BI-WEEKLY VISITS TO SEE MY DAD, my mother and I were alarmed by the soft whisper of a woman's voice in her ear. It came from the sister of Dad's business partner's wife.

It was dark in the women's waiting room where we took our seats on a wooden bench after the routine body search. Soon it would be our turn to be ushered into another room deep inside the prison compound. The woman's words sounded ominous: "Evelyn *Khanoum*, you need to be worried once again, for Youssef's name is back on the execution list."

It appeared that a group of factory workers claimed they found evidence that my father was sending funds to *Ghods*, the name Ayatollah Khomeini designated for the State of Israel, that so-called "demonic extension of the superpower, *Emrika*." So, there was my father, sitting inside a cauldron of hate while his workers tried anything within their means to paint him a Zionist, and therefore be typecast as an anathema to the powers that be.

There was a *mujahed* freedom fighter named Mohammad posturing as a liaison with the authorities in Evin. He was referred to my mother by the Italian-born wife of one of my father's cellmates, whose restaurant employees betrayed him as a *taghouti*—Westernizer. That friend eventually got out after three months. For the mullahs, a restaurant was far from being as politically sensitive as a factory which manufactured brake linings.

After months of precious negotiations and funds spent to no end, I decided it was time to step into the fray. In truth, I had long itched to brainstorm a strategy to get out from under my family's protection and be involved, but the decisive moment was placed on a silver platter by none other than Mohammad himself. "I have no choice other than to turn to you," he told me, "since your mother has a habit of turning numb with fear each time I plant her in front of the powerful figure of a mullah."

That didn't surprise me. My mother had been used to a protected life during better times, and, hard as she tried, was helpless to navigate her way into a coherent exchange with those turbaned medieval creatures, our *nouvelle aristocracie*. It wasn't as if we enjoyed no support at all from fellow community members. And, despite our awkward situation, I was grateful for the vital cushion of kindness we got from the only remaining friends of our family, since everyone else had fled upon learning about the Ayatollah's imminent return to Persia.

Edward and Margaret received us, mother and daughter, with open arms in their apartment every evening at dusk along with a dwindling handful of people from our once-prolific Iraqi Jewish community.

I chose to think of their hospitality as a sort of sanctuary far from the brave new world outside. But, then it was inevitably back to the perils of the job to get my dad out of harm's way each time we crossed the threshold of a third floor apartment they rented while Uncle Edward, the title we used in those days to call our elders, liquidated final assets before clearing his family out of Iran. Uncle Edward had run a major supermarket in a busy section of downtown Teheran's commercial district. Aunty Margaret's table was generously spread with delicious Iraqi Jewish dishes every time we showed up at their door. The first question she asked by default was about the latest developments on the prison front. They were a kind couple who asked nothing in return for the tough task of being perpetually present as our psychological sounding board.

One day, my mother and I boarded a pickup truck with Mohammad to travel to the medieval city of Qom. When we arrived at our destination, Mohammad had my mother stay at his mother's house, while he guided me on a visit to the famous gold-domed mosque of Qom. Sitting crossed legged on the marble floor amid the intricate tiles and mirror inlays of the surrounding walls, I followed the slender floral patterns dancing on the turquoise of the Persian tiles, admiring their perfect symmetry, while the *mujahed* opined solemnly on a subject that seemed very close to his heart.

"You see these poor souls? They come here to claim their share in a world that has allotted them nothing to call their own. That is why you see them at any time of day surrounded by all this beauty, the only luxury they can afford." My eyes wandered from one huge wall to the next, stopping at each one's magnificent speech of geometry, which spanned the entire distance from floor to ceiling. They caught each tiny inlaid piece of mirror work and each floral arabesque. One easily went dizzy just thinking of those twelfth-century artisans at work.

My mother and I had driven the distance to Qom from Teheran. I was to push a letter penned by Mohammad—and bearing my signature— into the judge's hand. Our mission was to track him down just before he arrived at a weekly-televised Friday prayer gathering, to which he made his way through a narrow dirt alley. The discreet path led to an open area where anxious spectators anticipated a new topic of discussion. My mother and I were asked to remain waiting in Mohammad's mother's living room until such time as Mohammad would show up to fetch me. There, my mother and I sat patiently, our legs folded in Islamic fashion on the Persian carpet. The room was devoid of any furniture, unlike our own living room back in Teheran, where many classically styled European pieces graced the eleventh floor condo apartment of a brand new French-engineered high-rise building. Mohammad may have figured, *a little introduction about the local customs can help her get her mother accustomed to the scene and perhaps begin to feel at home during this maddening pause.*

I remember that, as an aside, he let me know that his mother had frequently called him a rabble-rouser who cleverly frittered precious time away on dangerous pursuits. When I learned that he was thirty-seven years of age, I inwardly corroborated with her view.

He told me he had been kidnapped as a young boy, and that he grew up in a military camp in Palestine with a number of other young boys. These cradle-snatched kids were raised as trained foot soldiers steeped in the military arts to fight the Jewish state. Years later, I read about Ottomon sultans, suspicious of their own generals, who had young boys abducted in Greece and kept in special barracks, trained and bred— and trusted—to safeguard their hegemony over a sprawling empire. I had chanced upon a book in my sister's library by Noel Barber called

Lords of the Golden Horn. In it the adult Janissaries were described as "privileged troops drawn from captured Christian boys, welded into the Empire from an early age, swaggering in their white turbans, loose jackets and yellow boots."[14] They protected their Ottoman masters' hegemony over Greece, parts of Eastern Europe and huge swathes of Arab lands.

When significant losses had been incurred throughout the Empire, the British foreign secretary at the time turned the sultan's attention to the Janissaries' lack of skill in the way of European military standards and methods, fearing that a possible Russian takeover would be disastrous to British interests in India.[15] Sultan Mahmud eventually issued an edict, lured the restless Janissaries into a massive revolt and crushed them into complete annihilation at the hands of secretly prepared battalions led by an unscrupulously devoted officer named Kara Djehennem, or *Black Hell.*[16]

Looking back, one would think that history's lessons wouldn't be lost on the well-read Mohammad, who carried a different book with him each time he came to my sister's home to meet with her and my mother bearing news about developments concerning our father's case.

In his mother's humble home, Mohammad's letter sat on my lap the whole while as my mother and I awaited his return in silence. As it was someone else's handwriting, I daresay I felt as one on the verge of getting caught cheating at a grammar test, for it was composed with an eloquence I was unable to match. As a graduate of an American school with only an hour of Persian a day under my belt, I was humbled by his eloquence and noticed that my thoughts were now centred on wondering whether the poetry of the ancient Sufi masters would become lost on future generations. One forcibly came to sense the erudition of this "rabble-rouser."

---

[14] Noel Barber, *Lords of the Golden Horn: From Suleiman the Magnificent to Kamal Ataturk*, 22-23.

[15] Ibid, 113.

[16] Ibid, 115.

Indeed, that was the first time I had felt badgered by a sense of inadequacy on account of our predominantly American curriculum at the "Little United Nations" that was our Community School in Teheran.[17] Beyond that, it remained that if anyone in the family were sufficiently equipped to act as Mohammad's collaborator, it would have to be me. One thing school had imprinted upon us was a set of tools for critical thinking and the importance of relying on one's own judgment. It was no wonder on that fateful day that my thoughts were on a much loved institution that had been run by a Presbyterian mission—soon to be—if not already, dissolved by a fanatical regime that rained terror over our poetic, picturesque Persia, as it had done, with the virulent gusto of sand in a desert storm.

My story is only half told without an account of the part assured by another player in our midst, as mother and daughter awaited destiny on a Persian carpet in medieval Qom.

Mohammad's mother's was a traditional Iranian home. Persian carpets covered the entire surface of each room; the only furniture was a row of cushions that leant against the modest walls. As the door opened, my heart skipped a beat for fear of being overcome by revolutionary guards. I looked up from behind a pair of weary, blinking eyes that met

---

[17]   J. Richard Irvine, 2009. *Community and Iranzamin Schools, Tehran, Iran.* [essay] The following parts of the 18-page essay were extracted from the original Word version emailed to the editor on the occasion of an alumnus reunion held in Montreal, August 2009. The essay describes the founding and history of the schools discerned by the American Presbyterian Mission's "view of the future brought to fruition (by) Dr. (Samuel Martin) Jordan's intention to bring the 'best Western methods to the needs of the country' while 'retaining all that is good in their own civilization.'" … "Community and Iranzamin Schools where boys and girls from more than fifty countries and nearly every cultural and religious tradition studied together in harmonious mutual esteem; bequeathing to us a marvelous extended family which truly celebrates genuine community amidst the world's diversity" (page 14). "Sarah McDowell, speaking for the Mission's School Committee, stated the objective of the school as 'helping the individual student to find his or her place in our turbulent world and to fill him with a sense of responsibility, an understanding of peoples who come from many cultural backgrounds, and a conviction that life has purpose and meaning'" (page 5).

the figure of a kindly-looking woman who stepped over the threshold, a large, round aluminium tray of food motionlessly balancing on her head.

Suddenly it looked too good to be true, and I shuddered at the thought she may be expecting a party of guests, I flinched at the prospect of having to share our space with strangers. But, to my surprise and amazement, generous portions of steaming white rice and kebobs graciously landed and were being carefully placed on the floor. She smiled at our gaze and turned back into her world, gently closing the door behind her. We ate heartily.

After the dishes were cleared and Mohammad's mother returned with the welcome sound of tiny chinking glasses of tea served in the true Persian way, we spent the rest of our time anticipating how long it would take Mohammad's goatee to show up once again at the white painted wooden frame of the glass door that separated the kind woman's living room from the dreaded world outside.

Counting the minutes, I sensed the presence of someone else in that space besides the mother-daughter duo that we were.

The sun shone bright outside, and stillness reigned within. The brilliant summer light that filtered through the glass pane induced a peculiar emotion that may have peaked, perhaps during better times. It was heavy and blinding. I searched my heartstrings to detect any sign of fear, but touched upon wonderment instead. There was truly another being with us, but I got the sense that I alone was aware of its presence. It didn't take longer than half a minute before I recognized the person who was communicating from a different dimension, a sort of plane that I was obviously connecting onto.

A question was being asked of me, and I got the sense that this presence wasn't going away without an answer anytime soon. I looked toward my mother, whose utter silence likened her to the biblical figure that had turned into a pillar of salt, as it seemed she had no desire to speak a single word or give out as much as a sigh! She seemed to have stepped out of her usual personality for a sort of chosen segment in time.

So, I shifted my focus away from looking for clues from the living, for it was clearly the departed who now kept me company—in a room drowned in silence, where one may have heard a pin drop, even as it could have softly landed on the kind woman's thick, wine coloured Persian carpet.

"Where is Youssef?"

I realized that I was in the presence of someone I knew, and even, who was close of kin. But, then perhaps it was I who tarried in *his* presence. *How did you find me?* Then I realized that, if ever I was going to fathom what this was all about, this was the perfect opportunity to seize the moment—in silence. So I used my thoughts as a channel. I began to sharpen my focus, and I answered him with my thoughts. I replied to my grandfather's spirit that I had suffered my father's absence for long enough. My grandfather had passed away about a decade earlier. I was thirteen when he left our world, succumbing the way he had at the age of 87 to colon cancer.

"Where is Youssef?"

I told him that our grandmother had gone to her grave taking with her the dreaded thought that her beloved eldest son was dead.

A third question mark was minted by a repetition of the phrase, "Where is Youssef?"

He is in Evin ... and ... I am in pain.

"Go and get him."

Me? ... Little, powerless me, overwhelmed most of the time, and spending the rest of it talking about my father? Truly a bore!

But, wait! Help me! Use me if you can! I will be your tool. Guide me Bababozorg! Guide me, Grandpa ... if you can ... to the right place! ... at the right time. Can you help me make all that happen?

"Go and get him."

That was the second time he'd said that.

Further sharpening my focus, my thoughts blurted out: *"I'll do whatever it takes."*

"Go and get him."

That was the third time!

It was empowering. Someone had given me the key to a chest of treasures. Truly!

If God had been watching over us, I had for many months become numb to the feeling. There was a time, some time after our country had turned itself upside down, when I remember feeling that the mullahs were mightier than the Almighty. But, who was nudging me with encouragement in a medieval city many kilometres to the south of our capital city? Who was this lofty spirit elbowing me to bigger things than my cup was able to handle without overflowing or getting jinxed in the process?

Surely, my grandfather made of himself a messenger to inspire and imbue his loved ones with the spirit of better days. During his time within our realm, he loved with unmatched fervour. Was there a reason to question his concern for those who knew him as their patriarch, such as something so immaterial, apparently as far as he was concerned—as the fact of being deceased? And, yes, if there were a lesson to be learned that afternoon, it definitely was that there *truly was* one! What a strange and yet wondrous thought!

What a lesson in self-confidence, indeed! I decided to take the conversation a step further and engage my grandfather in a friendly—and less serious—exchange. How special it was to have a chance to enjoy my grandfather's company indefinitely, now that I had him within *thinking* distance. *We could have seized the opportunity together to reminisce*, I thought, *upon former days when the whole family was reunited under yours and Nanati Grandma's roof for Passover or Roshashana?*

Wait…! no sooner had such thoughts infiltrated my mental space, than I was forced to make sense of his withdrawal, and it dawned upon me that he was ready to exit from that other dimension that seemed to be my abode for a brief segment of time. Alas! Abandonment wasn't the word. It was more like water disappearing from a tub after someone had pulled the stopper.

Bababozorg (grandfather in Persian) unsuspectingly retreated into the realm from whence he had come. Our conversation had lasted long enough—just long enough—to establish reconnaissance and leave me with a mission before withdrawing into the void.

Pacing back nostalgically down memory lane, there I found *Bababozorg* with his small, classic, leather-bound transistor capturing Arabic tunes from Iraqi radio while crickets pinched the night air with song in the watered garden below. We trickled down, my siblings and I, to watch *him* play solitaire and listen curiously to Iraqi tunes from across the border. My cousins and siblings and I took turns on his lap as pieces of pitted watermelon hung suspended a few excruciating moments on a fork above our expecting palates. That was the magic of a typical summer night on the balcony of the downstairs level which my grandparents and *Nanati's* sister, *Khaleh* (maternal aunt in Persian) occupied below our upper level home.

He clobbered us one by one in the game of cards to which we succumbed, each time without exception, and to *Nanati's* dismay. She had a habit of brokering concessions on our behalf, saying that there was no shame in allowing us even half a chance. He, however, was unrelenting, knew his role to awaken the young and unprepared ahead of life's challenges, and, as with anything else he accomplished in his 87 years, he went about it passionately…soulfully.

The voice in the sunlit room convinced me that there were forces ready and willing to help in the course of my journey. I was certain that my grandfather was the higher power I had been seeking to elbow me into action. All that remained to be done was to do—*or die!*

After our two hours of silence, Mohammad showed up once again at the wood-framed glass door of his mother's house. I received my cue to get up and follow him, since the judge was now making his way to the famed Friday prayers. Clad in my white *chador,* Persian for the Iranian body-length veil, I briskly skipped, then trudged along a narrow, dusty alleyway. In a heartbeat, I lost sight of the adventurous *mujahed* whose tall, slender and agile figure surreptitiously slipped behind the mud wall of a nearby home and found myself following the precise instructions he had painstakingly trained me to stick to.

As the big brown *abaya*—the mullah's attire—drew closer, I reminded myself to avoid eye contact or the exchange of even a syllable with the turbaned figure. I slipped the letter in his hand and scurried back on my tracks, not knowing where I was in relation to the house we had left moments earlier. The turbaned figure had passed out of our field of vision, and I was overrun by relief when Mohammad suddenly made himself visible once again, after anxiously awaiting my return. Needless to say, the mission was accomplished, and a sense of victory swept over both of us. *We're inching,* I dared to imagine, *almost head to head with an answer to the question of our ceaseless wait for an overdue verdict on a factory related court case.*

Purportedly, a sort of leniency had crept into the judge's attitude toward my father shortly after the outset of the trial—or so my father told us from behind the glass pane of our visitation booth. For my part, I just lived and breathed simply through my mother's hopes—hopes that wove and strove their way into her heart and consciousness, as days turned into months and months into years. They were entirely based on my father's reassurances during visitation. As such, and unbeknownst to me at the time, he was in all likelihood exempt from the prospect of facing a firing squad.

There was a flip side to her optimism. Further false testimony by a band of frenzied workers turned our dilemma into two years of agony over the phone after the trial, with the only answer to my mother's pleas being, "*Khahar*, Sister, call back next week ... *hafteyeh ayandeh*."

As the number of executions increased, families lost loved ones to administrative blunders. There was a serious risk that my father's file could get mired in the melee. A counter-revolution was foiled. Members of the failed coup were being mowed down by the firing squad at the rate of twenty per night for two consecutive months. How did we know? They were neatly lined up on our television screens while a prosecutor fired questions from behind a camera, a warning to anyone at large who may have been cooking up a similar project.

At the southern tip of Teheran is an old edifice dating back to the era of the *Shahanshah*—King of Kings—where I was headed on a winter morning. It was imperative to meet with a contact of Mohammad's at the *Kakh-é-dadgostari* city courthouse in the *Maidan-é-Sepah* Square, formerly *Maidan-é-Toopkhaneh*. He had been briefed on the details of my father's case. He was going to be my mentor, and through him, I was entrusted to carve my own path of access to his contact in the office where the archives were kept at Evin.

I watched the city I loved pass by as the packed bus jolted me against a windowpane, my shoulder leaning with all the strength it could muster. It was like going through a time machine, and though I wanted the illusion not to dwindle, I was soon catapulted back by the discomfiting sight of slush and signs of the bitter winter outside, as a reluctant mass of humanity pressed against my white chador with each jerk. *Could they not have purchased brakes from my father's factory for that wobbling thing they called a bus?* Since the West's economic embargo, spare parts were hard to come by. Nevertheless, I believed with every ounce of muscle that each jolt was bringing me closer to the object of my mission—and the brave new world outside.

Once inside the courthouse, I spotted the famous German-educated Mullah Beheshti busily crossing the wide marble floors of the upper level where Mohammad's contact would meet with me. Ayatollah Mohammad Beheshti was the main figure of the Islamic Republic Party (IRP) whose creation was approved by Khomeini in February 1979 just after the revolution. He held a Ph.D. in religious studies from Teheran University, spoke English and German, and had been appointed in the seventies by the shah's government to head the Islamic Centre in Hamburg. The IRP "had ties to armed paralegal forces like the Revolutionary Guard [*pasdaran*], created by Khomeini in May 1979, and the violent groups called hezbollah" [party of God in Persian], which disrupted demonstrations and attacked dissidents. To entrench his power to cover every region, "Khomeini appointed IRP-endorsed *ulama* as Friday prayer leaders in nearly all cities and as his representatives in government bodies,"[18] My father's judge, whom I met in the dirt alleyway in Qom, was one of them.

Dr. Beheshti was an ex student of Khomeini. He took opposing views against Bani Sadr, Iran's President and armed forces commander during the Iran-Iraq war, whom Khomeini dismissed after being criticized by him for his leadership. From hiding, Bani Sadr, who never tried to create a party or coalition, called for an uprising, and sided with the Mujahedin. When the latter rallied against Bani Sadr's impeachment, Hezbollah killed some of them, which instigated an armed struggle against the regime. In June 1981 Ayatollah Beheshti, leader of the clerical regime's judicial system, was among seventy men killed by a bomb at an IRP leadership conference. This event and the assassination of the chief of Teheran's main prison was blamed on the Mujahedin, and fierce repression was followed by thousands of executions.[19]

I felt the muscles of my face flinch at the sight of the life figure of the black cloaked, though scholarly looking figure cross the broad marble squares below his sweeping gait, then quickly bent my face to glimpse at the suite number jotted on a paper stub in my hands, which remained miraculously dry despite the messiness of the morning's journey across town. Still stunned at having caught a glimpse of Beheshti, *or was it an apparition?*, I quickly spotted the same number on a door to my right.

I knocked with a slight hesitation and entered to find Mohammad's courthouse contact greet me from behind a glass-topped desk.

---

[18]   Nikki R Keddie, *Modern Iran: Roots and Results of Revolution*, 243-44.

[19]   Ibid, 253.

How strange that it was so clear of any clutter, or anything at all, for that matter. Wasting no time, he quickly got down to business and said I had two choices: I was either to trust him—and if that were the case, he expected me to follow his instructions to the letter—or there was nothing in his power that could possibly get me closer to my goal.

When I gave him the assurance he needed that I could be a good listener, he said that he knew a good person, a well-meaning young man inside Evin's compound stationed in the office that housed the prison files and archives. The young man had helped other women just like me ... women who had come to him as a last resort. As if to assure himself that I understood his solid intentions, he offered phrases in a manner I still remember, uttered as one does a dirge, with a solemn tone that laced every word almost mechanically, in order to express the essence of what I needed to comprehend: "I have seen many like you, all of them mothers, sisters, daughters ... and the list goes on. You have to trust me or remain at your own risk."

And so, after the Qom excursion to meet the judge who had his own Friday prayer—and the more esoteric details of which I hid from anything that had ears, and now that the meeting with this city courthouse bureaucrat friend of Mohammad too had crystallized, the mujahed was ready with a folder he had prepared for me to take inside the prison compound.

This time, I would meet his friend's contact in the room with the prisoners' files and archives. Inside the folder was a two-page spread of a newspaper article and copy of the letter I had given the judge in the dusty alley in Qom. The letter essentially highlighted the article from Teheran's daily, *Kayhan*, which accused my father and his partner of all kinds of wrongdoings, even as there was yet no judgment delivered since the time of a court hearing two years before it was published. The time had arrived to deliver Mohammad's carefully prepared folder to the bureaucrat's contact in Evin.

My new assignment began at seven in the morning one spring day of that same year. I was told to come back at two in the afternoon, so I sat under the scorching sun until the start of regular visitation hours, which began promptly at the designated time. Picking myself up from the dusty knoll outside the prison gate, I made my way toward it once again, this time mentally rehearsing what the guard needed to hear. Mohammad had told me to paint him a verbal picture of what it may be like to live without a male guardian in such dangerous times. *Was the judge able to imagine a similar scenario for his own daughter, to live in fear and fret for her mother's safety every night?*

He looked above my head, and I figured that was either because my grandfather's spirit was hovering over my head with the most beautiful bright light, or because he wasn't allowed to look a woman straight in the eyes.

Frightened to the bone lest he discover the file under my chador, I made it to the women's physical search quarters right next to the entrance. As the old woman approached to frisk the front of my body, I slid my father's file—a standard egg white–coloured folder—against my lower back. As I surreptitiously slid the file folder forward to hug my belly, I felt the smelly hands of the old woman checking me from behind. *She either didn't have the smarts, or simply stuck to the regime's rules of prudishness,* I thought as my sister, Maureen's label of 'the bitch of Buchenwald' came to mind. She didn't make me take off the white *chador,* my long veil! I chuckled to myself at Maureen's label, which so accurately described her bat-like figure. It approached us before each visitation in order to perform the dreaded task of frisking for firearms at the women's entrance.

I figured anything was possible once that ordeal was behind me. I focused my thoughts on my brother, a college student in Boston trying to make it to the finish line with meagre funds from whatever our mother was able to scrape together. I thought of Maureen and her husband and their children—their life in Teheran was at a standstill awaiting my father's return from the jaws of hell. I thought of my sister, Cynthia, whose days were riddled with worry for our father while taking care of her husband and daughters in her new home in Naples, Italy. But, most of all, I thought of my mother, who cried every evening before going to bed thinking of her husband, and of my brother most probably going to bed hungry on many nights in far-off Emrika – which the Teheran clerics had labelled the big Satan, *Shaytaneh-Bozorg.*

Life was a relentless procession of waiting rooms. Then, up in the administration's filing room there stood, indeed, a kindly-looking young man. He came forward introducing himself, and then asked my name, and finally politely confirmed that he had received word of my visit from Mohammad's contact in the *Kakh-é-dadgostari* courthouse building.

I stood in the midst of desk after desk piled high with prisoner files, bursting with suspense for the next stage in my seemingly unending quest for Eldorado. The young man recalled the countless women—mothers, sisters, daughters alike—who regularly sought him out for assistance. They were all victims, he said, and they all deserved to be treated as human beings. He said he was quite aware of the extent of our suffering and was willing to do whatever it took to help us. His main concern was to get on with the task of identifying my father's file with utmost discretion. He stressed that it needed to remain under strict supervision to avoid accidentally steering an innocent loved one into harm's way.

I remember only now the way he looked with agitation toward the pile of folders that buried my father's file. He spoke of his frustration at seeing the guards come in and have their way with the documents, sometimes taking one folder from the top of the pile and sliding it between some others at the bottom.

As he said this, he saw bewilderment on my face. So he repeated the explanation, this time going through the motions, mimicking the gestures of somebody pulling a file from the top of a stack and slipping it somewhere toward the bottom. He told me that he tried to keep a tab on my father's file, that he remembered the name on it, but that he distinctly noticed that the folder with that familiar name kept eluding him, and that it was none of his own doing. He assured me that this time he would mark the folder I had brought underneath my white chador in such manner as to recognize its edges from among the stacks of other files. My head spun with rage and confusion as he went on, and I was unable to hang onto his words.

After expressing amazement at how I managed to pass through security with my folder intact, he told me that my next step and only hope was to speak to the judge! He allowed me to digest the thought.

Then, after some reflection, I asked the kindly young man when the judge was normally scheduled to arrive at Evin and what his vehicle looked like. I studied the image of tall piles of folders standing on several desks next to his, and noticed that I was gripped by certain fear for his safety while he attempted to help families like ours. If people on our side of the cruel spectrum were looking for kindness in a world where evil had taken charge, I now knew there were truly some precious souls who wished kindness upon us, even though they were part of the cruel apparatus of the mullahs. I recalled the mental torture and the rotten phrase, "*Khahar,* Sister, call back next week … *hafteyeh ayandeh,*" and looked wide-eyed with wonderment as he repeated the ordeal of how, time and again, my father's file eluded him, because someone had placed it out of view back under the heap each time it managed to make its way to up the top. It seemed that some people in the factory paid the prison administrators to keep the file under, thereby barring the partners from their plant.

My efforts on Dad's behalf culminated in a stunning incident before the prison gate. It was a sunny afternoon again, on the day I made it back to Evin. The idea of remaining anchored to my mission was cemented onto every cell of my body. Suddenly, I intercepted our judge's bullet-proof Peugeot as it pulled up to the huge cast-iron door. In a split second, there were only two thoughts that crossed my mind: Youssef Koukou had been good to his workers, and we had nothing left to lose!

I was banking on the fact that my father was a kind soul, and the Universe surely had better things in store for the gentler among humankind. After all, I was a product of the Community High School of Teheran, trained by a curriculum that encouraged intellectual rigour. A Presbyterian mission under the tutelage of a dynamic American principal and primarily American teachers, it was the place and time when we were taught to believe in a better world, and I was about to make it so, at least for my family.

There I was with my right hand outstretched, index finger pointing straight ahead. The judge's smoked glass windshield made it difficult to make out his turban from where I stood just ahead of the olive green Peugeot station wagon. Was it my white chador billowing as it did like a peace flag in the summer breeze?

To be sure, the events that followed convinced one that this ironclad persistence could hardly have been camouflaged by a long white veil, the same one which the judge would have recognized as having followed him on his way to deliver Friday prayers to a regularly huge crowd in Qom!

As I stood immobile by the fender, I allowed the veil to communicate an unspoken message toward the vehicle that there was business to settle with the big guy in the back. Thus far, he was still mine, though soon to be swallowed by the opening doors of the prison grounds behind.

Once again I tried to make out exactly where he was seated in the rear of the station wagon, unsure which figure I was pointing at. My right arm struck out like a scarecrow's from my, by then, billowing white chador, index finger pointed toward the smoked glass. My twenty-three-year-old frame stood resolute against the likely stolen or confiscated vehicle. A crowd consisting of awestricken family members on visitation quickly formed around the judge's heavily armoured, luxurious looking French Peugeot.

Suddenly, a *pasdar* revolutionary guard jumped out of the back of the vehicle and pointed his rifle in my direction. With my eardrums packing a solid pounding, I thought, *Oh, dear, perhaps this whole idea of go-and-get-him is all for naught—and what, pray tell, was I thinking?* Besides pounding a tune of a thousand and one, my heartbeat sounded louder than I had ever heard before, clamouring to be heard…saying, *"I'm still here!"*

It also seemed too late to turn back!

My eyes caught sight of a glistening object. Approaching me was the shiny edge of the *pasdar's* rifle. My first thought was not to overstay my welcome and confusedly let myself be whisked away from the green cast iron prison door that still towered above us. A nearby female voice approached and whispered, *"Khanoum, is that how it's done?"* The angry revolutionary guard slammed the prison door behind me, and the world quickly slipped into a haze as my mother caught my weight into her embrace.

The big green gate had by now shut behind the bullet-proof Peugeot of my father's judge, and I remembered very little from that point forward, other than the fact that we were back to square one … and perhaps even further behind.

Had I ruined everything? What were the consequences of hope and positive action in that backward world of chadors, turbans, and black beards? My shaking body regained consciousness inside the folds of my mother's black chador. I felt the terror stitched in her jaws, as she pleaded, "Sandra, have you any idea what you are up to?"

I slowly regained consciousness. The prison door came ajar. Out slipped the agile body of the previously furious revolutionary guard. He carried a different demeanour. His hands were free, and his calm gait made him look serene and approachable.

"Agha wants to see you. You will need to go inside. His car is standing not far behind the door."

Was this the beginning of the end? That question was answered soon after I made my way toward the green door, arms braided into my mother's. To my amazement, the right rear window of the car slowly came down to reveal the rock star features of a handsome face. It was topped with a turban that framed some of the most interesting features for one who was infamously known for his cruel methods. Blue eyes, milky white skin, and a well-trimmed red goatee turned a fascinated gaze in my direction to acknowledge my presence with a dignified nod. It felt as though he was nodding to all the Persians there were in the world with one sweeping gesture.

"Who do you have here?"

"My father."

"What is his name?"

"Youssef Koukou."

"Do you see that kiosk?"

I nodded.

"The person inside will give you a ticket." Then he added, "Who is with you?"

"My mother."

There seemed to be a fixed interest and determination in the judge's gestures. "The man in the kiosk will give both of you tickets. He will also give you directions to the second floor. That will be the administration department. Do you see the kiosk?"

I nodded again.

"Go then, he will give you two tickets which you will keep with you." I wondered what my father had done to the judge during his trial to have left such a lasting effect on him. Even though my dad had always been perfectly capable of charming ruffians into gentler tones, this was all too theatrical a scene for my waking eyes to digest, especially after having regained consciousness only seconds earlier.

At last, my mother and I were on the second floor where Agha stood in his dark brown *abaya* mullah's attire in the company of five male figures. Typically loyal to fanatical Islamic tradition, the absence of ties made them look like thugs in plain dark suits by the Western standards we were more accustomed to. They stood together in a row flanking the judge on either side.

"Who do you have here?" he asked again.

"Youssef Koukou," I answered to this larger audience.

"Where is the file?"

"It's here; I brought it myself a few days ago." I told him about the young man who took possession of the file in the archive room, and described the room in detail. I mentioned that I had seen lots of documents and that the desks were piled high with folders.

I had passed my veracity test! It was now clearer than ever that the man in whose hands life itself hung in the balance like a bead on a rosary had recognized the young girl who had followed him in the dusty alleyway in Qom—in her white chador. Without further ado, he sternly addressed the five stationary figures to his left and to his right without moving his neck. They resembled those figures on the chessboard of life that Mohammad described one day as he came away exasperated from a meeting he had set up for my mother with a certain mullah.

And then came the judge's orders: "The file must be on my desk promptly on Monday *Do-Shanbeh* at ten in the morning."

"When will I have a judgment?" I pressed on. After all, why leave important matters to hang in midair? Asked when our next visitation was, I quickly offered, "In two weeks, on a Wednesday!"

"Well, now that you know how to find me..."

His sentence hung in mid-air, and I spied the beginnings of a smile on the corner of his mouth, just enough for me alone to detect it from the new angle at which he stood. He left the sentence unfinished.

I let myself take a liking to this big authority figure standing as he did in his long brown robe. Without words, his role in the grand scheme of things came through loud and clear, and so did those of the men who flanked him on the chessboard of power. At last the two year mystery was clear as daylight: those were the very individuals who, for a fee, kept the file 'under' during my mother's endless months of 'Sister, call back next week.'

I paused to stare at them dumbfounded, but quickly grabbed at my mother's arm to leave, so as not to overdo the welcome. He asked me about the tickets I had been given at the kiosk, without telling us explicitly that without them my mother and I would never be allowed to leave the prison premises. I respectfully replied that I still had the two stubs. The air seemed thick with a fat, uneasy silence. I grasped the tickets tightly in my left hand and shook my hand slightly, ruffling the side of my chador to make sure what I had just said was correct.

My mother and I tugged against each other all the way back down the stuffy stairway that was so pregnant with the sigh of death. After making it down the last level of what I now recall as the stairway to hell, we found ourselves back in the courtyard. My only thought on the way down was to avoid looking back lest I, too, in true biblical fashion, would turn into a mere pillar of salt, if not physically, then figuratively, but most certainly—emotionally!

Two weeks passed, and I stopped the judge's car again at the appointed time. The driver opened the window and quickly blurted something that sounded like, "Come back in two weeks." Another fortnight passed, and I was determined to see the fruits of my endeavours. I showed up in front of the judge's car yet once again. Every window's smoky greyness masked the turbaned figure inside. In a mad panic, I crossed the courtyard back to our women's waiting room and flashed my gaze toward the guard at the glass entrance.

"The judge has a message for me, and the driver refuses to stop," I managed to blurt out between the anxious coughs, the dust in the air exacerbating the dryness in my throat.

The next thing I heard has remained as a drumbeat in my left ear ever since that sunny Evin afternoon: "I will help you!"

With that, the guard got another one to cover for him and turned to run in the direction of a seventeen-seater minibus that was just about to exit the first interior checkpoint of the prison compound. The judge's green vehicle immediately behind had about a hundred meters to go before reaching the main cast-iron gate that gave out to the street. The guard engaged the driver in conversation, buying me time. I knew the only thing left to do was to lower my head to allow the judge to recognize me from his back seat. Sure enough and to my wide amazement, the reluctant driver of the vehicle, forced as he was to open his window once again, instructed me to meet him at the tall green main gate at the street exit.

It was like standing at the apogee of snow-capped Damavand, that perfectly cone-shaped mountain just outside of Teheran, which was believed to be a live volcano. For once, I was *not* feeling ridiculously immaterial in the face of the powers that be. For once, *they* were less powerful than God! There I was at the summit of success in my attempt to harness the attention of the ultimate decision maker at Evin. Exhilarating?

To be sure, it may not have been the same feeling looking up from the feet of snow white Damavand, which everyone and the poets had likened to a bride. I was positioned at the head of a snaking line of cars in a queue deep inside the womb of a prison compound, next to our blessed women's waiting room, and a *pasdar* was willing to abet me in my scheme.

In short, I had reached home base. I was, essentially, poised to squeeze a judgment out of the turban in charge!

Outside the prison gate, the *pasdar* who had come out from the seat next to the driver's welcomed me with a look of disdain and blurted out a few broken phrases, as though spitting verbal diarrhoea. "Mr. Engineer—what's his name?" (I hadn't a clue.). "Two years, *do-sal.* Mr. Monabaty the partner, three years, *seh-sal.* Mr. Koukou, is that your father?"

Silence. Bewildered silence. "That is your father, isn't it?"

"Yes ... Youssef Koukou is his name."

"Five years, *panj-sal.*"

As the vehicle sped away, an avalanche of emotion overtook my senses from head to toe, and I stood awash with a feeling of gratefulness that our months of agony reached the finish line. Soon we learned of my father's transfer to Ghezel-hesar, far from the sound of the executioner's fire. An hour's drive from Teheran on a road that drove past my father's factory, this other prison was a safer place for him to mete out a pre-determined—not *un*determined—period of time as a guest of one of the cruellest regimes in history.

Six months later, I serendipitously found myself ambling into a newspaper outlet to grab off the stand one of the last copies of *Time* magazine to appear anywhere in the country. When I reached the "People and Milestones" section, one particular entry caught my attention about a widely feared, high-ranking cleric of the ruling regime in Teheran. I rubbed my eyes to make sure I had read properly. The name belonged to our red-haired judge who had sentenced his twenty-something son to the will of the executioner. The young man had opposed his father's sentences on the heads of those counterrevolutionaries we had watched for two months on television. The members of the *mujahedeen-e-khalgh* organization were alleged Communist sympathizers, an eyesore to the regime. Their coup to topple the political apparatus of the supreme leader of the Islamic Republic of Iran had just been foiled, henceforth the appearance before the camera in groups of twenty each. By next dawn they were no more.

As for Mohammad, the *mujahed*, he told me I was unique among the young women who came back to Iran from studies abroad, in that I had remained a truly Persian girl. I watched with disdain as he gave himself reason to confiscate a self-portrait I have painted in oils during the heady high school days. It was a major piece that meant a lot to me—along with our Golden Age that had already stepped out the door. I had learned all about oil painting at a private studio owned by a local artist and his father. My art instructor's oil paintings were of mythical figures such as Mithra and other ancients from Persian literature; they seemed to have walked onto his life size canvases with delicate steps to show us all the rich tapestry woven by Persian mythology.

Riding a cab one day, I sat shell shocked in the seat in the back, recognizing the man in the front sitting next to the driver and deeply regretted what happened next. Instead of risking betrayal by the cab driver to the morality police, I remained silent, wondering what Persia's artists were doing to survive in a world parallel to that which the mullahs had modelled for us.

4

JOURNEY TO THE OTHER SIDE OF HELL

THAT WAS MY BELOVED DAUGHTER, SANDRA'S ACCOUNT of events as they unfolded outside the walls of Evin. At the onset of my disappearance, my wife, Evelyn, learned soon enough that, in the name of God, our factory was confiscated by the Islamic court, and a freeze was placed on our family's real estate. We passed the time by telling stories and keeping in a relatively positive frame of mind. Whenever an inmate was depressed, there was a buddy to remind him to make better and ensure a more enjoyable stay "because outside those walls there lays an even bigger prison."

One day my former cellmate, the restaurant owner, met with my wife after finding out that one of his employees had contacts within the system. He obviously pulled a few strings and was able to obtain my release six months before the end of my five-year term. I was free to go home. After being told my time had ended, I was transferred back to Evin to sign some release papers, and along with another inmate in his eighties I was led to the exit door at its main gate.

Everything was strange to us outside. We had no chance of finding a taxi, but a private car showed up and I signalled to the driver. I asked him to take us home for whatever he was willing to charge. Once inside the car, the good man asked us where we were heading. We each gave our addresses. He thought for a while and looked blankly back at us: Teheran had no streets that went by those names. He was amazed at our apparent lack of orientation. We later understood that the new regime had changed the names of most streets, mostly naming them after the martyrs of the revolution. One street's name had become "Khalid-e-Islambuli," after the assassin of President Anwar el-Sādāt of Egypt, who had signed a peace treaty with Israel.

I resorted to physically showing him the way to my home, and his kindness was such that he accepted nothing in return. During our short journey the driver asked the reason we did not know our way home. We told him we had just been freed from doing time in Evin, and we knew little of what had been going on outside. When he asked my companion the reason he had been jailed, he replied that he had composed a poem against Ayatollah Khomeini; the poem had been found in a drawer of his desk in his office. The good man excitedly asked him to recite the poem, to which the old man replied, "No thanks, I've already done time in jail."

I am forever grateful to the courage of my wife, Evelyn, and dedication of my daughters, Maureen and Sandra, who remained in Iran as long as it took for me to know freedom once again.

Jews were not allowed to leave the country—they were kept as hostages in their own countries, much as they were in Syria and other countries whose legislation was hostile to minorities. There were special circumstances, however, in which it was necessary to visit an immediate relative or get medical treatment for an ailment. In such cases, an exit visa came on the back of a guarantor's signature as a promissory note for their return.

The administrative body responsible for issuing exit visas was run by inexperienced *pasdars*, those dreaded revolutionary guards, who conducted their operations inside a small, confiscated house. It was no coincidence that long lines of applicants formed outside the building. People were showing up on average twice a week over two months in a row before being allowed to get in to sign the necessary paperwork.

During one of our excursions, I noticed a group of *pasdars* joking about the anguish of some of the Jewish applicants outside. They were pleading to be allowed inside. I felt so degraded watching that scenario and called upon what courage as I had, got out of my car, and approached them. I greeted them respectfully and reminded them that these people were the descendants of their Persian ancestors of 2,500 years ago. I told them that amongst the thousands of prisoners in the country, one hardly found a Jewish killer, rapist, bank robber, or such, and they deserved better treatment. I got no answer from them—and one by one, they went back to duty.

I went back to my car slightly heartened. While my wife was still inside filing a request for her exit visa, I reflected on Cyrus the Great, the Persian monarch who in biblical times played a phenomenal role toward the liberation of Jews in captivity, and whose name was "unconditionally praised" and mentioned twenty-two times in The Book. "Cyrus the Great (ca. 600 – 530 B.C.E.) was a towering figure in the history of mankind. As the 'father of the Iranian nation,' he was the first world leader to be referred to as 'The Great.' Cyrus founded the first world empire – and the second Iranian dynastic empire (the Achaemenids) – after defeating the Median dynasty and uniting the Medes with the other major Iranian tribe, the Persians." The Circle of Ancient Iranian Studies (online) further relates that his conquests triggered the age of empire building, not only by his successors, but later by the Greeks and Romans. The famous Cyrus Cylinder, housed in London's British Museum, has been hailed as the world's first declaration of human rights. Inscribed in Akkadian cuneiform and discovered in 1878 in Iraq, it details his conquest of Babylon in 539 B.C.E. and his subsequent humane treatment of the people who came under his rule. The Cyrus Cylinder explains how this benevolent ruler established peace and abolished forced labour: "The people of Babylon . . . the shameful yoke was removed from them."[20]

I continued to ruminate over the Bible's unambiguous portrayal of Cyrus as a righteous ruler, a "'shepherd of Yahweh'" who tolerated diversity within the imperial fold, and who, in keeping with such a policy, issued a decree in 538 B.C.E. to allow the Jews to return to Jerusalem and rebuild their Temple. Cyrus' proclamation promptly encouraged Jews remaining in Babylon to finance the venture, and had even gone as far as pledging the return of the sacred vessels that Nebuchadnezzar had removed from the Temple and placed in those of the local Babylonian gods. Abba Eban cites from the Book of Ezra where an even more generous pledge was made. Persia not only paid for the rebuilding of the Temple, but supplied even the animals and other

---

[20]   Circle of Ancient Iranian Studies, The (CAIS),1999. *Cyrus the Great, the Father and Liberator.* [online] Available at: <http://www.cais-soas.com/CAIS/History/ hakhamaneshian/Cyrus-the-great/cyrus_the_great.htm>. [Accessed 10 September 2011].

means for the sacrifices to resume there,[21] as had been the tradition before the Babylonian conquest of Jerusalem.

> *Moreover I make a decree what ye shall do to the elders of these Jews for the building of this house of God: that of the king's goods, even of the tribute beyond the river, forthwith expenses be given unto these men, that they be not hindered.* (Ezra. 6:8)

In 537 B.C.E. a prince of Judah named Sheshbazzar led a small group of Jews back to the City of David. Unsurprisingly, only a minority of the Babylonian Jews chose to make this journey. "By this time the Jews were well established in Babylon, with their own distinctive commercial, political, and religious institutions, and had little reason to fear their new Persian rulers. Babylon for the Jews was the America of ancient times."[22]

My family descended from those Jews who chose to remain even after being governed by the new rulers, the Persians, for more than 200 years at the time in Babylon, known today as modern Iraq, where they had once been brought as captives from Jerusalem. My family remained in Babylon for roughly 2,500 years up until the 1930's, when my father moved our family to Isfahan in central Iran when a contact at a car dealership opened the path to a new business opportunity.

As these and similar recollections flooded my mind, I was finally called upon to sign the paper of guarantee for my wife's return. The *pasdar* asked me if I was sure my wife would come back.

"What does it matter to the Islamic Republic if she returns or not?" I asked. He coldly instructed me to sign the document and leave.

Soon after, I was able to see Evelyn off at Teheran's Mehrabad Airport where she stood on Persian soil for one last time. She flew to Naples in Italy where our daughter, Cynthia, lived with her husband, Eli, and two

---

[21] Abba Eban. *Heritage: Civilization and the Jews*, 70-71.

[22] Ibid, 71.

daughters at the time. My daughter, Maureen, and her family eventually found their way to the United States. Sandra married an expatriate Belgian engineer at the company where she worked. I was promised and then denied a leave of absence to be present at a small reception in our home. She and her husband, at the end of his contract, left to Belgium about a year before my release from prison.

After working at a government job for some time, I too abandoned the soil of Persia for good, to adopt a homeland far from that of my biblical ancestors and all that my family had cherished over the half century we lived in Iran.

Through some friends, I was introduced to a smuggler who regularly transported his clients across the border to Pakistan. Our contract was a verbal agreement; payment was required in full and in advance—in hard cash. I was told to await further signals for the next step in this clandestine operation. Like all my fleeing compatriots, I once again needed my unwavering trust in God. There was no written contract with these experts in contraband who charged fortunes—at times one's entire life savings—to guarantee the safety of the many desperate Iranians who chose to leave their beloved homeland. One was never certain that they were not, in fact, placing their lives and possessions in criminal hands. This thought often gave one pause to ponder the wise admonishments of my prison inmates to bide the time as best we could, since the world outside was a much bigger prison than the one we were locked inside.

Days passed until the smuggler finally called to detail plans to arrange my flight down to Zahedan, the province in the south-east on the border of Pakistan, at which point a certain individual was to signal me to follow him.

At the Zahedan airport, a man took me to a cottage where I met up with a group of Jews possessing the same itinerary as mine. We ate a hearty dinner. Soon after our meal someone entered the cottage to tell us it was time to leave. We were herded into a pickup truck and laid low on its flatbed totally hidden from view. We remained in that position all the way until the truck reached the city limits. The truck's bumpy, nightlong trek along a dirt road took us close to the border, guided by a full moon as our headlights.

It was cold. Since I had drunk a lot of liquid at the meal prior to our trek across the desert terrain, nature's call pressed hard. I passed a message to the driver to stop for a moment, but for reasons of safety, he refused. An hour passed before I repeated my plea. The driver gave me two minutes. I stepped down from the truck only to find out that my system refused to evacuate, forcing the impatient driver to wait a few more arduous minutes until I finally relieved myself and got back on the truck.

At about six o'clock in the morning, we reached a mountain close to the Pakistani border. We were instructed to climb up the hill while a couple of mule drivers carried our belongings. It took us three hours to reach the summit, where we were told that we had reached our destination. Two Pakistani station wagons awaited us. After eating a humble breakfast, we were delivered to Quetta, the border city where a United Nations office provided temporary passports for refugees to facilitate the issuance of visas by consulates in several other countries. Our place of rest was a two-star hotel in Quetta, where I was able to call Evelyn, who was still in Italy with our daughter, Cynthia, anxious to receive news of my escape. With valid passports in our pockets, we were flown into Karachi and lodged in an inn, whereby we were left to fend for ourselves from that point forward.

The verbal package deal made with my smuggler covered all expenses up to that point, at which time he returned all the valuables he had withheld from us at the start of the journey. He asked me if all had been satisfactory, and I showed my thanks by telling him that he would remain in my memory forever as a real gentleman.

Once in Karachi, I called Evelyn one more time, and learned that a visa was ready to be stamped on my passport at the Swiss Consulate. After getting my passport stamped with the visa, I booked a flight to Zurich which was scheduled to leave the following day.

At Karachi's airport, everything was okay up to the point of boarding, when a well-dressed officer asked to see my papers. He claimed that I needed an exit permit from the foreign ministry! "Yes and no," I said. "I am your guest here in transit from Iran, expecting your help."

The answer was, "As a dear guest you can stay in my house tonight and get your papers done tomorrow."

Aware that I had to think quickly before losing my flight and possibly face another chain of murky events, I added, "I think I have another paper," and discreetly placed a fifty-dollar note under the passport. He told me it wasn't enough. Relieved that money was the solution, I added another thirty dollars, whereupon he led me into the plane and wished me a safe journey.

As the plane took off for the free world, a Swissair hostess asked if I wanted a drink—and I struggled to overcome utter shock at being offered an alcoholic beverage after being deprived of such a simple pleasure, one that we had taken so much for granted during better times. I asked for champagne and sipped with glee while silently repeating a prayer in my heart. For it was faith that had given me one end of a rope, and just as the plane lifted off the runway, I was certain that God was pulling at the other end. How good it was to have kept my trust in Him, for He had driven me through the valley of the shadow of death and verily delivered me from evil!

As for my partner and I, we both eventually ended up in "God Bless America" and remained good friends until several years later, in 2003, when I was saddened to learn that he had passed away from heart failure.

I obtained political asylum in the United States and met many other signs of God's grace, and many people—some devout, others agnostic, still others who turned away from their roots. Most people fell into one of two categories: they were either on the far right following dogma to the letter, or had moved away from religion altogether. More than a few asked me what made me so enthusiastic about my faith. From a host of discussions I shared with many on the topic of spirituality and faith, I sensed a growing urge compelling me to share the essence of my own personal convictions. I had gained so much insight joyfully studying that page-turner that I call The Book.

I continued to read and reread the written word.

My studies eventually culminated in a moment of clarity, where Scripture seemed much simpler to understand than many interpretations may have had us believe. I continued to search deep into my heart while reading on and found much solace in directly rediscovering the words of the prophets and feeling the beauty of God's message. I decided there was no better time to write about an epiphany that slowly but surely crouched into my soul with such clarity.

It was during a walk in the park under the shade of some of Great Neck's thick vegetation that I was, for a reason unbeknownst to me compelled to write, for what it was worth. Something compelled me to synthesize what stood out, for me, as key in unlocking the towering theme of the Hebrew Bible. Skimming through the rest of my book, its pages may seem overlade with quotes from the Bible. But I assure the reader, there is cohesiveness, a reason and an inspiration behind each selected biblical passage. Various passages are expanded upon in greater or lesser detail. Invariably, they can be followed by a reading of the full episode in its original biblical text.

It is a personal journey into the story of my ancestors as told in The Book.

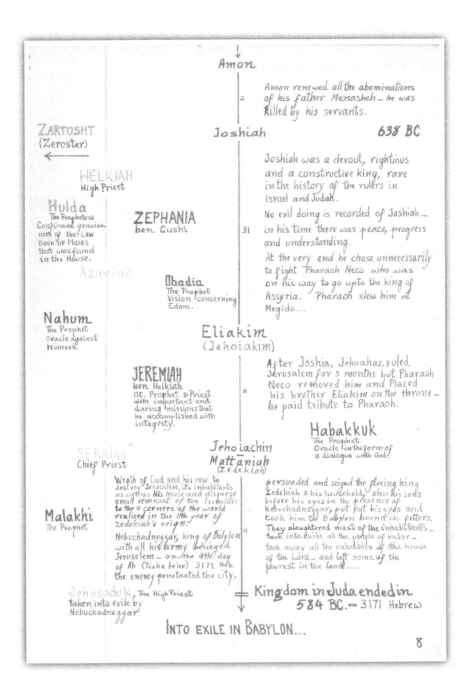

Amon

Amon renewed all the abominations
of his father Menasheh — he was
killed by his servants.

2

Joshiah   638 BC

ZARTOSHT
(Zeroster)
←

HELKIAH
High Priest

Hulda
The Prophetess
Confirmed genuine-
ness of the LAW
Book of Moses
that was found
in the House.

Azariah

ZEPHANIA
ben Cushi

31

Joshiah was a devout, rightious
and a constructive king, rare
in the history of the rulers in
Israel and Judah.

No evil doing is recorded of Joshiah —
in his time there was peace, progress
and understanding.

At the very end he chose unnecessarily
to fight Pharaoh Neco who was
on his way to go upto the king of
Assyria. Pharaoh slew him at
Megido...

Obadia
The Prophet
Vision concerning
Edom.

Nahum
The Prophet
Oracle against
Nineveh.

Eliakim
(Jehoiakim)

JEREMIAH
ben Helkiah
Gt. Prophet & Priest
with important and
daring missions that
he accomplished with
integrity.

11

After Joshia, Jehoahaz ruled
Jerusalem for 3 months but Pharaoh
Neco removed him and placed
his brother Eliakim on the throne —
he paid tribute to Pharaoh.

Habakkuk
The Prophet.
Oracle in the form of
a dialogue with God!

SERAIAH
Chief Priest

Jehoiachin
Mattaniah
(Zedekiah)

Malakhi
The Prophet

Wrath of God and his vow to
destroy Jerusalem, its inhabitants
as well as His House and disperse
small remnant of the Isrhelites
to the 4 corners of the world
realized in the 11th year of
Zedekiah's reign.

Nebuchadnezzar, king of Babylon
with all his army besieged
Jerusalem — on the 9th day
of Ab (Tisha be'av) 3171 Heb.
the enemy penetrated the city,

11

persuaded and seiged the fleeing king
Zedekiah & his household, slew his sons
before his eyes in the presence of
Nebuchadnezzar, put out his eyes and
took him to Babylon bound in fetters.
They slaughtered most of the inhabitants —
took into exile all the people of valor —
took away all the valuables of the house
of the Lord — and left some of the
poorest in the land....

Jehosaduk, The High Priest
taken into exile by
Nebuchadnezzar

Kingdom in Juda ended in
584 BC. = 3171 Hebrew

INTO EXILE IN BABYLON...

8

Page 8 from Volume I of four manuscripts handwritten by the author
prior to his definitive departure from Iran.

PART II
SEEKING CLUES FROM BIBLICAL HISTORY

5

IN SEARCH OF ESSENCE

Remember the former things of old:
for I am God, and there is none else; I
am God and there is none like me,
declaring the end from the beginning,
and from ancient times the things that
are not yet done, saying, My counsel
shall stand and I will do all my
pleasure. (Isaiah 46:9–10)

DOMINANT IN THE BOOK IS A COMMON THREAD THAT BECKONS the discerning eye of seasoned readers from the first page in Genesis, and runs through to the very last page of the final chapter, Malachi.

I found that the story of revelation given by God to man has followed a plot and a central theme that has been told and retold from generation to generation. I found that understanding The Book as one with a plot helps reveal its essence ... its intrinsic message. Readers searching for a central theme may have touched upon it through the plot of a storyline that set the stage for actual events fulfilled by history. Seen in this light, readers of the Scripture may perhaps not have ended up with disappointment. They may perhaps not have turned away from further study of the written word.

An intimate reading of the Scripture can reveal several underlying ideas that are tightly interconnected.

The first is the absolute dominance of God as apparent throughout The Book. He is in full command over the Universe. This theme is consistent throughout the Scripture, specifically when there is a moral to be learned through a particular turn of events. Already in the first of the Ten Commandments, He declares: *"I am the Lord thy God ... Thou shalt have no other gods before me"* (*Exodus 20:2-3*).

The second is that God shapes events and designs the destiny of nations to actualize precisely as they have.

Third, for reasons we may never know within our own lifetimes, it was God's will to build the nation of Israel, distinctive in many ways from other nations, His will to elevate its people to prominence in the Holy Land, only to disperse them to the four corners of the world with the promise of a return, as history continues on its path.

Fourth, and unique to The Book while present in no other on Earth, is that God speaks to man face to face, not only as an individual, but as a people that gathers itself into a kingdom, a nation with an unforgettable memory of witnessing divine revelation with all its members sharing in the experience collectively. The message that comes down from that experience is then heard and heard again in unison within each family, with each generation passing it down to the next.

6

A RARE VISIT

ABRAHAM, THE ARCH FATHER OF NATIONS, was visited by three passers-by:

> *And he lifted up his eyes and looked, and lo, three men stood by him: and when he saw them, he ran to meet them from the tent door, and bowed himself toward the ground, and said, My Lord, if now I found favor in thy sight, pass not away, I pray thee, from thy servant: Let a little water, I pray you, be fetched, and wash your feet, and rest yourselves under the tree. And I will fetch a morsel of bread, and comfort ye your hearts; after that ye shall pass on: for therefore are ye come to your servant. And they said, So do, as thou hast said.* (Genesis 18:2–5)

Academicians generally perceive the three men visiting Abraham to be angels, but a closer read of the events that follow reveals that one of the visitors is God, Himself, accompanied by two attendants.

Food was prepared: *"… and he stood by them under the tree, and they did eat"* (Genesis 18:8).

Then: *"… they [the attendants] said unto him, 'Where is Sarah thy wife?' And he said, 'Behold in the tent'"* (Genesis 18:9).

That question is simple enough for the two attendants in order to open some dialogue and conversation. But, the next question is asked by the Supreme: *"And he said, 'I will certainly return unto thee according to the time of life; and lo, Sarah thy wife shall have a son.' And Sarah heard it in the tent door, which was behind him"* (Genesis 18:10).

Abraham and Sarah were old; and the manner of women had ceased to be with Sarah, "*Therefore Sarah laughed within herself, saying, 'After I am waxed old shall I have pleasure, my lord being old also?'* " (Genesis 18:12).

"*And the Lord* (YHWH) *said unto Abraham, 'Wherefore did Sarah laugh, saying, Shall I of a surety bear a child, which am old? Is anything too hard for the Lord? At the time appointed I will return unto thee, according to the time of life, and Sarah shall have a son*'" (Genesis 18:13–14).

From this passage, one may understand that God can—and does—create anything that the mind can imagine.

Sarah, fearful of being disrespectful, denied having laughed; but He said, "No, you laughed indeed!"

Thereafter, God sent His two companions off on a mission to the city of Sodom. He stayed behind in Abraham's tent and began to tell of His plan to bring down the two cities whose entire populations are same-sex oriented. God then weighed the choices in front of his host, Abraham, who pleaded with Him to evaluate the possibility of an alternative plan to that of their final destruction.

> And Abraham drew near, and said, Wilt thou also destroy the righteous with the wicked? Peradventure there be fifty righteous within the city: wilt thou also destroy and not spare the place for the fifty righteous that are therein?… And the Lord said, if I find in Sodom fifty righteous within the city, then I will spare all the place for their sakes. (Genesis 18:23–26)

Abraham dared to ask God's pardon for forty-five righteous men—then he pushed his luck for forty, thirty, twenty, and finally: "*And he said, Oh let not the Lord be angry, and I will speak yet but this once: Peradventure ten shall be found there. And He said, I will not destroy it for ten's sake*" (Genesis 18:32). Abraham's concern was also about Lot, his nephew, and his family, inhabitants of Sodom. "*And the Lord went His way, as soon as He had left communing with Abraham: and Abraham returned unto his place*" (Genesis 18:33).

What makes this visit special? We may have noticed that, in all other encounters between God and humankind in the Scripture, God took the tone of supreme commander, or that of a father who instructed and educated his children, or a boss who demanded results—as when He punished Moses for disobeying his instruction, and hence forbade him passage to the Promised Land alongside the people he had led out of Egypt. In His visit to Abraham's tent, it is clear that God was positioning Himself as a guest. In the saga of Sodom and Gomorrah, although His decision was already made as to the imminent destruction of the two entire cities, God discussed the matter in the form of negotiation. He seemed to be desirous to appear as a guest who tarried in Abraham's dwelling.

This affection toward Abraham singled him out from among all other figures in the Scripture, in that nowhere else does The Book demonstrate evidence of a rapport with God in such a uniquely intimate way as that by which He shared those special moments with Abraham described above.

Meanwhile, the two angels went on their way to carry out their mission and utterly destroy the cities of Sodom and Gomorrah along with their entire populations, except for Lot and his two daughters, whom they guided into safety, "*For we will destroy this place, because the cry of them is waxen great before the face of the Lord and the Lord hath sent us to destroy it*" (Genesis 19:13).

Lot's wife was unfortunate to have not heeded the angel's advice, who warned against turning back to take a last look at the fallen city of Sodom. "*His wife peered behind him and she became a pillar of salt*" (Genesis 19:26). Symbolically, it can be understood that she was unable to let go of the past to apply her energies to the pressing needs of the present. She lacked faith that all was working in her family's favour.

That calamitous episode in ancient history took place in a city located in the vicinity of the Dead Sea, which happens to be the lowest point on Earth. Here, we may pause to ponder the deeper message about Creation going forward, about history and the type of society that was envisioned at its core, which comes through the story of the wholesale destruction of Sodom and Gomorrah.

7

GOD'S INTENT UNFOLDS

SOME READERS MAY BE PUZZLED BY JACOB'S DISGUISE as his elder brother, Esau, to receive his father's blessing. This, and many similar incidents in the Bible, can frustrate the reader who sets The Book aside, only then to read further with more frustration.

Jacob's dilemma for the blessing took root when his mother, Rebecca, conceived and was told by God: *"Two nations are in thy womb, and two manner of people shall be separated from thy bowels ... the elder shall serve the younger"* (Genesis 25:23). This declaration reveals that God Himself planned—or better yet, programmed—the creation of the two nations even before the two chromosomes shaped in Rebecca's womb.

Rebecca delivered twins. The first one, red and hairy, was called Esau; next emerged the twin holding on to the heels of Esau, and they called him Jacob.

The lads grew up, and as Jacob was cooking a stew one day, Esau returned from hunting, hungry and exhausted. He asked Jacob to give him some of the red stuff to drink. Jacob asked him to sell his birthright in return for the soup. Esau, near collapse, agreed.

Esau was his father's favourite, but the young lads' mother, remembering God's words to her while she was with child, favoured Jacob. Father Isaac, who was by now dim of sight, asked Esau, his first born, to hunt for game and prepare his favourite dish *"that my soul may Bless thee before I die"* (Genesis 27:4). As Rebecca listened behind the scene and heard Isaac's words for Esau, she told Jacob to bring two young goat kids for a delicious meal, and to take it to his father for a blessing. Jacob told his mother that, since Esau was hairy and markedly different from himself, his father may discover the deception, but she assured him not to worry, and that all would be well.

So, Jacob covered his arms and neck with a lambskin, and brought his blind father a delicious meal. His father was puzzled: "*And Jacob went near unto Isaac his father; and he felt him, and said; The voice is Jacob's voice, but the hands are the hands of Esau*" (Genesis 27:22). Isaac's dilemma slowly faded, and he finally found no other choice than to place a blessing upon Jacob: "*See, the smell of my son is as the smell of a field which the Lord has Blessed … Cursed be every one that Curseth thee and Blessed be he that Blesseth thee*" (Genesis 27:27–29). The important point to remember is that Isaac seems to have given a blessing despite his better judgment. Having sensed his own confusion, unable to differentiate between his two sons, he also may not have been aware of the implications of the blessing he had just placed on the head of his youngest son. Was it then a Higher Source that placed every one of the words he pronounced as he blessed Jacob?

We may ask how the patriarchs can be taken seriously with such acts. Yet, if we are able to see them as part of a bigger design, we may just have found a key to deciphering the message of The Book. According to Jewish tradition, major blessings are given to the first-born son. In this case, God's intent is elsewhere and remains steadfast to his promise to Rebecca before the birth of her twins: "*Two nations are in thy womb … the elder shall serve the younger*" (Genesis 25:23).

Jacob was then named "Israel," a title that eventually marked the symbol of a nation. We will discuss in a subsequent chapter the patriarch Jacob's warning to his sons about the shift in leadership of the growing tribe of Israel. It suffices for our intents and purposes simply to mention at this juncture that Jacob's statement as a father to his sons was premonitory, a prediction that crystallized into actual history many centuries later, during the time of the kings and the prophets. Details about the outcome of Jacob's premonition will be discussed further along in tandem with the sequence of events as they unfold in The Book.

At this juncture, however, we delve into a statement further down the line, which leads us to look back upon Isaac's blessing on his youngest son, as a symbol or a signpost that ultimately followed him as he surpassed himself from the realm of the individual to the patriarchal, a model that served as a blueprint for a people who walked into their own becoming as a nation: *"And he said unto him, What is thy name? And he said Jacob. And he said thy name shall be called no more Jacob, but ISRA-EL: for as a prince hast thou power with God and with men, and hast prevailed"* (Genesis 32:27–28).

8

MAJOR ELEMENTS OF THE HEBREW SCRIPTURES

A STORY WORTHY OF BEING PRODUCED FOR STAGE or screen requires a powerful script with a powerful plot and dialogue to capture imaginations. It also needs a skilful director and carefully selected actors to embody their respective roles. Then there are various professionals who create the appropriate attire and settings and manage the props to support the scenes, and so on.

The history of the Jews of the Hebrew Scriptures can be likened to a carefully scripted play in which God emerges as the director. The play unfolds according to His design, and each individual, unbeknownst to him or her, performs a part on a predetermined script beginning with Adam and Eve, and moving on to Noah, Abraham, Isaac, Jacob, Moses, and Aaron ... all the way down to the kings such as David and Solomon, to the erection of the Temple of Jerusalem, to the priests, the great prophets such as Elijah and Elisha, on down to the destruction of Jerusalem and the Temple in her midst, and to the going of the Hebrew nation into exile, where they witness the word of the prophets such as Isaiah, Jeremiah, and Ezekiel.

Moses, Judaism's foremost revered prophet, was leading a humble life in Midian by the time he reached the ripe old age of eighty. In Midian, a remote desert land far from his birthplace in Egypt, he shepherded his father-in-law's flock of sheep with hardly an ambition to do more with his life. It was then that God caught him by surprise, spoke through a bush that seemed to be burning, and instilled in him the power to lead an enslaved nation out of bondage, in spite of a speech defect and fears of not being up to par for such a colossal task. Chapters three and four of the Book of Exodus deal with Moses' discovery of his new mission.

God handpicks ordinary individuals such as Moses, and despite their plea of ineptitude, empowers them, bewildering us with the enormity of their accomplishments. But, what is even more bewildering is that these actors on the biblical stage are ordinary folk; they are there to help us realize just who is in command! We see that, of such a man, advanced in age, having fled Egypt many years prior to that time because he had killed a slave master, God made someone capable of taking the stairs up to Pharaoh's domain to demand the freedom of a nation—basically to tell him what to do. The rod that is activated and the sea that is made to allow passage by foot are divine acts.

One of the props in this divine production is the tabernacle, a mobile temple to serve as a reminder of God's presence in the midst of the camp of the Israelites:

> And Moses said unto the children of Israel, See the Lord hath called by name Bezalel the son of Ur ... he hath filled him with the spirit of God, in wisdom, in understanding, and in knowledge, and in all manner of workmanship ... to work in gold, and in silver and in brass ... he, and Aholiab, the son of Ahisamach ... Them hath he filled with wisdom of heart to work all manner of work. (Exodus 35:30–35)

Two artisans were selected from among the crowd for their workmanship and labour to produce quality artefacts. One such item was the Ark of the Covenant that carried the two tablets of the Ten Commandments. The menorah was another symbolic object, since its focus was to light up the tabernacle. Yet another detailed part of the scene was the high priests' vestments, such as their headwear and breastplates, whose functions and designs were detailed by divine instruction. The altar, of course, was an important prop, for it was the place from which the high priests stood to perform their symbolic sacrificial functions through the act of animal sacrifice as an offering to God.

An interesting aspect of the breastplates is that they are affixed with gemstones called the Urim and the Thummim. These gemstones were the vehicle of interaction between the high priests and God. The priest's role as an oracle was to interface with God when making important decisions. The gems lit up, or remained inactive, depending on whether they received divine signals or revelation, the whole intended for the protection of the nascent Jewish nation.

"And He [Joshua] shall stand before Eleazer, the Priest, who shall ask counsel from him after the judgment of Urim before the Lord: at his word shall they go out, and at his word they shall come in…." (Numbers 27:21). These were God's instructions to Moses to prepare Joshua for his new mission to lead the Jews to the Promised Land.

At first glance, it may appear trivial or inappropriate to liken an act of God to the handiwork of man in a theatrical production. Upon further reflection from a different vantage point, we find that it is man who follows in the ways of God: *"And God said, let us make man in our image, after our likeness…."* (Genesis 1:26).

That being said, we observe two constants that remain the primary components throughout The Book: the omnipresent Creator of the Universe, who maintains His Creation and keeps the heavens together with what we see as unfathomable perfection, whose name is YHWH; and the Nation of Israel, *A'am Israel*. These are the two phenomena in The Book that remain constant, everlasting, and, for the sake of clarity, intentionally set apart as distinct from all other components of the history of humankind.

All other variables throughout the Scripture, including Moses, the prophets, the kings, the high priests—the good guys and the bad—seem to be directed from above to perform their specific part in making Israel what it is. They seem to be operating as a harmonious whole in order to bring mankind to a level desired by Him alone. He wants men and women to get to know Him the way He wants to be known—as a father—and to love Him with all their heart and all their soul, to fear Him, trust Him and follow His commandments, as one does with regard to one's parents. It is a relationship with the divine unique on Earth among nations, inasmuch as wherever the people meet with trial and error, with challenge and adversity, they do so as a nation, resilient, possessing the will to survive as one family. This sense of identity is one of a child whose father is a protector, a theme that remains central throughout the passing millennia. At the core of any Jewish sense of identity, the notion of belonging remains universal and surpasses all physical, geographical, and chronological boundaries.

This theme resonates consistently throughout The Book, whether during times of revelation and prophecy, or during those when God reveals hardly any signs, but instead leaves it to the people to search Him out, until such time as He will choose to show His countenance again, to establish peace and harmony, not for the Jewish nation alone, but for the benefit of all mankind.

"I will hide my face from them, I will see what their end shall be" (*Deuteronomy 32:20*).

9

FEAR OF GOD

KORAH, THE SON OF IZHAR, A LEVITE, was the richest member among the Israelites camping in the Sinai Desert. Besides his enormous wealth, Korah had many followers including influential leaders in the camp like Dathan and Abiram. Along with two hundred and fifty supporters, Korah rose and confronted Moses and Aaron with an eye to grab the leadership at the helm:

> *Ye take too much upon you, seeing all the congregation are holy, everyone of them, and the Lord is among them: wherefore then lift ye up yourselves above the congregation of the Lord? (Numbers 16:3)*

> *And Moses said unto Korah, Hear, I pray you, ye son of Levi: Seemeth it but a small thing unto you, the God of Israel has separated you from the congregation of Israel, to bring you near to Himself to do the service of the tabernacle of the Lord,... and seek ye the priesthood also? For which cause both thou and all thy company are gathered together against the Lord: and what is Aaron, that ye murmur against him? (Numbers 16:8–11)*

Further talks with Korah and his supporters yielded more of the same blind opposition. *And the Lord spoke unto Moses and unto Aaron, saying, separate yourselves from among this congregation, that I may consume them in a moment"* (Numbers 16:20–21).

Confrontations arose and dragged on between the two camps until ...

> *And the Earth opened her mouth, and swallowed them up, and their houses. And all the men that appertained unto Korah, and all their goods ... went down alive into the pit,*

> and the Earth closed on them: and they perished from among
> the congregation. (Numbers 16:32–33)

God's severe punishment was inflicted upon Korah and his followers because they were contending with God Himself, who had ordained Moses and Aaron as His ambassadors to the nation. One can only imagine the fate of Moses and Aaron had they faced angry crowds alone without God's intervention. Korah's story bears a message similar to a Psalm of David, where it is said, *"The fear of the Lord is the beginning of wisdom: a good understanding have all they that do His commandments: His praise endureth for ever"* (Psalm 111:10).

Korah's story reminds us that God appoints men of quality to lead and to create momentous change, and not necessarily men of wealth and influence. The message that comes down to us about the fate of Korah and his henchmen resounds clearly with an idea earlier discussed.

God is the power behind the play. God seems to be scripting the plot as it unfolds in The Book. We are perpetually reminded of where we stand in relation to our Creator. Indeed, Korah's own descendant, many generations down the line, goes by the name of Samuel, a superb national and religious leader (see I Chronicles 6:7–12). He is called upon to anoint the very first two kings of Israel, King Saul and later David. His story in Samuel I and II relates the early history of the Jewish nation.

Samuel was a man of God, clean handed and with no record of wrong doing in all his tenure. We see that God, even as He took away from Korah, was the benevolent giver who compensated the bad reputation of Korah in the hearts and minds of later generations by Samuel's appointment to the task at hand. This question deserves reflection, since the saga of Korah is read in a separate Torah portion from Chapter 16 of the Book of Numbers, called *parasha*, on the same Sabbath every year in synagogues the world over. It seems fair to consider this *parasha* as a message of God's absolute authority.

10

WHAT CAN WE LEARN FROM THE KINGDOM OF ISRAEL IN BIBLICAL TIMES?

WHEN THE ISRAELITES ENTERED THE PROMISED LAND, each one of the twelve tribes settled a region ordained to it. In those days, there was no federal government, and no central authority or leadership to safeguard the collective interest against surrounding forces.

At that time, Samuel, a man of God acting as a seer, helped the people in their new land solve day-to-day issues. The twelve tribes of Israel learned that each of the neighbouring states was ruled by a king. They approached Samuel and stated their concern that they, too, needed the leadership of a king to rule over the land.

Samuel placed the issue before God. *"And the Lord said unto Samuel, Hearken unto the voice of the people in all that they say unto thee: for they have not rejected thee, but they have rejected me, that I should not reign over them"* (I Samuel 8:7).

Samuel delivered God's word to the people and warned of the downside of a kingdom. He admonished that a king was likely to use the people's income and efforts to glorify himself, and surround himself with courtiers and officers who may uphold their own interests at the expense of the people. But, the people persisted. So, God instructed Samuel to anoint Saul, the son of Kish, a Benjaminite. Saul was a young man of choice, taller than his people, who barely reached his shoulder in height. *"And Samuel said to all the people, See ye him whom the Lord hath chosen, that there is none like him among all the people? And all the people shouted, and said, God save the king"* (I Samuel 10:24).

Saul's first experience was to defeat the Ammonites who encamped against Israel, but the biggest test came when he was assigned by God to destroy the Amalekites. It all began when Samuel conferred with Saul, saying the following:

Thus saith the Lord of hosts, I remember that which Amalek did to Israel, how he laid wait for him in the way, when he came up from Egypt. Now go and smite Amalek, and utterly destroy all that they have, and spare them not; but slay both man and woman, infant and suckling, ox and sheep, camel and ass. (I Samuel 15:2–3)

Along with two hundred thousand footmen and ten thousand men of Judah, Saul marched to battle against the Amalekites and captured their king, Agag, sparing his life, but killing all his people—men, women, and children. He also spared the best of his sheep and the oxen and all that was good of his possessions. Saul's error in deviating from God's command led to his downfall, and he died in battle against the Philistines.

Readers can follow King Saul's full story in I Samuel, Chapter 19 and further. In doing so, they will read passages that clearly demonstrate a recurring theme in the Scripture; namely, that God's word is final. He makes it clear from the start that He alone is King, and brought the message home again when Saul's defeat was the consequence of his deviation from God's intent.

And, the time had arisen to appoint a new future ruler for Israel. God ordered Samuel to fill his horn with oil and go to Jesse, the Bethlehemite, to anoint one of Jesse's sons as Israel's new ruler king. At the meeting, Jesse introduced seven of his sons, all present in that meeting, but they were all rejected by God.

And Samuel said unto Jesse, Are here all thy children? And he said there remaineth yet the youngest, and, behold, he keepeth the sheep. And Samuel said to Jesse, Send and fetch him: for we will not sit down till he come hither. (I Samuel 16:11)

Then Samuel took the horn of oil, and anointed him in the midst of his brethren; and the Spirit of the Lord came upon David from that day forward. (I Samuel 16:13)

We will see why it was David, youngest son of Jesse at the time busy shepherding his father's sheep when called upon to be anointed by the prophet Samuel, who was chosen to be future king of Israel.

Israel under King Saul was at war with the Philistines at the time. David used to bring food to his three brothers at the battlefront when he noticed a fearsome warrior known as Goliath in the Philistine camp. The giant-like Goliath called out for someone from among the Israelites to meet his challenge. The challenge was that the people of the befallen warrior were to be brought as slaves to the victor's camp. Upon hearing the threat of Goliath, David volunteered to come forth and meet his challenge.

David's brother, Eliab, considering the lad to be a minor, was angered by his audacity. *"Why camest thou down hither? And with whom hast thou left those few sheep in the wilderness? I know thy pride, and the naughtiness of thine heart; for thou art come down that thou mightest see the battle"* (I Samuel 17:28).

Having heard David's intention to bring down the Philistine monster, the people brought the lad before King Saul. *"And David said to Saul, let no man's heart fail because of him; thy servant will go and fight with this Philistine"* (I Samuel 17:32).

Saul was as desperate for help, as he was astounded by the boy's offer. *"Thou art not able to go against this Philistine to fight with him: for thou art but a youth, and he a man of war from his youth"* (I Samuel 17:33).

As Saul took confidence in David's wilfulness, he offered him his personal battle gear. David instead decided to engage the monster in his ordinary state, armed with the simple boyish tools of a stick and a sling.

And the Philistine said unto David, Am I a dog that thou comest to me with staves? ... Come to me, and I will give thy flesh unto the fowls of the air ... Then said David to the Philistine, thou comest to me with a sword, and with a spear,

> *and with a shield: but I come to thee in the name of the Lord*
> *of hosts, the God of the armies of Israel whom thou hast*
> *defied. This day will the Lord deliver thee into mine hands;*
> *and I will smite thee ... that all the Earth may know that*
> *there is a God in Israel. (I Samuel 17:43–46)*

> *And David put his hand in his bag, and took thence a stone,*
> *and slang it, and smote the Philistine in his forehead ... and*
> *he fell upon his face to the earth ... but there was no sword*
> *in the hand of David ... David ran and stood upon the*
> *Philistine, and took his sword and drew it out of the sheath*
> *thereof, and slew him, and cut off his head therewith. And*
> *when the Philistines saw their champion was dead, they fled.*
> *(I Samuel 17:44–51)*

In this adventure, one witnesses the will of a child armed with faith alone. One also witnesses the will of God. The image projected by a ruddy lad who commits himself with a stick and sling in a challenge against a giant armoured to the tooth presents the essence of what we are seeking to understand from the Scripture. There is much to be learned about the power that gave a teenage boy the faith, and the means, to overcome a threat made upon an entire people.

David grew to become a great leader in Israel, a warrior who fought the enemy on all fronts and united the twelve tribes of Israel. He captured Jerusalem from the Jebusites and established it to become the capital of Israel. David's total devotion and submission to God—his trust and fear of God—his fairness and humility in position of power, was unequalled in Jewish history. Yet he, too, was depicted in The Book as a mortal with all-too-human flaws. However, his faith was so strong that God promised and granted David and his descendants a leadership role in Israel, despite a grave mistake he committed in his personal life.

David's unfortunate mistake was to seduce Bathsheba, a beautiful married woman whose husband, Uriah the Hittite, was an officer serving in David's army at war. When she sent word to David that she was with child, David ordered Uriah back from the warfront in order to camouflage the child's identity.

Uriah returned. The king summoned him and told him to go home to his wife. Uriah answered by pleading: "*The arc, and Israel, and Judah, abide in tents ... and the servants of my lord, are encamped in the open fields; shall I then go into mine house, to eat and to drink, and to lie with my wife? As thou livest ... I will not do this thing*" (II Samuel 11:11). Tragically, David isolated Uriah to die in battle, and thereafter claimed Bathsheba as his wife.

Because of David's numerous noble qualities such as a complete trust in and deep devotion to his God, his rule was lengthy, and he is generally seen as a just and fair-minded king of Israel. His legacy became a cornerstone in the heart and mind and soul of Judaism. Is not David qualified to serve as a specimen candidate who demonstrates well the concept that, even those elevated souls possessing the noblest of qualities—faith, fair-mindedness, and courage—are prone to err? Readers are strongly encouraged to read the captivating story of David and Bathsheba in II Samuel, Chapter 11, and further. In reading the full story, they discover that the son born to Bathsheba out of wedlock fell ill and died early in childhood, but Bathsheba later delivered another son to David. He was none other than Solomon, future king of Israel.

David made his mark in history as a great poet and songwriter. A loving musician, he wrote most of the poetry and music that became the Book of Psalms, filling it with praise for God and precious advice to his kinsmen, which he delivered so eloquently in the following psalm:

> *Blessed is the man*
> *that walketh not in the counsel of the ungodly,*
> *nor standeth in the way of sinners,*
> *nor sitteth in the seat of the scornful.*
> *But His delight is in the law of the Lord;*
> *and in His law doth he meditate day and night.*
> *And he shall be like a tree*
> *planted by the rivers of water,*
> *that bringeth forth His fruit in His season;*
> *His leaf also shall not wither;*
> *and whatsoever he doeth shall prosper.*
> *(Psalm 1:1–2)*

David shone as a man who embodied model human characteristics and a decent nature that pleased God. Several passages in the Scripture describe his successive confrontations with King Saul and the events that led to an extraordinary accession to the throne. Readers are encouraged to follow the full text of David's life in the books of I Samuel, chapters 16–31, followed by II Samuel, chapters 1–24 and I Kings, chapters 1–2, and further on in I Chronicles, chapters 10–29.

According to God's promise to David, leadership in the kingdom was by inheritance. Thus it was David's beloved son, Solomon, whom he appointed to succeed as king in Israel.

Solomon, the son of David, was but a child when he inherited his father's throne. It happened that his elder brother, Adonijah, constantly conspired against him for kingship, although David had meant from the start to appoint Solomon as his successor. The immediate task at hand was to do away with Joab, who was the top military brass, and Abiatar, the chief priest, both of whom sided with rival brother Adonijah. Above all, Solomon had a nation of twelve tribes to rule, all of them coming with a long list of expectations.

It was in such circumstances that God appeared to Solomon in a dream, telling him to state his wish. And Solomon said:

> *O Lord my God, thou hast made thy servant king instead of David my father: and I am but a little child: I know not how to go out or come in. And thy servant is in the midst of thy people which thou hast chosen, a great people … Give therefore thy servant an understanding heart to judge thy people, that I may discern between good and bad: for who is able to judge this thy so great a people? (I Kings 3:7–9)*

> *And God said unto him, because thou hast asked this thing, and hast not asked for thyself long life; neither hast asked riches for thyself, nor hast asked the life of your enemies; but hast asked for thyself understanding to discern judgment; behold, I have done according to thy word: lo, I have given thee a wise and an understanding heart; so that there was*

none like thee before thee, neither after thee shall any arise like unto thee. And I have also given thee that which thou hast not asked, both riches, and honor: so that there shall not be any among the kings like unto thee all thy days. And if thou wilt walk in my ways, to keep my statutes, and my commandments, as thy father David did, then I will lengthen thy days. (I Kings 3:11–14)

Solomon's story delivers a key to the reader of The Book as to how a country with no constitutional government can be ruled by a child sitting on a throne soon to be the envy of its contemporaries, so much so, that *"there shall not be any among the kings like unto thee all thy days"* (*1 Kings 3:13*). To go on, God gifted Solomon with all that He promised him, above all forty years of tranquillity and peaceful borders, unseen throughout the millennia in Jewish history. Yet, this gift of peace and prosperity had not even been requested by Solomon from God in his legendary dream.

Solomon's first call to judgment was to arbitrate between two conflicting women; each had given birth to a son. One of the infants died when his mother mistakenly lay upon him at night, and she tried to claim the other woman's child as her own. When the case was brought before Solomon, he ordered to cut the living child in two—with half to be granted to one woman and the other half to the second.

Then spoke the woman whose the living child was unto the king, for her bowels yearned upon her son, and she said, O my Lord, give her the living child, and in no wise slay it. But the other said, Let it be neither mine nor thine, but divide it. Then the king answered and said, give her the living child and in no wise slay it: she is the mother thereof. (I Kings 3:26–27)

The people soon heard the news and feared their king, for they saw that he was blessed with the power of judgment and the wisdom of God.

Solomon's achievements were many. Firstly, he authored the books of Proverbs, Ecclesiastes, and the Song of Songs. Then, as was promised to his father, King David, God privileged Solomon with the building of the Temple, a feat that his father had wanted to achieve but was unable to during his own reign. God told David that the building of the Temple of Israel was to be accomplished by his son in II Samuel 7:4–7, where He messaged David through the Prophet Nathan on events to follow. As it happened, the temple was erected, and in it was placed the Arc of God, which held the two tablets along with the tabernacle and all its holy artefacts.

In an emotional inauguration speech, Solomon asked God to accept any prayer of those who pray facing in the direction of the Temple. From that time onwards, Jews from all four corners of the globe continue to pray facing toward Jerusalem.

But, Solomon, too, was not spared from committing several grave mistakes. Indeed, in the Book of Deuteronomy, God declared just what a king's obligations toward Israel were: *"He shall not multiply horses to himself, nor cause the people to return to Egypt … neither shall he multiply wives to himself, that his heart turn not away: neither shall he greatly multiply to himself silver and gold" (Deuteronomy 17:16–17).*

Yet, finding himself privileged and at the height of achievement and successes beyond his wildest dreams, Solomon amassed enormous wealth and indulged himself in luxury. He imported horses from Egypt and kept a huge number of court attendants at the toil and expense of the taxpayers. Against such violations of decent conduct, God answered with silence and solemnity. Solomon kept many women, most of them from foreign lands including Pharaoh's daughter, women from among the Moabites, the Ammonites, the Edomites, the Sidonites, and still others. He went as far as worshiping their gods—building a high place for Chemosh, the god of Moab on the Mount of Olives facing Jerusalem for his foreign wives (I Kings 11:1–8).

> So God said to Solomon: *"Forasmuch as this is done of thee, and thou hast not kept my covenant and my statutes, which I have commanded thee, I will surely rend the kingdom from thee [change of course], and will give it to your servant. Notwithstanding, in thy days I will not do it for David*

thy father's sake: I will rend it out of the hand of your son. Howbeit, I will not rend away all the kingdom: but will give one tribe to thy son for David my servant's sake, and for Jerusalem's sake which I have chosen." (I Kings 11:11–13)

The reader may recall at this juncture, a premonitory phrase about such a change of course, only touched upon very briefly in Chapter 7 of this book, precisely where Jacob is seen offering his sons a prediction about things to come concerning the leadership of the Jewish people.

About 750 years before Solomon was made aware of God's desire for a shift in the leadership of the Jewish people, Jacob, at an old age in Egypt, had gathered his twelve sons to bestow upon them his blessings. From those twelve brothers came the twelve tribes of Israel, Jacob's descendants. Jacob's blessing for his son Judah, the forefather of the Davidic Dynasty, was: *"Judah, thou art he whom thy bretheren shall praise ... Judah is a lion's whelp ... who shall rouse him up? The scepter shall not depart from Judah, nor a lawgiver from between his feet, until Shiloh come...."* (Genesis 49:8–10).

Readers are cautioned to pick up a message discernable from within the next quoted passage in relation to Jacob's blessing on the head of Judah. Shiloh, written down in the passage by the scribe in the above verse from Genesis, is mentioned more than seven centuries down the line, as we shall see in the verse taken from I Kings. Scribes simply recorded actual events as they went down in history. The point to be made is an obvious link between Jacob's blessing above and the verse from I Kings below.

By the same token, it seems fair to say that Jacob, too, had no clue as to the ultimate significance of Shiloh in the greater scheme of things. Yet, the veracity of Jacob's blessing above, seems clearly to be self-fulfilling, some 750 years down the trodden path of history, where indeed The Book demonstrates the meaning of Shiloh with respect to Jacob's prophetic blessing on the head of his son, Judah; thus we read with amazing clarity:

And it came to pass when Jeroboam [Solomon's servant] went out of Jerusalem that the prophet Ahijah the Shilonite

> *found him in the way ... and he said to Jeroboam, take thee*
> *ten pieces: for thus saith the Lord, the God of Israel, Behold*
> *I will rend the kingdom out of the hand of Solomon, and will*
> *give ten tribes to thee. (I Kings 11:29–31)*

We have just established that the scribe who notarized the meeting between Ahijah, the Shilonite, and Solomon's servant, Jeroboam, may not have been aware that he was dealing with a previously encrypted code from events dating back several centuries within the same family line. That was the house of Judah, from whom King David came to the throne followed by his son, Solomon. Jacob, for that matter, may not have known the precise details of what was in store somewhere along the line for the descendants of his son, Judah, when he said *"until Shiloh come"* (Genesis 49:8–10).

By conducting a spiritual journey through a close reading of The Book, one may conclude that the central theme is God as screenwriter and director and we as human actors on His stage. The parts seem to relate interdependently within the whole, much like a work of art that hangs in a gallery.

Scripture is loaded with a wealth of wisdom expressed through poetry intertwined with prose. The intention behind writing this work is to help readers, the new as well as the disinterested, to benefit from their reading of The Book, or at least to be inspired to delve deeper so as to avoid the pitfalls of losing interest altogether. Readers may experience unnecessary confusion and choose to abandon the Bible, it having been subjected to interpretations that meandered beyond the original intent of the written word, as we shall see in relation to King Solomon's *Shir-ha-Shirim*, the Song of Songs.

Portions in scriptural text can be appreciated on their own, but their ultimate meaning and beauty results from their relationship to the sum of the parts as they build up into a unified whole. In this author's view, the Hebrew Scriptures offer a message that comes through with full authenticity only when seen as a sum of connecting parts that transcend time and space, such as in the example of Jacob's prophetic blessing on Judah. In much the same way that any authentic work of art succeeds as a sum of its parts, the Tanakh is no different in that respect. While a picture that hangs on a wall in a gallery is the creation of a skilled artist, Scripture is inspired by the will and design of the ultimate Creator.

The Book of Ecclesiastes (meaning *The Preacher*) was written by Solomon. It begins with a telling verdict by the author on his former lifestyle: *"Vanity of vanities, says the Preacher, vanity of vanities! All is vanity!"* (Ecclesiastes 1:2).

We hear this verdict from a man who, throughout his life, placed earthly pleasures and pursuits high on his list of priorities. While God punished him, albeit only slightly, for his excesses, He granted Solomon a measure of grace on account of a promise He had made toward his father, Israel's beloved King David. That being said, in this author's view there has been much attributed to the Song of Songs that is simply absent from the author's original intent.

For example, it is widely accepted that the Song of Songs—*Shir-ha-Shireem*—was written as a metaphor for a love between God as husband on the one hand, and the nation of Israel as a beloved bride on the other. We have just pointed out, however, King Solomon's sentiment toward women, the fact that he had several wives and concubines, most of them having brought with them replicas of their own gods. It seems almost absurd in the eyes of this writer to interpret such a sensuous poem about earthly passion and desires to symbolize a relationship between God as husband and Israel as a bride. Placing this poem on a platform beyond its reach seems far-fetched, given King Solomon's excessive propensity for worldly pleasures. A more critical eye would be wary of interpretations of this nature, especially since they seem to have led inexperienced readers of the Scripture into confusion—and away from further study of The Book!

Solomon's own words in the book of Proverbs, which he himself authored, resound with clarity: *"Every word of God is pure: he is a shield unto them that put their trust in him. Add thou not unto his words, lest he reprove thee, and thou be found a liar"* (Proverbs 30:56).

So, how does one go about arguing the fact that the Song of Songs is not about a metaphor for a marriage between God and the nation of Israel, and simply a love song to one of Solomon's many concubines? We can start by considering the following verse in Solomon's Song of Songs: "*I have compared thee, O my love, to a mare among Pharaoh's chariot horses*" (*Song of Songs 1:9*).

For one thing, God forbids kings in Israel to look back to Egypt, let alone import horses from whence he delivered his people out of four centuries of bondage (Deuteronomy17:16). Elsewhere, when giving a number count for his lovers, Solomon chants, "*There are threescore* [60] *queens, and fourscore* [80] *concubines, and maidens without number*" (*Song of Songs 6:8*).

Furthermore, let us consider the Queen of Sheba, one of King Solomon's lovers, who comes all the way from Ethiopia with an abundance of gold, spices, precious stones, and other valuable items to meet him (I Kings, Chapter 10). In the following song Solomon reflects upon her sentiment toward him: "*I am black, but comely, oh, ye daughters of Jerusalem, as the tents of Kedar, as the curtains of Solomon. Look not upon me, because I am black, because the sun hath looked upon me*" (*Song of Songs 1:5–6*).

In all likelihood, the Queen of Sheba was simply challenging those fair daughters of Jerusalem in her quest to capture the king's heart.

Similarly, certain strategic details must not be lost on the critical reader of this song of Solomon, such as the massive precautions taken to ensure the king's measures for nocturnal safety and privacy: "*Behold his bed, which is Solomon's; threescore valiant men are about it, of the valiant of Israel. Behold, they all hold swords, expert in war; every man his sword upon his thigh, because of fear in the night*" (*Song of Songs 3:7–8*). In those days, security was a deep concern, since darkness fell on many moonless nights with no electricity.

Further reading reveals that, in contrast to the modest ways of his father, David, Solomon engaged in self-glorification:

> *King Solomon made himself a chariot of the wood of Lebanon. He made the pillars thereof of silver, the bottom thereof of gold, the covering of it of purple, the midst thereof*

being paved with love, for the daughters of Jerusalem. Go forth, O ye daughters of Zion, and behold King Solomon with the crown, wherewith his mother crowned him in the day of his espousals and in the day of the gladness of his heart. (Song of Songs 3:9–11)

Solomon praises the daughters of Jerusalem as often as eight times in the Song of Songs. It therefore seems clear that he is only referring to a personal relationship involving a lover—and not a special relationship between God and the Jewish nation.

The Song of Songs is a beautiful piece of literature in its own category, the expression of a passionate love between a man and a woman, performed in lyrics as the title indicates, and it is to our great loss that we have no access to the original musical intonations as performed by the author.

King Solomon's writing style in the Song of Songs is eloquent and easy to understand by any standards. In the same way, Proverbs and Ecclesiastes, his two other personally authored works, are characteristically packed with dense philosophical content and sometimes problematic for the average reader to comprehend. This same thread is laced throughout the Song of Songs, and, in this author's view, calls for a literal interpretation, instead of one which attributes meaning beyond what is purely narrative of love between earthlings, and thus leading to confusion.

Had the intent been to suggest a metaphor for the relationship between God and the Nation of Israel, Jerusalem, and the Temple, Solomon may well have scripted a more appropriate, respectful, and distinguished style—eloquently comprehensible to any reader. But such a simple style is clearly missing from the song. The inherent complexities characteristic of Solomon's writing described above provide enough evidence to refute any notion that God is being portrayed as an actor on a stage alongside a betrothed Jewish people.

From what has been made available to us, we can presume that, in all likelihood, Solomon authored his three books at different stages in his life: the Song of Songs at the height of his physical prowess, the Proverbs when he reached the apogee of his intellectual achievements, and finally the Book of Ecclesiastes in which the excesses of former times came full circle to haunt him at an advanced age.

Bible commentators traditionally have attempted to justify the sins and wrongdoings of various personalities in the Scriptures; they have, in this author's view, done The Book disfavour. By attempting to somehow elevate the moral standards of these individuals and adjusting their image to fit into a preconceived model, they miss the more profound message about humanity and the fragility of life. The problem with this kind of over-interpretation is that it creates a distortion that only serves to throw readers off track, where they were solely and simply looking for truth.

On the other hand, let us assume for a moment that God purposefully placed those sins into the hearts and minds of precisely those characters He chose, and that those individuals committed various acts as we have seen described in the Scripture. A picture emerges from the words to give life to what it means to be ethical in the sense that God intends us to be, such that:

- No human being is perfect, no matter whom he or she happens to be.

- No individual is above God's law, and no sinner goes unpunished.

- We do not need to try those tested sins we witness in the Bible. We need to reflect upon the notion that every act bears consequences.

- We can live as though telling our neighbour through our cautious choices and actions that life is too short for self mastery to be learnt solely on the basis of one's own set of trials and errors.

Instead of reading too much into the Song of Songs, we can look beyond it to see what else Solomon has to share with us of his experiences as a man of justice and a man who was also capable of sin. Similarly, we can readily benefit from those who have trodden the beaten path. Some of the most important biblical characters who go through the test and are dealt God's justice may serve as the best models. We are the beneficiaries of their experiences, provided we take the time to read the written word without adding onto it or taking away from it so much that it loses the intrinsic meaning, and hence its value.

Verily, one can follow the plots and subplots throughout The Book on one's own in order to get a full picture that portrays God's intent for His children. Perhaps it is only through a complete reading of the Scripture that one can seize its yield through a personal grasp of its content—as a whole—as is the case with any work of art. The Tanakh is intended as an integral whole. It is, after all, a monumental piece of literature unsurpassed in history in terms of how widely it has been read. Also, it has been my experience along with many before me, and undoubtedly many who have yet to discover, that a healthy knowledge of history helps one circumvent the errors of the past.

11

THE PROPHETS

GIVEN THE PEOPLE'S PROPENSITY TO COMPROMISE in following God's commandments, the prophets appeared at various points in biblical times to bring them back to the straight path. They were high-level envoys entrusted by God to advise the people to correct themselves. Prophets were empowered through miracles as a demonstration of God's love and concern for His children. Their role was to rekindle the people's faith and trust in Him. It was also their divine mandate to warn, to admonish, and to foretell. The prophets were the people's moral compass.

The prophets' role was critical in the sense that they were the moral weathermen of their time. Communication between God and His prophets came through visions or dreams.

Of all the prophets on Earth, Moses was the greatest exception. In a very personable way, God talked to Moses and listened to his questions. *"And there arose not a prophet in Israel like unto Moses, whom the Lord knew face to face" (Deuteronomy 34:10).*

After Moses, the greatest prophets in The Book are Elijah, Elisha, Isaiah, and Jeremiah; they prophesied in Israel in the era of the Kingdom. After them came the priest Ezekiel, who encountered several visions while in captivity in the land of the Chaldeans.

During the time of Elijah, in the ninth century B.C.E., the ruling power in Israel was split into two kingdoms: the Davidic kingdom in the south with its capital city Jerusalem, and the Kingdom of Israel in the north, in Samaria. It was during Elijah's time that Ahab became king in Samaria and married the Sidonian princess, Jezebel. After she became first lady, Jezebel lost no time in diverting Ahab toward worshiping her god, Baal, and encouraging him to prostrate himself to Baal. Jezebel also brought into the land over 450 Baal prophets to spread idolatry throughout Israel.

"And Elijah the Tishbite, who was of the inhabitants of Gil'ead, said unto Ahab, As the Lord God of Israel liveth, before whom I stand, there shall not be dew nor rain these years, but according to my word" (I Kings 17:1).

It then happened that a severe drought and famine brought devastation upon Samaria and its inhabitants, until *"it came to pass after many days, that the word of the Lord came to Elijah in the third year, saying, Go, show yourself unto Ahab; and I will send rain upon the Earth"* (I Kings 18:1). And, while Elijah had gone into hiding, Ahab all the while placed a search on his life throughout the duration of the draught.

It happened that Obadiah, who was in charge of Ahab's household, was on the road when Elijah appeared in front of him and said, *"…go tell thy lord, Behold, Elijah is here!"* (1 Kings 18:8).

Ahab was quick to confront Elijah, and the first thing he told him was:

> *Art thou he that troubleth Israel? And he answered, I have not troubled Israel; but thou, and thy father's house, in that ye have forsaken the commandments of the Lord, and thou hast followed Baalim. Now therefore send, and gather to me all Israel unto mount Carmel, and the prophets of Baal four hundred and fifty, and the prophets of the grove four hundred, which eat at Jezebel's table.* (I Kings 18:17–19)

> *Ahab gathered them all at Mount Carmel: "And Elijah came unto all the people, and said, how long shalt ye between two opinions? If the Lord be God follow him: but if Baal, then follow him. And the people answered him not a word"* (I Kings 18:21).

The decisive moment occurred when Elijah addressed the Baal prophets and demanded that they choose one of two bulls that were brought before them. He instructed them to cut one up and place it on a wooden plank, and to ask their god to send fire over it from above. He told them that he intended to take the other bull in the same manner and call for fire in the name of Yehovah. Whichever God responded with fire was obviously the Almighty. The people agreed.

The Baalists went to work calling their god—dancing and cutting themselves with swords and spears until blood spurted on them. At day's end there was no response—and there was no listener.

Then Elijah called the people to draw near to him. With twelve stones that symbolized Israel's twelve tribes, he built an altar to honour God's name. Then he placed wood on the altar and cut the pieces of the bullock and placed them on the wood. He told the people to pour four jugs of water over the wood—and they repeated this process three times, until the water poured evenly around the altar, and even filled a trench circling it.

> *And it came to pass at the time of the offering of the evening sacrifice, that Elijah the prophet came near, and said, Lord God of Abraham, Isaac, and of Israel, let it be known this day that thou art God in Israel ... that this people may know that thou art the Lord God, and that thou hast turned their heart back again. Then the fire of the Lord fell, and consumed the burnt sacrifice, and the wood, and the stones, and the dust, and licked up the water that was in the trench. And when all the people saw it, they fell on their faces: and they said, The Lord, He is the God; the Lord, He is the God. (I Kings 18:36–39)*

> *And Elijah said unto them, take the prophets of Baal; let not one of them escape. And they took them: and Elijah brought them down to the brook Kishon, and slew them there. And Elijah said unto Ahab, Get thee up, eat and drink; for there is a sound of abundance of rain. (I Kings 18:40–41)*

What followed was a flurry of clouds and heavy rains. The Scriptures in the Book of Kings recount this and further spectacular events in Elijah's life in I Kings, Chapters 17–22 and II Kings, Chapters 1 and 2. Elijah was the only prophet on Earth who ascended to Heaven alive in a whirlwind. He left his mantle behind for his servant Elisha to succeed him as another distinguished prophet to the nation. The point is that God, by means of several similar miracles throughout Elijah's lifetime, had warned Israel against idolatry and corruption by bringing close to home the message of whom they needed to see as their Saviour. He created those wonders to warn the people to exercise caution and not stray away from the straight path he had graciously laid down for them.

Jewish people believe that Elijah is the harbinger of the Messiah who will return to redeem Israel and establish peace on Earth. These are the very last words of the Hebrew Scriptures: *"Behold I will send you Elijah the prophet before coming of the great and dreadful day of the Lord: and he shall turn the heart of the fathers to the children and the heart of the children to their fathers, lest I come and smite the earth with a curse"* (Malachi 4:5–6).

The Prophet Elisha (850 B.C.E.) spent most of his life helping people in distress. He travelled between various cities and taught the law; he also delivered judgment over disputes that arose within communities. On a political level, the kings also sought counsel with Elisha when faced with the challenges of dealing with enemy forces. Elisha's unique prophetic style was that he induced the powers of prophesy by stepping into a trance while listening to joyful music.

The Book of II Kings tells the story of Naaman, a commander of the Aramaian army, who was inflicted with leprosy. A series of events led him to the entrance of Elisha's house in search of a miracle cure. *"And Elisha sent a messenger unto him, saying, 'Go and wash in Jordan seven times, and thy flesh shall come again to thee, and thou shalt be clean'"* (II Kings 5:10).

Naaman was enraged and left, because the man of God did not let him in for a visit; he therefore ignored Elisha's advice, especially since previous attempts to immerse himself in the good rivers of Damascus had given him no relief. But Naaman's deputy suggested that he follow Elisha's advice and try bathing himself in the Jordan, just as the man of God had directed him to. When Naaman immersed himself seven times in the Jordan, his flesh became as that of a young boy. *"And he returned to the man of God … and he said, Behold now I know that there is no God in all the Earth, but in Israel: now, therefore, I pray thee, take a blessing of thy servant"* (II Kings 5:15).

But, Elisha refused to take anything in return and told him to go in peace. This was only one of Elisha's many miracles, and numerous others are described in II Kings, Chapters 2 through 13, bringing forth the powerful message that God is the Ultimate Master of the Universe, and that there is no event that is too miraculous for Him to perform through his prophets in order to unveil the truth of His omnipotence. If we pause to reflect on their significance in isolation, the miracles may not seem like much. But, when we see the tireless work of the prophets as a string of events that tie into a bigger plot in the theatre of life, we see that The Book itself is prophecy in its entirety—and that history as we shall see it unfold in later chapters is the fulfilment of that prophesy.

Among the prophets, it was no other than Isaiah (619–533 B.C.E.) through whom God revealed His future plans for earthlings, delivering with astonishing clarity: *"Behold the former things are come to pass, and new things do I declare; before they spring forth, I tell you of them"* (Isaiah 42:9).

In another passage of the Book of Isaiah, God proclaimed: *"Declaring the end from the beginning, and from the ancient times the things that are not yet done, saying, My counsel shall stand, and I will do all my pleasure"* (Isaiah 46:10).

The book of Isaiah begins with a reprimand to Israel for a lack of appreciation toward God's blessings: *"Hear, O Heavens, and give ear, O Earth: for the Lord hath spoken; I have nourished and brought up children, and they have rebelled against me. The ox knoweth his owner, and the ass his master's crib: but Israel doth not know, My people doth not consider"* (Isaiah 1:2–3).

Here is an instance in which the Jewish nation is seen wandering away from God's commandments. It may help to remember that, when Israel peopled and gained sovereignty over the Holy Land, they were mostly shepherds and farmers, and they often intermingled with Canaanites, who practiced idolatry. At the early stages in the evolution of Judaism, this phenomenon was unavoidable. In the absence of any central hub of culture, literature, and centres of learning, it is hard to imagine that for the most part, they had managed well to keep consistent with their relatively new elevated spiritual persona. So, it happened that their better selves became the prey of the many idolatrous belief systems they encountered among the peoples with whom they came into contact. More importantly, the kings and religious leaders were often themselves corrupt. Whereas their role was ideally to maintain the burden of responsibility to shepherd the people within the realm of divine principles, they often led them astray.

However, we see that the greater part of Isaiah's prophesy is given to a vision of the future. It is expressed in a futuristic and foretelling mode, and with much emotion. Isaiah's words paint a picture of a God of compassion, and we see in the following excerpt from chapter 60 of the Book of Isaiah, that in the midst of His people's betrayal, God had already set the stage for Jerusalem to become the spiritual centre of the world.

> *Arise, Shine; for your light has come, and the glory of the Lord is risen upon you ... Lift up your eyes all around and see, they are all assembling and coming to you; your sons will arrive from afar and your daughters will be raised at (their) side ... Who are these that fly as cloud, and as doves to their windows? ... and the ships of Tarshish in earlier times, to bring your children from afar? (Portions of Isaiah 60:1–9)*

Who *are* these who are flying as cloud? And, what can be made of the *windows?* What does the image of doves suggest in this passage? It may be appropriate first to explore what is meant by the ships of Tarshish.

There are many clues from Scripture that point to the geographic positioning of the ships of Tarshish on the Mediterranean Sea, known in Scripture as *yam gadol,* the great sea. They brought silver and other valuable goods possibly from places as far off as Spain, along trade routes that linked to the Phoenician trading city of Tyre in Lebanon: *"For the king's* [King Solomon's] *ships went to Tarshish with the servants of Huram: once every three years the ships of Tarshish used to come bringing gold, silver, ivory, apes, and peacocks"* (2 Chronicles 9:21).

"Every three years" suggests that the journey to Tarshish was a long ways from the Phoenician port city of Tyre in Lebanon, from whence also came the timber for the building of Solomon's temple in Jerusalem. *"And Solomon purposed to build a temple for the name of the Lord, and a royal palace for himself.... And Solomon sent word to Huram the king of Tyre: 'As you dealt with David my father and sent him cedar to build himself a house to dwell in, so deal with me'"* (2 Chronicles 2:1-3).

Another Biblical reference to Tarshish comes from the Book of Jonah, where God instructs Jonah to arise and go to the city of Nineveh to decry its corruption, *"...for their wickedness has come up before me. But Jonah rose to flee to Tarshish from the presence of the Lord. He went down to Joppa and found a ship going to Tarshish, away from the presence of the Lord"* (Jonah 1:2-3).

According to the online Jewish Encyclopaedia, one source even mentions Tarshish as denoting Italy or the coasts of Europe to the west of Greece, while another links the name to the coastal city of Carthage.[23] David Abulafia, in *The Great Sea: A Human History of the Mediterranean*, describes Tartessos as a wealthy land known from the time of Herodotus—a place that has been argued over by scholars going back to antiquity. He relates that, while some see Tartessos as a city, or a river, it more recently has been accepted to refer to a kingdom or region in southern Spain populated by native Iberians. Tartessos, and the lands located on both sides of the river Guadalquivir, were known for their silver deposits. Abulafia further mentions that it was the Phoenicians, and not the Iberians, who transported the silver eastward to Greece and Asia. The Phoenicians taught the Tartessians to extract, refine and process metals, since as early as the eighth century.[24]

The Phoenicians' outreach was such that their activities heavily influenced and lifted the political and economic life of that distant land to another level. "They were beginning to transform the entire Mediterranean." Abulafia adds: "Tartessos has often been equated with the metal-rich land of Tarshish mentioned again and again in the Hebrew Bible. Jonah, fleeing from God, set out from Jaffa for Tarshish, which

---

23   The unedited full-text of the 1906 Jewish Encyclopaedia. *Tarshish.* [online] Available at: <http://www.jewishencyclopedia.com/articles/14254-tarshish>. [Accessed 20 August 2011].

24   David Abulafia, *The Great Sea: A Human History of the Mediterranean*, 78-79.

the author of this story clearly understood to be somewhere extremely remote, the furthest one could go across the seas."[25]

Connecting the dots between ancient and more recent times, it seems appropriate to view the Isaiah prophesy above in the light of recent Jewish history. In 1948, as the Jewish nation state struggled to be reborn just before the declaration of a newly formed Israel, its shores were landlocked by belligerent Arab neighbours. As a result, the immigrants' sole point of entry to their Promised Land was by air or by sea.

In *"Operation Babylon, The Story of the Rescue of the Jews of Iraq,"* Shlomo Hillel described the logistics that were being put into place to airlift 150,000 Jews, the world's oldest Jewish community, out of their ancient Babylon soon after an edict was issued allowing them to leave the country on condition that they renounce citizenship and leave wealth and possessions behind: "I knew that we might yet need their goodwill to iron out some of the technical aspects of getting our immigrants to Israel, such as obtaining permission to fly via Cyprus (which was still a Crown Colony), or, preferably *purporting* to fly to Cyprus while actually going directly over Jordan (which was under strong British influence.)"[26]

Hillel recounts the modern day Exodus of the Iraqi Jews from their home of 2,600 years to the refugee camps of Israel. After a worldwide outcry was bellowing throughout all the major news channels about the hostage status of Iraqi Jews, the Iraqi government had no choice but to issue a decree that they can finally be allowed to leave the country, with the condition they renounce citizenship and leave all their wealth and belongings behind. Because it was inappropriate in the Arab view to have any direct ties with the fledgling Jewish state, and to save face for the Iraqi leaders, the airlifting operation necessitated a detour through Cyprus along the Mediterranean Sea—the Sea of Tarshish of old.

Mordechai Ben-Porat, an Iraqi Jew who helped organize the mass immigration between 1949 and 1951, brainstormed the plan in "an

---

[25]   Ibid, 79.

[26]   Shlomo Hillel, *Operation Babylon*, 239.

amazingly forthright letter" to the Minister of Interior to propose that his country's Jews be flown "'from Baghdad and Basra direct to Lydda [airport in Israel], where the passengers will be disembarked. The aircraft will then be flown to Cyprus, where the papers will be cleared and the aircraft returned to Baghdad and Basra to pick up fresh loads.'"[27] In this way, there would be no trace of a direct flight between Iraq and the fledgling state of Israel.

While Hillel's airlifting operations raced the clock to evacuate the disinherited Jews of ancient Babylon, farther to the north—in Europe—operations to set up camps to temporarily put up holocaust survivors were in full throttle in preparation for their transfer by sea to Palestine. Many camps were being built near the big cities such as Milan, from which they made their way in vast numbers by train or on foot over the mountains, and however else it was possible, to get to the seaside cities along the southern and western boot of Italy: Genoa, Naples, Bari and others. Bracha Habas, a major Israeli author and journalist, described in *"The Gate Breakers"* how one Yehuda Arazi, a member of a party organized to search for Jews, together with Ada Sereni, who managed to get herself to Italy to find her husband at the end of 1945, negotiated with ship owners for their ships, with the aim of transferring emaciated Jews from the death camps of "Dachau, Ebensee, and so on" to Palestine.[28] With great difficulty, Arazi along with several young recruits constructed sleeping quarters and basic amenities on a vessel called Pietro. In his words, "'The ship was also repainted before its clandestine journey across the Mediterranean. The white coat with the green stripe was replaced with a pale blue-gray color that would make the ship hard to distinguish against a background of sea and sky.'"[29]

Further still, we may recall, that through Isaiah, God saw it fit to set the stage for Jerusalem in a way befitting the ancient city to be considered, in some ways, a spiritual capital of the world. In what is quoted below, a keen linguist may be able to detect an interesting relationship between

---

[27]   Ibid.

[28]   Bracha Habas, *The Gate Breakers*, 367-68.

[29]   Ibid, 369.

prophecy and history; should the linguist also be an avid reader of The Book, the word for violence in Hebrew may flash like a light bulb in the passage below from Isaiah. The reader is cautioned to keep in mind the word "*hamas*," which in Hebrew denotes "*violence:*"

> *The sons of foreigners will build-up your walls and their kings will serve you. In my wrath I smote you, but in my favor I had mercy on you. Your gates will be opened continuously— day and night they will not be closed, to bring you the wealth of nations, and their kings under escort. For the nation and kingdom that does not serve you [refers to Jerusalem] will perish.... The glory of Lebanon shall come to you, the fir tree, the pine tree, and the box together, to glorify the place of My Sanctuary; and the place of my feet. The sons of your oppressors shall come bending unto you, and all who scorned you will prostrate themselves at the soles of your feet; they will call you "City of The Lord, Zion of the Holy One of Israel".... Violence ["hamas" in Hebrew] shall no more be heard in your land, nor plunder and calamity in your borders.... Your people will all be righteous; they will inherit the land forever; the shoot of My planting, My handiwork, in which to glorify.... I Am The Lord, in its time I will hasten it. (Portions of Isaiah 60:10–22)*

As we delve deeper into Isaiah, we find that Jerusalem is an integral part of prophesy in the Scripture:

> *For behold, I create new heavens and a new Earth: and the former shall not be remembered, nor come into mind. But be ye glad and rejoice for ever in that which I create: for, behold, I create Jerusalem a rejoicing, and her people a joy. And I will rejoice in Jerusalem, and joy in my people: and the voice of weeping shall be no more heard in her, nor the voice of crying. (Isaiah 65:17–19)*

But, even before the above declaration, God reveals unconditional love and forgiveness and compassion toward His people:

In a little wrath I hid my face from thee for a moment, but with everlasting kindness will I have mercy on thee, saith the Lord thy redeemer. For this is as the waters of Noah unto me: for as I have sworn that the waters of Noah should no more go over the Earth; so have I sworn that I would not be wroth with thee, nor rebuke thee. For the mountains shall depart, and the hills be removed; but my kindness shall not depart from thee, neither shall the covenant of my peace be removed, saith the Lord that hath mercy on thee. (Isaiah 54:8–10)

There is yet another prophet who distinguished himself as among the great ones in Israel. He, too, assumed the role of spokesman for the Almighty. His name was Jeremiah (600 B.C.E.), who at a young age experienced a strange vision:

The word of the Lord came to me saying, Before I formed thee in the belly, I knew thee, and before thou camest forth out of the womb I sanctified thee, and I ordained thee a prophet unto the nations. Then said I, Ah Lord God! Behold, I cannot speak: for I am a child. But the Lord said unto me, Say not, I am a child: for thou shalt go to all that I shall send thee, and whatsoever I command thee thou shall speak. Be not afraid of their faces: for I am with thee, saith the Lord. (Jeremiah 1:4–8)

Jeremiah's mission is clearly stated in The Book: "*See, I have this day set thee over the 'nations' and over the 'kingdoms;' to root out, and to pull down, and to destroy, and to throw down, to build, and to plant*" (Jeremiah 1:10).

Centuries back, in the desert, before the end of his mission, and just as the Israelites were about to cross a threshold of history into the Holy Land, Moses' words came as a sort of warning instead of a fanfare of praise and welcoming. He addressed the people with the stern message that they had no idea about what they were about to experience:

I call heaven and Earth to witness against you this day, that ye shall soon utterly perish from off the Land whereunto you go over Jordan to possess it; ye shall not prolong your days upon it, but shall utterly be destroyed. And the Lord shall scatter you among the heathen, whither the Lord shall lead you. And there ye shall serve gods, the work of men's hands, wood and stone. (Deuteronomy 4:26–28)

Jeremiah's appointment came at a time when the people of Judah, royal families and religious leaders alike, were deep into corruption. They had turned their backs on ethics and moral principles, stubbornly worshiping idols. The time was ripe for Moses' declaration to crystallize into living history. The reader of The Book can easily grasp Jeremiah's deep sense of pathos and sadness as he uttered the same stern warning delivered by his predecessor back on the sands of the Sinai wasteland.

Jeremiah's mission started with God sending him to people of all ranks and levels to instruct them to repent, to return to God and thus avoid annihilation. *"Run ye to and fro through the streets of Jerusalem, and see now, and know, and seek in the broad places thereof, if ye can find a man, if there be any that executeth judgment, that seeketh the truth; and I will pardon it"* (Jeremiah 5:1).

And, at one point, God sent the prophet to a potter:

The word which came to Jeremiah from the Lord saying: Arise and go down to the potter's house, and there I will cause thee to hear my words. Then I went down to the potter's house, and, behold, he wrought a work on the wheels. And the vessel that he made of clay was marred in the hand of the potter: so he made it again another vessel, as seemed good to the potter to make it. Then the word of the Lord came to me saying: 'Oh house of Israel, cannot I do with you as this potter?' saith the Lord. Behold, as the clay in the potter's hand, so are you in my hand, oh house of Israel. (Jeremiah 18:1–6)

Now Jeremiah found himself cornered into a task from which he could find no way out: *"Oh Lord, thou hast deceived me, and I was deceived: thou art stronger than I and hast prevailed: I am in derision daily, everyone mocketh me"* (Jeremiah 20:7). Jeremiah's frustration accumulated at the people's lack of interest to hear about God; he sensed their desire to see him hobbled. *"Wherefore came I forth out of the womb to see labour and sorrow, that my days should be consumed with shame?"* (*Jeremiah 20:18*).

Jeremiah had the unhappy task of prophesying that his people were about to face a calamity predestined by God. The book of Jeremiah testifies to the atrocities that were soon to befall the Jewish nation. In his book of Lamentations, Jeremiah narrated the enormity of the siege of Jerusalem: *"How doth the city sit solitary, that was full of people! How is she become as a widow! She that was great among the nations and princess among the provinces, how is she become tributary"* (*Lamentations 1:1*).

The siege of Jerusalem by Nebuchadnezzar, king of Babylon, spread famine throughout the city. His armies breached the surrounding wall of Jerusalem, pillaged and burned the house of the Lord, the king's domain, and the homes of all its leaders. The atrocities committed by the ferocious Chaldean army are recorded in detail in Chapter 54 of the Book of Jeremiah.

In his book of Lamentations, Jeremiah laments that Moses' prophecy regarding the Holy Land's future destruction has verily come to pass: *"The Lord hath done that which he had devised; he hath fulfilled his word that he had commanded in the days of old"* (*Lamentations 2:17*).

However God kept watch over Jeremiah's safety throughout the ensuing turmoil to ensure that he carried on with his mission: *"Now Nebuchadnezzar king of Babylon gave charge concerning Jeremiah to Nebuzaradan the captain of the guard saying, 'Take him, and look well to him, and do him no harm; but do unto him even as he shall say unto thee'"* (*Jeremiah 39:11–12*). *"Be not afraid of their faces: for I am with thee, saith the Lord"* (*Jeremiah 1:8*).

Just as the prophet had a mission, the Creator had a promise:

> *Thus saith The Lord which giveth the sun for a light by day, and the ordinances of the Moon and of the stars for a light by night, which divideth the sea when the waves thereof roar; The Lord of hosts is His name: If those ordinances depart from before me, saith the Lord, then the seed of*

> *Israel also shall cease from being a nation before me for ever.*
> *(Jeremiah 31:35–36)*

As much as Jeremiah's chapter in history is pregnant with gloom and doom, it eventually transforms into an ebullient offering of hope, for he emerges unambiguous in his conviction that an eternal bond was alive and well between God and the seed of Israel. Similarly, Jeremiah's significance on the historical stage as the messenger of hope is close to the prophetic vision of Isaiah, which will be examined further down. In the next passage, he prophesies the redemption of Israel in days to come.

> *Hear the Words of the Lord, O nations, and declare it in the isles afar off, and say, He that scattered Israel will gather him, and keep him, as a shepherd doth his flock. For the Lord hath redeemed Jacob, and ransomed him from the hand of him that was stronger than he. Therefore, they shall come and sing in the height of Zion, and shall flow together to the goodness of the Lord, for wheat, and for wine, and for oil, and for the young of the flock and of the herd, and their soul shall be as the watered garden; and they shall not sorrow any more at all. Then shall the virgin rejoice in the dance, both young men and old together: for I will turn their mourning into joy, and will comfort them, and make them rejoice from their sorrow. And I will satiate the soul of the priests with fatness, and my people shall be satisfied with my goodness, saith the Lord. (Jeremiah 31:10–14)*

By the time the Book of Ezekiel was written, we witness the redemption and rebuilding of the Temple in Jerusalem. Ezekiel (c. 622 B.C.E.) was born into priesthood, or a *Kohen* lineage of the patrilineal line of Ithamar. He was the son of Buzi, a priest, who was among the captives taken to Chaldea, modern day Iraq, and settled by the river Chebar.

Kohens (כֹּ הֵן, plural: כוהנים, *kohanim*) were, and remain to this day, direct descendents of the Biblical Aaron. A subgroup within the tribe of Levi, they were known as Priests whom Jewish law stated were responsible for offering the sacrifices, allowed only to be done in the

Temple of King Solomon, built about 950 B.C.E. It was from the tribe of Levi that the spiritual leaders and teachers were appointed.[30] It is interesting to note, too, that Ezekiel was only twenty-five years old when he and some 3,000 among the highly trained and wealthier Jews were exiled to Babylon. My family descended from those Jews, having chosen to remain in Babylon even after the Persian King Cyrus allowed them to return to Jerusalem and rebuild the Temple. My ancestors have remained in Babylon for over two thousand years, up until a series of persecutions uprooted the Iraqi Jewish community and provoked the mass exodus in 1950 earlier described, although my father had earlier crossed the border to Iran for business opportunities, in the 1930s (Chapter 4, Part I).

> *The hand of the Lord was upon me, and carried me out in the Spirit of the Lord, and set me down in the midst of the valley which was full of bones. And caused me to pass by them round about: and, behold, there were many in the open valley, and lo, they were very dry. (Ezekiel 37:1–2)*

> *And He said unto me, Son of man, can these bones live? And I answered, O Lord God, thou knowest. Again He said unto me Prophesy upon these bones, and say unto them, O ye dry bones, hear the word of the Lord. Thus saith the Lord God unto these bones; Behold, I will cause breath to enter into you, and ye shall live. And I will lay sinews upon you, and will bring up flesh upon you, and cover you with skin, and put breath in you, and ye shall live; and ye shall know that I Am the Lord. (Ezekiel 37:3–6)*

> *So I prophesied as I was commanded: and … there was a noise, and behold a shaking, and the bones came together, bone to his bone. And when I beheld, lo, the sinews and the flesh came up upon them, and the skin covered them above: but there was no breath in them. Then said He unto me, Prophesy unto the wind … and say to the wind. Thus saith the Lord God; Come … O breath, and breathe*

---

[30] Rabbi Joseph Telushkin, *Jewish Literacy: The Most Important Things to Know About the Jewish Religion, Its People, and Its History*, 61.

upon these slain, that they may live. So I prophesied as He commanded me, and the breath came into them, and they lived, and stood up upon their feet, an exceeding great army. (Ezekiel 37:7–10)

Then He said unto me, Son of man, these bones are the whole house of Israel: behold, they say, Our bones are dried, and our hope is lost ... therefore prophesy and say unto them, Thus saith the Lord God; Behold, O My people, I will open your graves, and cause you to come up out of your graves, and bring you into the Land of Israel.... And I shall place you in your own land: then shall ye know that I the Lord have spoken it, and performed, it saith the Lord. (Ezekiel 37:11–14)

Toward the end of his book, Ezekiel's script bears witness to the fact that the hand of God came upon him and ...

In the visions of God, He brought me into the land of Israel, and set me upon a very high mountain ... and behold, there was a man, whose appearance was like the appearance of brass with a line of flax in his hand, and a measuring reed; and he stood in the gate. And the man said unto me, Son of man, behold with thine eyes, and hear with thine ears, and set thine heart upon all that I shall show thee ... declare all that thou seest to the house of Israel. (Ezekiel 40:2–4)

In that vision, the man with the linen cord and a measuring rod took Ezekiel on a tour of a future Temple in Jerusalem. In his vision Ezekiel was able to pick out every architectural detail of the temple to be: its pillars, an inner and an outer court, gates, a hall, an altar, the Holy Chamber, with all of its compartments. It is the draft of a monument with a holy chamber where only the *kohen gadol* (high priest) would be allowed to pray. Ezekiel's vision depicted all the details with the painstaking accuracy of an architect's craftsmanship, ready to be handed over to the builder.

Visit by the Supreme:

> *Afterward he brought me to the gate, even the gate that looketh to the east. And behold, the glory of the God of Israel came from the way of the east: and his voice was like a noise of many waters: and the Earth shined with his glory ... and I fell upon my face. And the glory of the Lord came unto the house by the way of the gate whose prospect is toward the east. So the spirit took me up, and brought me into the inner court; and, behold, the glory of the Lord filled the house. And I heard him speaking unto me out of the house; and the man stood by me ... and He said unto me, Son of man, the place of my throne, and the place of the soles of my feet, where I will dwell in the midst of the children of Israel for ever, and my holy name, shall the house of Israel no more defile, neither they, nor their kings, by their whoredom, nor by the carcasses of their kings in their high places. (Ezekiel 43:1–7)*

In the same vision, Ezekiel was briefed on the Temple's administration—the new law and order. He then recorded the vision's description of the various responsibilities that were to be delegated to the *kohanim*, to the Levites, and to the princes.

The man with the measuring rod ushered Ezekiel back to the Temple entrance, where water emerged from under the threshold.

> *And when the man that had the line in his hand went forth eastward, he measured a thousand cubits, and he brought me through the waters; the waters were to the ankles. Again he measured a thousand, and brought me through the waters; the waters were to the knees. Again he measured a thousand, and brought me through; the waters were to the loins.*
>
> *Afterward he measured a thousand; and it was a river that I could not pass over: for the waters were risen, waters to swim in, a river that could not be passed over. (Ezekiel 47:3–5)*

Now when I had returned, behold, at the bank of the river were very many trees on the one side and on the other. Then said he unto me, These waters issue out toward the east country, and go down into the desert, and go into the sea ... and there shall be a very great multitude of fish ... exceeding many. (Ezekiel 47:7–10)

It is important to note that the Holy Land has always been vulnerable to draught and low levels of precipitation, despite the fact that its entire western border is a coastline running north to south along the Mediterranean Sea.

Israel's scorching sun can easily vaporize seawater into rainfall. From what we have been handed down through prophecy, we know that scarcity of water appears to be linked to the will of God, and we note that according to the above vision, God promised a lasting peace in a time to come, when water would come forth in abundance to sustain the whole region.

The miracle of Israeli agriculture is in the technique her farmers use to compensate for the desert's scarce vital resource: water. Israel's drip technology ensures that plants and crops are fed in amounts that are spread incrementally over space and time. A well-controlled distribution system irrigates the soil below through water reaching it not by an open hose method, but one drop at a time! Such a method of irrigation ensures little to no waste of precious moisture while keeping the soil constantly nourished.

Still, we can pause to reflect, albeit on a symbolical level, between what we have understood from chapter 47 of the Book of Ezekiel in the above-quoted verses, on one hand, and Israel's achievements in making the desert bloom, on the other. Even with the miracle of modern technology, water is still scarce in the region. Governments regulate this vital resource, and the ultimate miracle seems to be forthcoming only upon the will of God.

The Tanakh is a window into the past, the present, and the future. It offers insight into much of modern history with the fulfilment of numerous warnings delivered by the prophets. It is thus difficult to ignore their counsel—that whatever occurred in the past and whatever will occur in future is entirely in the hands of God alone. The Hebrew Scriptures are not only ancient history, sometimes expressed through symbols, at other times through storytelling or poetry. The Scripture also encourages us to use our deeper capacities and conscience to the benefit of all. This is the essence of the Golden Rule.

The Scriptures bring to life a theatre of events, each concerted precisely into a program that only He knows and understands. This is the critical contribution of Jewish prophets on the historical stage. Understanding this fundamental aspect of the Tanakh can help us deepen our understanding of the human condition and of our times. The Book, then, can be read as a prophecy for our times, and an intimate reading can lead us to an observation that Jewish history is prophecy—fulfilled!

12

THE JEWISH NATION IN EXILE

IN 587 B.C.E. THE BABYLONIAN KING, NEBUCHADNEZZAR, breached the wall surrounding Jerusalem, the last stronghold of the kingdom of Judah, after a prolonged siege. His ferocious army killed, destroyed, and pillaged whatever lay in its path, leaving the poor behind and taking with them the nobility, the religious leaders, the doctors, the lawyers, the tradesmen, and professionals—in other words the educated class—which he took as captives and deported to Babylon. While it is most unusual for an enemy to conquer and deport a people to their land as refugees, numerous clay tablets housed in London's British Museum have been translated and found to be a testimony to the Babylonian king's desire to bring the learned folk from Jerusalem in order to elevate his own realm with their skill and technology.

Meanwhile, Jerusalem's Temple was plundered and burnt to the ground. Zedekia, Judah's last king, was caught during flight and brought before the king of Babylon. His sons were slain before his eyes, after which he was blinded, bound in fetters, and taken to Babylon.

Looking to a larger view of the picture can help us see the Almighty's intent for the deportees as twofold. One reason seems akin to putting the land to rest:

> And I will remember the land. The land also shall be left of them, and shall enjoy her sabbaths, while she lieth desolate without them, and they shall accept of the punishment of their iniquity ... because they despised My judgments, and because their soul abhorred My statutes. (Leviticus 26:42–43)

The other reason was to help them keep the torch of faith burning while coming into an appreciation of what was previously taken for granted:

> *Thus saith the Lord of Hosts, the God of Israel, unto all that are carried away captives, whom I have caused to be carried away from Jerusalem unto Babylon. Build ye houses and dwell in them; and plant gardens and eat the fruit of them. Take ye wives, and beget sons and daughters; and take wives for your sons, and give your daughters to husbands, that they bear sons and daughters; that they may be increased there and not diminished. (Jeremiah 29:4–6)*

I was often asked by my children why the Islamic Revolution in Iran placed such heavy emphasis on Israel's presence in the Middle East. Ever since imprisonment uprooted my family, I felt compelled to make sense of any connection that may have justified so much vilification and hatred toward a land located miles away, a land whose recent—and not so recent—history was so separate from that of my native Iran. I wasn't able to come up with any rational connection besides that which came from ancient history from The Book about the Jews of Babylon.

When Cyrus the Great, the Persian Emperor, vanquished the Chaldeans in 539 B.C.E., he allowed the Jews of the realm to go back and rebuild the Temple of Solomon. Through the leadership of Ezra and Nehemiah, a few Jews in Babylon returned to Jerusalem and rebuilt the Temple, but most of the Jewish inhabitants of Jerusalem returned to Babylon or emigrated to other countries.

> *Now in the first year of Cyrus king of Persia, that the word of the Lord by the mouth of Jeremiah might be fulfilled, The Lord stirred up the spirit of Cyrus king of Persia, that he made a proclamation throughout all the kingdom, and put it also in writing, saying, Thus saith Cyrus king of Persia, the Lord God of heaven hath given me all the kingdoms of the Earth; and he hath charged me to build him a house in Jerusalem which is in Judah. Who is there among you of all his people? His God be with him, and let him go up to*

Jerusalem, which is in Judah, and build the House of the Lord. (Ezekiel 1:1–3)

As mentioned earlier, my ancestors belonged to the tribe of Judah. Some of that tribe's members chose to remain in their ancient Promised Land, and others returned to Babylon after the rebuilding of the Temple in Jerusalem. My family descended from those who remained in Babylon—modern day Iraq—all the way until recent political events uprooted the entire Iraqi Jewish population, all this after over two-and-a-half millennia in what my children's history books have referred to as the land of the Fertile Crescent. Even though the Persian Emperor Cyrus conquered Babylon and liberated the Jews, my ancestors were among those who chose to return to, or remain in, Babylon. When a massive Exodus was organized in 1950 to airlift a huge number of Iraqi Jews fleeing from persecution, it was coined Operation Ezra and Nehemiah after the Exodus that took place in biblical times.

Ezra and Nehemiah are the two chapters in the Bible that relate the story of the Jewish exile to Babylon. These two sages led the return for the rebuilding of the Second Temple in Jerusalem. Those who, like my Iraqi Jewish ancestors, chose to remain in Babylon, were much later—in the middle of the twentieth century,—forced to leave, twenty-five centuries after an ancient deportation uprooted them from a paradise lost to another paradise they were forced to leave behind:

> The prisoners of Nebuchadnezzar have left a country where they had lived for twenty-five centuries. They were there before the Christians or the Muslims. To preserve the Book, they studied it, composing the Babylonian Talmud. And while they became integrated into a series of empires, caliphates and colonial powers, they remained Jews."[31]

The 1950 exodus resulted from mounting international pressure following an outcry of protests toward the widespread torture, killing, rape, confiscation from, and imprisonment of Iraq's Jews, causing much

---

[31] Naïm Kattan, Sheila Fischman, transl. *Farewell to Babylon: Coming of Age in Jewish Baghdad*, Foreword, 7.

embarrassment to the Iraqi government. In 1951, a year after passing the resolution to allow the heavily persecuted Iraqi Jewish population to leave the country, the government "shut the floodgates," having earlier declared that anyone who was registered to leave and renounce their nationality would have their money and property confiscated, although they had formally frozen all Jewish assets. Shlomo Hillel, an organizer of the modern Exodus to Eretz Israel (Land of Israel) in a personal account of the operations, described the new rule as a "nasty, nasty trick." Most of the 104,000 Iraqi Jews who arrived in Israel with Operation Ezra and Nehemiah came virtually penniless unless they had previously managed to transfer funds through relatives residing in Israel many years earlier.[32]

Over time, ancient Babylon, which later went down in history as Mesopotamia (the land between two rivers, the Tigris and the Euphrates), was named Iraq. This new chapter in the history of the ancient land was paged after the collapse of the Ottoman Empire in the early twentieth century and the drafting of political boundaries around a number of newly minted Arab states. For a time, what began as a land of exile for the Babylonian Jews evolved into a safe haven that provided the wherewithal for them to flourish, as God had proclaimed in The Book. For a time during the 1930s, there were no pogroms as in Russia, no inquisitions as in Spain, and of course there was no hint of the Holocaust that was soon to take place in Europe.

Iraqi Jews built businesses, held government jobs as civil servants, and contributed extensively in every sphere of their country's political, economic, educational, and cultural life. Even in the sphere of music, it was a couple of Iraqi Jewish brothers, Saleh and Daoud Al-Kuwaiti, who created most of the musical culture of Iraq as it has come to be known. After their departure amid the wave of emigration of nearly all the remaining Iraqi Jews in 1950, public knowledge of them was cleverly hidden for future generations: "Slowly but surely, their names disappeared from the radio programs, although the songs themselves were still played. The process came to a climax after Saddam Hussein came to power. In 1972 he established a committee in the broadcasting authority, and one of

---

[32]   Tamar Morad, Dennis Shasha and Robert Shasha, Ed. *Palgrave Studies in Oral History, Iraq's Last Jews, Stories of Daily Life, Upheaval and Escape from Modern Babylon*, 94.

its orders was to erase the names of the Al-Kuwaiti brothers from every official publication and from the curricula in the academy of music."[33]

My father, who immigrated to Iran in the early 1930s for business, never knew the hard times that ensued for Jews in Iraq, which slowly encroached upon them in the years before the Second World War, when the German Chancellor Adolf Hitler was in power and spread the Nazi creed among the Arabs. While my father's car dealership was flourishing and many other Jews of Iraqi origin made good business supplying materials to the Allied armies who used Iranian territory as a right of passage for the transport of military equipment to Russia, the atrocities in Iraq continued. They soon reached a peak when the independent State of Israel was proclaimed following a United Nations resolution.

At the onset of Operation Ezra and Nehemia, the new chapter in the history of Babylonian Jewry was being scripted. Hundreds of tent cities were erected to accommodate the new arrivals in the fledgling State of Israel, which absorbed immigrants even where food and housing were in severe shortage. Some crossed the border into Iran, where the former shah graciously granted them safe haven and facilitated their flight to Israel by El Al Airways.

> *And I will be found of you, saith the Lord—and I will turn away your captivity, and I will gather you from all the nations, and from all the places whither I have driven you, saith the Lord; and I will bring you again into the place whence I caused you to be carried away captive. (Jeremiah 29:14)*

Jeremiah's prophesy about a modern Exodus gives one pause to reflect upon the geographical positioning of the Holy Land, sitting as it does at a crossroads between East and West, and taking up a geophysical spot precisely at an intersection between the three great continents: Europe,

---

[33] Diwaniyya Dayan Center Podcast: Middle East culture, history and politics, 16 April 2012. *The Al-Kuwaiti Brothers: Iraqi Jewish Musicians.* [online] Available at: http://www.diwaniyya.org/2012/04/story-of-iraqi-jewish-musicians-al.html. [Accessed 12 June 2012].

Asia and Africa. *"Thus saith the Lord God; this is Jerusalem: I have set it in the midst of the nations and countries that are round about her"* (Ezekiel 5:5).

Because of its strategic geographic position and after falling under the dominance of the Chaldeans in 587 B.C.E., the land that had been promised to the people of The Book changed hands very often throughout history. Various empires and powerful conquerors each left their mark on this tiny strip of hotly contended real estate known as the Promised Land.

Chaldeans	587–539 B.C.E.
Persians	539–332 B.C.E.
Greeks	332–301 B.C.E.
Ptolemaics	301–200 B.C.E.
Seleucids	200–37 B.C.E.
Romans	37 BCE–638 C.E.
Arabs	638–1099
Crusaders	1099–1187
Salah-el-Din	1187–1244
Khwarizmi Empire	1244–1516
Ottoman Empire	1516–1917
British Empire	1917–1947
State of Israel	Since 1948

I discovered some interesting truths about the Jews in their Exile, after the Holy Land fell into foreign hands across a span of over 2,535 years.

The first insight that struck me was that, oddly enough, when the Jewish people were sovereign in their own land, they had a habit of deliberately turning their backs on the laws bequeathed to them by the prophets. They continuously solicited the strange gods of the idol worshippers. It was a sort of fad, an urge, perhaps an escapist tendency, and it occurred as common practice throughout all levels of society, from the royalty and members of the nobility down to the ordinary populace. This rebellious inclination to stray from Jewish roots took a different turn soon after the Jewish people lost their independence and became subjugated under foreign powers. While dispersed in exile among the many nations of the Earth, they once again strove to regain their true calling.

An oft-repeated passage from The Book is the lament of a deportee's song:

> *By the rivers of Babylon, there we sat down, yea, we wept, when we remembered Zion. We hanged our harps upon the willows in the midst thereof. For there they that carried us away captive required of us a song; and they that wasted us mirth, saying, sing us one of the songs of Zion.*

> *How shall we sing the Lord's song in a strange land? If I forget thee, O Jerusalem, let my right hand forget her cunning. If I do not remember thee, let my tongue cleave to the roof of my mouth; if I prefer not Jerusalem above my chief joy. (Psalms 137:1–6)*

Even though the Prophet Jeremiah had so much to lament over the situation of his compatriots, he nevertheless delivered strong words of consolation and hope from God:

> *But this shall be the covenant that I will make with the house of Israel; after those days, saith the Lord, I will put my law in their inward parts, and write it in their hearts ... for they shall all know me, from the least of them unto the greatest of them, saith the Lord: for I will forgive their iniquity, and I will remember their sin no more. (Jeremiah 31:33–34)*

Though the Greeks tried to crush the Jewish soul triggering the revolt of the Maccabees, and although the Romans incessantly tried to assimilate the Jews, the Torah remains till this day the nerve centre of Jewish life, just as it did in biblical times. Judaism has managed to survive forced conversions, inquisitions, pogroms, and a holocaust that decimated a large segment of its tiny global population. But, the challenges fell short of extinguishing the torch of a masterpiece called the Tanakh that was lit, inspired, and revealed by the God of Israel.

Over the last millennium and under Arab, Ottoman, and British rule, the Holy Land was under-populated throughout its occupation by foreign powers. By the end of World War I, the Jewish population in the Holy Land (which came to be known as Palestina, or more familiarly today as Palestine, a name coined by the Romans to divert it from any remaining connection to Jewish roots) counted a mere 55,000 souls. Again, the reason that the Holy Land remained desolate for so long seems connected hand in hand with the message scribed in The Book: *"The land also shall be left of them, and shall enjoy her sabbaths..."(Leviticus 26:43). And also "Ye shall be left few in number among the 'nations' whither the Lord shall lead you"* (Deuteronomy 4:27).

The total population of world Jewry following the Temple's destruction remained at all times below fifteen million. Throughout the centuries, religions were born whose paths intertwined with Judaism in various ways. Had the story of Judaism's survival to the present day been described as a miracle, then the first miracle may have been the Torah itself. And, whilst the people of The Book have been creating history over a period spanning close to 3,800 years, the destinies of other faiths have evolved in their own unique ways alongside that of the Jewish faith.

Jesus, a Jewish descendant, was born in Bethlehem Aphratah (most scholars say between 7 and 2 B.C.E.) when the Holy Land was ruled by the Romans. Four of his disciples, St. Matthew, St. Mark, St. Luke, and St. John scribed the Gospels. Many scholars date the writing of the Gospels between thirty and sixty years after Jesus' death. Paul (also Saul, or *Shaool* in Judeo-Arabic), a Jewish follower, took the school to Western Europe, from whence emerged the rapid spread of the Christian faith. The very first Christians who adopted their new faith were not inclined to consider Christianity as a factional component of Judaism. Although the Torah or Tanakh (Hebrew Scriptures) was considered an integral part of the Christian faith, the presence of Judaism represented a threat to the new school of religious thought; this exclusion consequently became a grave menace toward the security of the Jews. The Jews nevertheless held on to the Tanakh, which bestowed upon them God's revelation that His commandments are immutable and unchanging (Deuteronomy 4:2) and that the Jewish people will never lose their status as a nation (Jeremiah 31:35–36):

> *Ye shall not add unto the word which I command you, neither shall ye diminish aught from it, that ye may keep the commandments of the Lord your God which I command you. (Deuteronomy 4:2)*

> *Thus saith the Lord, which giveth the sun for a light by day, and the ordinances of the Moon and of the stars for a light by night, which divideth the sea when the waves thereof roar; the Lord of hosts is his name. If those ordinances depart from before me, saith the Lord, then the seed of Israel also shall cease from being a nation before me forever. (Jeremiah 31:35–36)*

Then, by the seventh century C.E., a man named Mohammad emerged in the Arabian Peninsula. Mohammad was an orphan brought up by his uncle Abu Taleb, who became in his youth the camel driver of Khadija, a rich widow who conducted business with Jewish merchants.[34] Mohammad, a highly intelligent person as it has been said about him, was attracted to the Jews and their principle of monotheism. The idea of a unique god led Mohammad to reiterate that belief in Arabic—*La illah'a il ullah*, a phrase to which was soon added *Mohammad Rasullulah*, meaning Mohammad is the messenger of God. After setting such a goal for himself, it is believed that the Jews helped Mohammad spiritually and materially to that end. In fact, whereas it was Jewish practice to face Jerusalem during prayer, Mohammad initially adopted that same ritual for Islam. When the Jews of Mecca resisted abandonment of their faith and failed to collaborate with the new prophet's repeated attempts to convert Jews to Islam, he modified this practice known as *qiblah*, and chose to face Mecca instead of Jerusalem during prayer.[35]

---

[34]   *Encylopaedia Judaica*, Volume 12, "Muhammad," 508.

[35]   Ibid, Volume 12, "Muhammad in Medina," 509.

Mohammad attracted followers both by his charisma and his sword in the name of God and Islam, to become the absolute power in Arabia. Jewish inhabitants of Arabia were counting on Mohammad's efforts to turn the pagans into God-fearing people, with whom they hoped to enjoy a peaceful life of coexistence. From his position of power, and contrary to their expectations, Mohammad decreed that Jews abandon their faith and adopt Islam. Some Jews, willingly or because of fear, converted to Islam and went as far as helping Mohammad further his ambitious plans to spread his faith. The majority—mostly the well-to-do who owned villages in Medina, Quraiza, and Khaibar—were unable to openly hold onto their Jewish identity. Those who showed open resistance to conversion were mercilessly massacred and their livelihoods looted.[36]

Nevertheless, throughout a period spanning more than 2,500 years of exile known as the Jewish Diaspora, the Jews met adversity by turning toward The Book for spiritual guidance and sustenance, and continued to struggle to survive as a people with a distinct calling:

> *And he said, It is a light thing that thou shouldst be my servant, to raise up the tribes of Jacob, and to restore the preserved of Israel: I will also give thee for a light to the Gentiles, that thou mayest be my salvation unto the end of the Earth. (Isaiah 49:6)*

---

[36]   Ibid, Volume 13, "Qurayza," 1436.

13

WHAT CAN THE BIBLE BRING TO LIGHT IN RELATION TO MODERN HISTORY?

IN MY QUEST TO UNDERSTAND GOD'S will for my people as written in the Scripture, I searched the five Books of Moses to seize the bigger picture, if any, of Jewish history since its inception at the time of the forefather Abraham. I found that God said to Abraham:

> *Know of a surety that thy seed shall be a stranger in a land that is not theirs, and shall serve them, and they shall afflict them four hundred years. And also that nation, whom they shall serve, will I judge: and afterward shall they come out with great substance. (Genesis 15:13–14)*

Three generations later, a turn of events took Jacob and his family to Egypt, where they increased in numbers. When the time came to be freed from slavery under the hand of the ruling pharaohs, Moses led them carrying all their belongings through the desert, where he delivered them a set of laws and prepared them to enter and take possession of the Holy Land.

Shortly before entering the land, Moses warned:

> *When thou shall beget children, and children's children, and ye shall have remained long in the land, and shall corrupt yourselves, and make a graven image, or the likeness of anything, and shall do evil in the sight of the Lord thy God, to provoke Him to anger…, that ye shall soon utterly perish from off the land whereunto ye go over Jordan to possess it … and the Lord shall scatter you among the nations, and ye shall be left few in number among the heathen, whither the Lord shall lead you. (Deuteronomy 4:25–27)*

Three important issues stand out from this declaration. The first is that the people in the land would become corrupt and worship other gods. That prophecy was fulfilled. The second is that the Jewish nation as a state would be destroyed and scattered among the peoples. That forewarning was precisely crystallized, as extensively described in the Books of Jeremiah, II Kings, and II Chronicles. The third point to remember is that "you will be left few in number among the nations." This, too, is confirmed by history. If we take the normal trend, the Jewish population may have been close to a billion by our present time in history. In comparison to other populations of the Earth, their sheer small number resembles a scenario of near extinction. There seems to be direct consistency between the historical facts and the Words of God in The Book: "*Declaring the end from the beginning, and from ancient times the things that are not yet done, saying, My counsel shall stand, and I will do all my pleasure*" (Isaiah 46:10).

Toward the end of his mission, Moses told the people, of the shape of their destiny after a Diaspora, and that Israel would be restored:

> *And it shall come to pass when all these things are come upon thee, the blessing and the curse, which I have set before thee, and thou shalt call them to mind among all the nations, whither the Lord thy God hath driven thee, and shalt return unto the Lord thy God, and shalt obey His voice according to all that I command thee this day, thou and thy children, with all thy heart, and with all thy soul; That then the Lord thy God will turn thy captivity, and have compassion upon thee, and will return and gather thee from all the nations, whither the Lord thy God hath scattered thee. If any of thine be driven out unto the utmost part of heaven, from thence will the Lord thy God gather thee, and from thence will He fetch thee: And the Lord thy God will bring thee into the land which thy fathers possessed, and thou shall possess it; and He will do thee good, and multiply thee above your fathers. And the Lord thy God will circumcise thine heart, and the heart of thy seed, to love the Lord thy God with all thine heart, and with all thy soul, that thou mayest live.*
> (Deuteronomy 30:1–6)

Moses' prophecy, uttered even before the entry of his people to the Promised Land, offers a trailer view of how the Jewish nation would be restored after dispersal to the four corners of the Earth. The question arises as to whether there are prophecies in the Bible that have not been fulfilled.

In the continuum of human events, there is room to ponder upon the words already presaged that have yet to be written down as history. We do know, however, that much of written history is a testimony to the words of the Jewish Prophets of the Hebrew Scriptures.

My Father, Heskel Abraham Koukou (Ezekiel in Hebrew) in his office in downtown Teheran. The year was 1960.

My mother, Naïma Koukou.

My Family in a photo taken in Isfahan. I was twelve years old. From left
to right: sister Violet, father Heskel, sister Flora, sister Loris, myself,
mother Naïma, and brother Anwar.

With Evelyn on our wedding day.

poor languages.

Samuel had a little shop in Malaga, next to the palace of Ibn Elarif, the wazir of king Habus. A slave of the wazir who frequently frequently furnished information to her master, regularly had her letters written by the poor Jew. These letters displayed so much linguistic and calligraphic skill that the wazir Ibn-Elarif became anxious to know the writer. He had Ibn Nagrela called into his presence, and took him into his service as his private secretary (1025). The wazir soon discovered that Samuel possessed great political insight, and consulted him on all important affairs of state, and as his advice was always sound, the wazir at length undertook nothing without Samuel's approval. When Ibn Elarif fell ill, King Habus was in despair as to what to do about his complicated relations with neighboring states. The dying wazir referred him to his Jewish secretary, confessed that his successful undertakings had been mainly due to Samuel's wise suggestions, and advised Habus to employ him as a councelor. The Berber king of Granada, who had fewer prejudices against the Jews than the Arab Moslems, raised Samuel Ibn Nagrela to the dignity of minister (Katib), and put him in charge of the diplomatic and military affairs (1027). Thus the shopkeeper of Malaga lived in the king's palace, and had a voice in all matters concerning the Pyrenean peninsula.

Diplomatic, wise, and always master of himself, Ibn Nagrela knew how to employ circumstances, and had the art of disarming his opponents. The gentleness with which he opposed his enemies is shown by an anecdote: Near the palace of Habus there lived a Mussulman

59

Page 59 from Volume IV of four manuscripts handwritten and illustrated by the author prior to his definitive departure from Iran.

PART III
RETURN TO THE SOURCE

14

WHAT'S IN A BLESSING?

THREE THOUSAND YEARS AFTER ISAAC'S BLESSING ON JACOB, the Israelites are still a nation, and although they are spread across the four corners of the globe and exist geographically apart from one another—rather than as distinct communities having lost the slightest thread of a common bond of kinship between one another—they miraculously hold strong to their Jewish identity as one, each mirroring the soul of a singular minded people, diverse in adopted language and culture, but singular in the sense of destiny as a nation.

The pages of their history are fraught with persecution in adopted lands, although peppered with periods of enlightenment where Jews were allowed to grow and their communities able to flourish. They produced leaders in every field of human endeavour. Repeated challenges that threatened their survival only served to strengthen their resolve. They remained anchored to their roots wherever their wandering led them, mindful of the divine revelations that God bestowed upon their early patriarchs. Having lost their homeland centuries earlier in the city of King David, its capital in Jerusalem, Jewish heritage in exile remained alive from one generation to another. Indeed, though the Greeks of antiquity, the Roman Empire, the Ottoman Empire and many others remain as such only on pages covered with ink, Jews hold fast to their common identity till this day.

One fight won against all the odds that threatened to annihilate the Jewish spirit occurred in Ancient Greece, when the Maccabees fought to preserve the soul of their religion against an empire that was hell bent on destroying their faith. The fact that Jews celebrate the victory of a small band of fighters against the oppressor every year at Hannukah attests to the resilience and stalwart devotion to Yahweh—the One God, and the Omnipresent.

What's in a blessing? *"Cursed be every one that Curseth thee and Blessed be he that Blesseth thee"* (*Genesis 27:27–29*). Seen in light of Isaac's blessing on his son Jacob, destined to be the forefather of a nation called Israel, the question arises: What, then, is in a curse?

In recent modern history, the challenge presents itself in the person of a man named Adolf Hitler, Chancellor of Germany during the early twentieth century. Hitler's rhetoric proposed a wholesale annihilation of men, women, and children of Jewish descent on the entire European continent. He also aimed to conquer and control much of the civilized world and beyond. Although his words were the death knoll of millions of Jews during the Second World War, he was eventually defeated by the Allied armies in 1945 and ended up shooting his favourite dog first, then asking his attendants to burn his own corpse before shooting himself in a final act of suicide. The curse that Hitler left behind was a scarred nation that for decades paid for crimes he instigated against humanity. Meanwhile, the tribe of Judah, which chose to remain in Babylon (otherwise known as modern day Iraq) from the time of their expulsion from the Holy Land until recently, faced the wrath of a challenger much farther to the East.

We now turn to a figure named Hassan Al Bakr, who acceded to power in Iraq in 1968, whose cousin, a man by the name of Saddam Hossein, was placed in the most powerful position within Al Bakr's Ba'ath government. Having forged close relationships with other party leaders at the time, he later betrayed many of these men to advance his own career.

Two years after Al Bakr staged an unsuccessful war alongside several other Arab states against the new state of Israel, and fearful of challenging once again the Hebrew nation on the battlefield, Saddam randomly picked nine prominent Jewish citizens and had them hung on 27 January 1969 in Baghdad's *Sahat El Tahrir*—Freedom Square—labelling them as spies for Israel. There was live TV coverage and announcements that the day of execution be declared a holiday for all Iraqis to rejoice. Hundreds of thousands were out in the street dancing in front of the hanging corpses without any show of remorse, respect, or value for these human lives."[37] He had made an open invitation to the inhabitants of the capital and outlying provinces to participate in the scene in order to celebrate the occasion. Everything worked according to schedule.

Saddam's rise to the most powerful position in the Ba'ath Party marked the beginning of routine arrests and torture of Iraq's remaining Jews. For decades, random bullying, murder on the streets of Iraqi cities, torture, imprisonment, rape, and expropriation of Jewish businesses and real estate led to the further dwindling of their once-huge population. Since the birth of the State of Israel, all but a handful of members of a once flourishing community remain. The country's former 140,000 Iraqi Jews, whose families had been citizens since 580 B.C.E., fled in droves, many of them by contraband through the rugged mountainous terrain spanning the border of neighbouring Iran. Most of them left much wealth behind. Where their first Exodus was from Jerusalem to Babylon in ancient times, this new one was away from the heart of Ancient Babylon. As refugees, they settled in lands spreading across the four corners of the Earth.

During the rescue mission called Operation Ezra and Nehemiah that airlifted hundreds to Israel, many families known to our Iraqi Jewish community of Teheran offered their homes to friends and relatives who crossed the border territory into Iran before heading off to join relatives in Europe, North America, Australia, India, China, and other parts of the globe. They rebuilt their lives, not as victims, but as parents desiring a better future for their children. At the same time as the number of Jewish refugees from Ancient Babylon emerged as a significant figure by any standards, Jews suffered a similar fate throughout other Arab lands in the aftermath of the establishment of a Jewish State. Another important factor in the tsunami of Jewish refugees from Arab lands was a consequence of the Six-Day War in 1967, which the Arab states imposed on the State of Israel. In all, the total number of displaced Jews in the Middle East came close to 800,000.

---

[37]   Morris Abdulezer, 19 February 2009. *"Baghdad hangings: remembering the horror,"* from a speech posted on *Point of No Return: Jewish Refugees from Arab Countries.* [online] Available at: http://jewishrefugees.blogspot.ca/2009/02/baghdad-hangings-remembering-horror-and.html. [Accessed 12 March 2011].

In 2003, the American President George W. Bush invaded Iraq, purportedly in search of weapons of mass destruction. Once again, one may ask the question: What is in a curse?

As for Saddam, who once ruled from amid nine palaces in the land of the Fertile Crescent known throughout written history as the Cradle of Civilization, he was hoisted by American soldiers, roughshod, from an underground rat hole, and exhibited to the world by satellite television with ropes tied around his neck in his final hour. His courtroom plea to the judge for execution by a shooting squad as political criminal was rejected. A man who once invited his fellow countrymen to be spectators on the scene of nine innocent Jews hanging from ropes in his capital's Freedom Square made of himself a tragic spectacle for his people and the world to watch.

I remember my father listening to Iraqi radio from his patio facing the garden of our property in the outskirts of Teheran. There was a longing in him, and all those who had once lived in Iraq, for the bygone days in their ancient homeland. Till this day, the food, the music, and the culture our fellow Iraqi Jews brought from our ancient homeland and kept alive through generations, are reminders of several millennia of cherished history, sometimes fraught with peril, but always grounded in a sense of belonging to the land from whence our arch father, Abraham, first made the journey from Ur onto the destiny that God had reserved for him.

Looking back to the Iraq that I left behind as a child—Cradle of Civilization—in which nestled such a wealth of spirituality, science, commerce and creativity, I can hardly help reflect upon the sovereign people of Arab lands, endowed as they have been with oil riches beyond their wildest dreams, having cursed Jacob's descendants, instead of channelling their windfall toward the common good. Their leaders looked to the destruction of Israel, though they could have benefited from peaceful cooperation, trade, and exchange of ideas through a partnership with their tiny democratic neighbour. Instead of engaging in the development of skills, they focused with stupor on the clash of ideologies. Amid the present turmoil that is the political landscape of Iraq, a huge number of Ishmael's descendants seem interested in a culture of death by taking their own lives and killing one another, and refusing to live peaceably alongside a tiny strip of land peopled by Jacob's descendants.

Indeed, when we study God's declaration about Ishmael, the son of Hagar, the second wife of Abraham, we find: *"And the angel of the Lord said unto her, Behold thou art with child, and shall bear a son, and shall call his name Ishmael; because the Lord hath heard thy affliction. And he will be a wild man; his hand will be against every man, and every man's hand against him..."* (Genesis 16:11–12).

15

ISRAEL: RETURN TO THE SOURCE

And I will be found of you, saith the
Lord—and I will turn away your
captivity, and I will gather you from all
the nations, and from all the places
whither I have driven you, saith the
Lord; and I will bring you again into
the place whence I caused you to be driven
away captive. (Jeremiah 29:14)

IT MAY SEEM OUT OF CONTEXT TO WRITE ABOUT MODERN HISTORY in a work whose purpose is to serve as a study of Scripture. Yet, the Tanakh not only relates the ancient history of the Israelites and how they came into their identity; it may also hold clues that can help the reader understand the rebirth of the Jews as a nation in modern times. If Einstein's famous saying about miracles is true, the miracle of a rebirth of a self-reliant modern State of Israel stands as a testimony to the notion that either nothing is a miracle or everything is. In the next chapters, we examine Jeremiah's prediction above in relation to current events. Readers are encouraged to remember the passage I have quoted as they progress toward the end of this book.

Palestine, in 1845, numbered fewer than 15,000 Jews. Most of them drew support for their survival from outside sources. They lived an impoverished life amid an arid and swampy environment under Ottoman rule.

It was at the persistence of the Russian pogroms and persecutions of the Jews in European countries that came to a peak during the Dreyfus Affair in France that a surge of sentiment emerged among the Jews of the mid nineteenth century to create a Zionist state in the ancient home of the patriarchs.[38]

The word *Bilu* comes from the Hebrew בִּיל"וּ; an acronym from Isaiah 2:5 for *Beit Ya'akov Lekhu Ve-nelkha* בית יעקב לכו ונלכה and translates as "House of Jacob, let us go up." It was named after a group of Jewish idealists that aspired to settle in the Land of Israel. They had a political purpose to redeem Eretz Yisrael, the Land of Israel, upon which they intended to re-establish the Jewish state. A wave of pogroms between 1881 and 1884 rocked many Jewish villages, and the anti-Semitic May Laws of 1882 introduced by Tsar Alexander III of Russia prompted masses of Jews to emigrate from the Russian Empire. Between 1871 and 1914, the average movement per year went from 4,100 between the years 1871 and 1880 to 75,144 by the period between the years 1911-1914. In the course of that period, about 1,749,000 Jews emigrated from Russia to the United States and overall the number of emigrants from the tsarist empire in the same period reached close to 2,285,000.[39]

Some decided to make *aliyah*, the term used to denote the immigration of Jews to the ancient land named in the Hebrew Bible as Eretz Yisrael.

The Biluim's dream to create modern firms in Palestine became a template for future arrivals from the Diaspora. At the same time, a Jew from Odessa by the name of Leon Pinsker issued a pamphlet entitled "Auto-Emancipation," giving birth to Zionism, the movement that aspired to the return of the Jews to Zion. He sought to synthesize the two main ideological camps of traditionalism and emancipation that were current at the time.

While emancipation was obviously the ethical and humanitarian answer to the problem of the Jews, Europeans were reluctant to wholesomely embrace the new climate of liberalism. Pinsker understood that going back to the ghetto was no longer an option, and that emancipation could no longer be pushed by the wayside. Already, a new generation had tasted a freedom it was unwilling to relinquish. The question was to find a

---

[38]   Abba Eban, *My People*, 319.

[39]   Antony Polonsky, *The Jews in Poland and Russia*. Volume II, 21.

model of emancipation that freed Jews from the entrapment of perpetual compromise and living at the mercy of others. Similar to other oppressed nationalities, the answer came to them in the form of "national liberation."[40]

Unaware of the existence of Pinsker and other likeminded thinkers, a man named Theodor Herzl who came from a well-to-do family in Budapest entered the picture to lead what soon became a bona fide socio-political movement. For, by 1897 he presided over the Zionist movement's first congress, which convened in Basle, Switzerland, where he delivered words that took fifty-one years to crystallize into reality: "At Basle, I created the Jewish State. In five years, perhaps, and certainly in fifty, everyone will see it."[41]

Herzl's dream was fulfilled in May 1948 when the tiny new nation state's first President, David Ben Gurion, proclaimed its sovereignty. Herzl's statement came at a time in the history of European Jewry when hopes were dim, and it was far from clear that any organized efforts offered a road to freedom from persecution and anti-Jewish discrimination. The popular image evoked by Abba Eban of each man pulling his cart out of the mud powerfully symbolized their pitiful condition. It was no tiny threshold in history when Herzl's idea for his people unified the "hidden resources of the Jews as a people, one people, wherever they might live."[42]

Herzl's genius lay not only in his stalwart faith and belief in an idea. He understood the fundamental principle behind nationhood—that of a common language. The Jews already possessed the language of the Tanakh. And, although his knowledge of Hebrew was limited to his study of The Book in preparation for Bar Mitzvah (a religious rite whereby every Jewish boy crosses the threshold of adulthood at thirteen), he understood its significance as glue that bound together the cultural components and basic traditions of the people of The Book—wherever they happened to live.

Herzl's initial concerns were threefold: (*i*) the urgent need to create a congress of representatives who were recognized as official spokesmen of

---

[40] Abba Eban, *My People*, 316-17.

[41] Ibid, 326.

[42] Ibid, 332.

world Jewry, *(ii)* the need for fundraising by a Jewish financial company, and *(iii)* the need to bring together men and women of science—engineers and technicians in all fields—in order to create an efficient model for a modern industrial state. He entertained a vision for the world at large, where it, too, evolved its own blessing of freedom through the liberation of its Jews: "And whatever we attempt there to accomplish for our own welfare, will react powerfully and beneficently for the good of humanity."[43]

Herzl left no stone unturned to obtain a charter from the Turkish government to legalize Jewish settlements in Palestine. But various meetings with the Turkish sultan and the anti-Semitic Kaiser Wilhelm II of Germany, Turkey's only European ally, yielded little.[44] At the sixth Zionist congress, Herzl's suggestion was to accept the British government's proposal of a Jewish homeland in Uganda, which was rejected unanimously by the Russian Jewish delegation, for their sights were solely set on Palestine.[45] However, in the months and years that ensued, further Jewish settlements were created, mostly owing to the local Ottoman government officials' practice of accepting bribes. Meanwhile, Herzl continued to secure financial assistance with the aid of Jewish philanthropists around the world.

Herzl's death from pneumonia in 1904 at the age of forty-four was followed by a funeral procession accompanied by 6,000 Jewish mourners. In 1949, one year after this dream of a modern Jewish state became living history, his remains were transported from his burial site in Europe to Israel and re-interred on a hill that faced in the direction of Jerusalem named Mount Herzl, after him.[46]

With Germany's defeat and the fall of the Ottoman Empire in World War I (1914 to 1918), Europe's political equation was totally reversed. The growing Zionist movement to settle Jewry in Palestine occurred in tandem with many other dynamics that were shaping the political landscape of the region. As France led the economic and cultural development of Syria,

---

[43]   Ibid, 329–30.

[44]   Ibid, 335.

[45]   Ibid, 337.

[46]   Ibid, 354.

England was quick to realize the importance of safeguarding its lifeline to India, the Suez Canal, from the territorial aspirations of other powers.[47]

It was in such a geopolitical landscape that the Zionist movement's need to produce a skilful leader was filled in the figure of a man named Chaim Weizmann (1874–1952).

Weizmann was born in a village named Motol near Pinsk located in the Russian Pale of settlement, isolated from the surrounding hostile world. Its inhabitants were entrenched in their Jewish traditions and the belief in a return to their ancestral homeland.

Early on, Weizmann showed great scientific talent, and in 1892, when it was almost impossible for a Jew to enter a Russian university, the young Weizmann enrolled at the Darmstadt Polytechnic in Germany and, after only two terms, moved to Berlin to study biochemistry at the Institute of Technology in Charlotenburg. His family fell on hard times, and he supported himself by tutoring the children of wealthy Jewish families in Hebrew and other subjects. He received his doctorate of science from the University of Freiburg in 1900 and went on to lecture in chemistry from 1900 to 1904 at the University of Geneva, and in biochemistry from 1904 to 1916 at the University of Manchester in England.

In his first encounter with several glittering Zionist intellectuals in Berlin, he was awed by Herzl's charisma and commanding presence and was soon drawn into the concept of the establishment of a Jewish State. Weizmann was also heavily influenced by a man named Ahad Ha-Am, who was busy building the body of work that went into forming a Hebrew-language Jewish cultural and spiritual lexicon destined for a new future country. As a proponent of the cultural objectives of the Zionist movement, Weizmann worked toward the creation of a Hebrew University in Palestine, which opened its doors in 1925.[48]

---

[47]   Ibid, 339–40.

[48]   Pinsk Stories. *Encyclopaedia of World Biography(c) on Chaim Weizmann.* [online] Available at: http://www.eilatgordinlevitan.com/pinsk/pinsk_pages/ pinsk_stories_weizmann.html. [Accessed 12 October 2011].

Theodor Herzl (1860 – 1904): "At Basle, I created the Jewish State.
In five years, and certainly in fifty, everyone will see it."
(Abba Eban, *My People*, 326)
[Illustration by Sandra Koukou]

Weizmann obtained British citizenship in 1910. He was befriended by a man named C. P. Scott, who was editor of the *Manchester Guardian*, and who, in January of 1915, introduced him to Lloyd George, later known as chairman of the munitions committee in Britain. When their laboratories encountered difficulties with the production of acetone, Weizmann found a new process to produce it, which became the big push in the war effort and cemented his friendship with Lloyd George, soon to become prime minister of Britain.

While working on a way to produce synthetic rubber, Weizmann, in 1915, developed a classic process of fermentation to produce acetone, a chemical urgently required for the war effort in Britain during World War I for the manufacture of a smokeless powder called cordite. It was Winston Churchill, the first lord of the Admiralty, who made the critical discovery of Weizmann's acid-resistant micro organism, called *Clostridium acetobutylicum*, available for widespread use in England, Canada, and the United States. The practice was rapidly taken from research laboratories to industry-focused facilities that handled microbiological processes. Weizmann's work was a key factor that led to the production of penicillin in World War II and many other modern biotechnological processes in the present day.[49]

Back in 1906, an interesting exchange occurred between Weizmann and James Balfour, which cemented the latter's dedicated support toward the Zionist cause. In 1917, as Lloyd George's foreign secretary, he created the Balfour Declaration, the first diplomatic act of international recognition of Zionism.

Why did the Zionists, Lord Balfour asked in 1906 during a meeting with Weizmann, refuse the British offer of a Jewish homeland in Uganda? Weizmann's autobiography by editors Meyer Wolfe Weisgal and Joel Carmichael[50] "contains a colourful account of that meeting," in which, as Abba Eban related, "the Zionist sought to show the British statesman why the Uganda offer, made during Balfour's tenure, was unacceptable:

---

[49]   Ibid.

[50]   See also: Meyer Wolfe Weisgal and Joel Carmichael, eds., *Chaim Weizmann: A Biography by Several Hands*.

"'Then suddenly I said: 'Mr. Balfour, supposing I were to offer you Paris instead of London, would you take it?'

"'He sat up, looked at me, and answered: 'But, Dr. Weizmann, we have London.'

"'That is true,' I said. 'But we had Jerusalem when London was a marsh.'"[51]

Weizmann worked tirelessly to attract support from other influential figures in London's political circles to align public opinion with the Zionist cause.[52] Ironically, strong opposition emerged from a number of Jewish dignitaries in England, who were concerned that recognition of nationhood for a state of Israel may compromise allegiance of Jews to their countries of citizenship. This recalcitrance on the part of British Jewry came as a surprise to Lloyd George's cabinet, and caused a frustrated Weizmann to resign as chairman of the British Zionist Federation. But it wasn't long before his mentor, Ahad Ha-Am, persuaded the weary Weizmann to stay firm to his ideals, by inspiring him to seize upon the gathering momentum, the new opportunities, and the huge responsibility that history had laid upon his shoulders.

As a result of Weizmann's efforts and despite opposition from certain members of British Jewry, which had caused some degree of hesitation within the British Cabinet, the Balfour Declaration was issued on 2 November 1917, addressed in a letter to Lord Rothschild, a member of the House of Lords at the time, declaring sympathy with the Jewish Zionist aspiration, and was approved by the Cabinet. It stated that Britain was in favour of the establishment of a national home for the Jewish people in Palestine, and would provide assistance toward the realization of that objective, it being understood that no prejudice shall befall the "civil and religious right of existing non-Jewish communities in Palestine, or the rights and political status enjoyed by Jews in any other country."[53]

---

[51] Abba Eban. *Civilization and the Jews*, 255-56.

[52] Abba Eban, *My People*, 92.

[53] Ibid, 357.

Chaim Weizmann (1874 – 1952): "But we had Jerusalem when London was a marsh."[54] [Illustration by Sandra Koukou]

---

[54]   Abba Eban. *Heritage: Civilization and the Jews*, 256.

In 1917, Jewish volunteers from England, the United States, and Canada collaborated with Jewish inhabitants of Palestine led by Vladimir Jabotinsky and Joseph Trompeldor to join the British forces to liberate Palestine from the Turks. As a result, Palestine became a mandate of Britain under General Allenby. On the basis of the Balfour Declaration and a newly liberated Palestine, all necessary conditions had thus been put in place for the Zionist Movement to: (*i*) facilitate immigration of millions of Russian and East European Jews to the Holy Land, (*ii*) obtain vital funding from Jewish philanthropists worldwide to buy land for settling the immigrants, and (*iii*) build and provide civic infrastructures progressively in pace with the region's needs.

The foundations of a new nation state had already been laid by early pioneers who had settled in communal and private farms (*kibbutsim* and *moshavim* respectively) in various parts of Palestine. At the same time, the emphasis was to build statehood around the unifying, and almost centrifugal, force of Hebrew as the national language, the language that was commonly spoken in the days of the Prophet Moses. And when Haifa's Technion University was inaugurated in 1913 with German as its official language, teachers and students alike went on strike until their cause was met to use Hebrew as the common cultural currency going forward.

If development was moving at breathtaking speed in the domain of education, the early settlers were frustrated at the pace at which the new territories grew. Palestine was still a British Mandate. Then, due to opposition from the Arab world—and Britain's own geopolitical interests in the region—scores of restrictive measures were applied to curtail Jewish immigration to Palestine, or at least bring it to a minimum; then came the Arab ban on the sale of land to Jewish people. Notwithstanding, Jewish immigration continued with the legal purchase of lands and the founding of new settlements, although at a much slower pace than expected.

Weizmann remained the indispensable Jewish leader of the British Zionist Federation, respected in Britain and amongst most European diplomatic circles. In 1918, he crossed the Aqaba and met Amir Feisal, the undisputed Arab Nationalist leader, son of Sharif Hossein of Mecca, who made written pledges to recognize the Zionist project in Palestine, provided that the aims of Arab nationalism were achieved in Iraq and Syria. The two leaders forged the first and only mutual understanding ever written in black-and-white print between Arabs and Jews until this day. In November of the year 1918, the World Zionist Organization congratulated Feisal on his coronation as Syria's king, and Jewish leaders met in London with Feisal, who issued a statement which was published in *The Times* of December 12th of that year.

His statement underlined the mutual understanding between what he called "the two main branches of the Semitic family, Arabs and Jews," and expressed hopes that the Peace Conference would foster a spirit of self-determination and nationality for each nation in the way of achieving its aspirations. He said that "Arabs are not jealous of Zionist Jews, and intend to give them fair play" and that the Zionist Jews had given their assurance to the Nationalist Arabs that they too intended to engage in fair play. He pointed out that despite Turkish intrigue in the region which generated "jealousy between the Jewish colonists and local peasants," he was confident that the Arabs and Jews understood each other and this mutual understanding of their respective aims would overcome any remaining "former bitterness, which indeed had already practically disappeared even before the war, by the work of the Arab Secret Revolutionary Committee."[55]

British vacillation overshadowed the small window of opportunity of that grace period to forge a mutual agreement between Arab nationalists and Jewish settlers in Palestine. Eventually, the plan was jeopardized by British dominance in Iraq on the one hand, and an action by the French to expel Amir Feisal from Syria on the other. The far-sighted Arab leader, a descendant of the Prophet Mohammad's own bloodline, soon became isolated among his own people. Shortly after, two things fell through the cracks as a result of European hampering of progress at a critical juncture in the political abacus of the time: the Arabs were denied any hope for Allied help to "secure their big Arab state," and they were no longer bound by the obligation to "concede little Palestine to the Jews."[56]

---

[55]   Ibid, 376.

[56]   Ibid, 376.

In July 1918, with the sound of guns yet resounding in the distance, the foundations for the Hebrew University on Mount Scopus near Jerusalem were laid down with an opening speech by Weizmann in the presence of the British General Allenby and his staff, and representatives of the Allied armies and Moslem, Christian, and Jewish dignitaries.[57]

The opening ceremony of the University took place on the 1st of April, 1925 in its scenic amphitheatre in the presence of distinguished guests from the world over. Lord Balfour, the arch supporter of the Zionist Movement, white haired and dressed in the ceremonial scarlet Cambridge robe, delivered a speech that may perhaps bring back to mind a unique moment in modern history. He pointed out that despite "the magnificence of the view" which was stretched before an audience of ten thousand strong, it was the consciousness that the inauguration of the occasion marked "a great epoch in the history of a people who have made this little land of Palestine a seed-ground of great religion, and whose intellectual and moral destiny is again, from a national point of view, reviving..."[58]

Lord Balfour pointed out that the world was witnessing a new experiment in the adaptation of Western methods and a Western system of education in an Asian setting, the whole in an Eastern language, Hebrew. He stated that, "...unless I have ... profoundly mistaken the genius of the Jewish people, the experiment is predestined to an inevitable success," and that, Jews and non Jews "who share the common civilisation of the world, will have reason to congratulate themselves..."[59]

---

[57]   Ibid, 369.

[58]   Ibid, 370.

[59]   The Earl of Balfour, *Speeches on Zionism*, 74.

16

ARAB NATIONALISM:
THE TURNING POINT

THE FLOW OF JEWISH IMMIGRANTS endeavouring to re-root themselves in what they saw as their historic homeland alarmed the Arab world, and the Arab inhabitants of Palestine in particular. Arab nationalism's leaders—large landowners, Moslem holy men, and the wealthy professionals whose power structure had strengthened itself within oligarchic patterns under Turkish rule—dominated the Arab community. The Arab nationalist organizations' unbalanced class structure was soon to become an expression of sympathies and orientations directly aligned with the aims and policies of Europe's dictators, Mussolini and Hitler. Their demand became the abolition of the Balfour Declaration, sovereignty in Palestine to be granted exclusively to the Arabs, and zero political privileges for the Jews. The leading opposition figure was Haj Amin al-Husseini, grand mufti of Jerusalem and president of the Supreme Moslem Council.[60]

The designation *mufti* is derived from the word *fatwa*, an irreversible verdict, and is a title reserved for a recognized Moslem mullah who adjudicates on religious matters." To Palestinian Arabs it was a bombshell. After all, they asked, by what right do the British, who have no legal standing in Palestine,… give what is not theirs to a people who represent a minority of the population of Palestine? Just a little more than five weeks later, the unthinkable happened." Jerusalem's surrender to the British on 11 December 1917 ending Ottoman Turkish rule, "put the Holy City under the control of non-Muslim authorities for the first time since the Crusades."[61]

---

60   Eban, *My People*, 376–77.

61   David G. Dalin and John F. Rothman, *Icon of Evil*, 11-12.

For al-Husseini, at the heart of the matter stood the ancient and yet ever self-renewing issue of religion. Coming from a family of religious leaders during the Ottoman Empire in what is now modern-day Turkey, he quickly seized the moment and lost no time to elevate himself to political leadership of the Arabs in Palestine and beyond, and used his veto power of *fatwa* in all Palestinian affairs. One may pause to reflect, flash forward to 1979, that, on some level we may recall the religious model adopted by Ayatollah Khomeini, supreme leader of Iran's Islamic Revolution, whose emphasis on Islam *as* politics helped him launch the wholesale de-secularization of Iran.

When, in the late 1920s, al-Husseini befriended Adolf Hitler, Germany's future *führer* promised loftily about a future liberation of the Middle East. But, the mufti and his followers never stopped to consider that Middle Eastern oil was an easy target for the German armies to obtain at a cost of zero cents to the barrel, had the *führer* eventually gained access to the geopolitical heart of the Arab world. Indeed, that was the plan behind Rommel's push through the Saharan sands before his campaign was cut short by the Allied armies at El Alamein in Egypt.

"There are many devices in a man's heart; the council of the Lord that shall stand" (Proverbs 19:21).

Had the grand mufti used his religious authority to align political aspirations for his people with that of the Zionists, he may have elevated their standards of living in tandem with that of the Jews, who were then deep into transforming desert waste and marshland to one that maximized the yields of agriculture in one of the world's most thirsted regions. But democracy and the tribalist character of Arab society were as mutually repellent to each other as oil and water, a concept that resonated with Hitler's hidden agenda. Whereas the Western modelled system of governance Dr. Weizmann proposed to the well meaning—but deposed—King Feisal, dreamt up a future where two peoples could carry a nation into the twentieth century as two horses that powered the same chariot, tragically, Husseini's oligarchic paradigm aligned itself with the emerging ideology of Europe's Nazi *führer*.

Winston Churchill's biographer, Martin Gilbert, in an historical account of Jews in Muslim lands entitled *In Ishmael's House*, describes when the seeds of Nazi ideology were first sown in the Middle East. As early as in 1935, four years before the outbreak of World War II, a pro-Nazi society with branches in Basra and Mosul established its headquarters in Baghdad, naming itself *al-Muthanna*, after Muthanna bin Haritha, who led the Muslim conquest of Iraq in the Seventh Century.[62] "...as Hitler began courting Arab support in opposition to the British and French, Nazi influence gradually took hold in the Middle East. At the end of 1937, Hitler prudently suggested omitting his racial ladder theory from the forthcoming Arabic translation of *Mein Kampf*."[63] Gilbert points out that the Arabs had earlier been wary of Germany's *führer*, since his book *Mein Kamf*, first put to print in 1925, had "placed them on one of the lowest rungs of the 'racial ladder,' just above the Jews."[64]

Mein Kampf gradually achieved the status of a household name in the Arab world after the 'racial ladder' revision took place, a process that took hold through the wholesale dissemination of Nazi propaganda minus the former anti-Arab rhetoric. In Vichy-ruled French North Africa, anti-Jewish sentiment climbed up a steep tangent. There, as in Iraq, many Muslims stood by to protect and assist their Jewish compatriots, a fact that testifies to a once naturally organic preference for peaceful coexistence between all faith groups and denominations. The changing political trajectory, however, was shaped by a strengthening machine of Fascist propaganda. Gilbert's account of the political climate in the aftermath of anti-Jewish riots in the Tunisian city of Gabès quotes from the French Resident-General in Tunisia, Admiral Estéva's telegraph to Vichy.

After the Vichy police put an end to the anti-Jewish riots, murders and tortures in view to avoid a possible collapse of their control, the

---

[62]   Martin Gilbert, *In Ishmael's House*, 176.

[63]   Ibid, 175: "Letter from German Propaganda Ministry, Berlin, to the German Foreign Ministry, 10 December 1937: Lukasz Hirszowicz, *The Third Reich and the Arab East*, pages 45-6."

[64]   Ibid, 175.

Admiral telegraphed Vichy to explain that the rise of German prestige following victories in the Balkans, North Africa and the Atlantic, led Muslims to believe more and more that they were getting the upper hand on the Jews, the latter having kept confidence in Britain and America. "The presence of German soldiers in Gabès, Estéva noted, 'has without doubt, even without intervention on their part, let the Arabs believe they would be protected in the case of riots.'"[65]

Flash forward several decades, one may stop for a moment to consider the economic boom that flourished after Israel took control of the West Bank of the River Jordan in 1967, undefeated after a pre-empted war imposed upon the tiny State of Israel by a handful of powerful Arab nations. A brief period of prosperity emerged that lasted until 1987, ending at the heels of what became known as the Oslo Accords. What the media called *occupied territory* became a boom region that created jobs and unprecedented growth and prosperity for the local Arab population; an unprecedented growth in GNP miraculously maintained its mind-boggling annual reach of 30 percent. Israeli entrepreneurship provided economic opportunity for the many Palestinians who flocked into the region and found educational and employment opportunities in ever growing numbers. Indeed, the local Palestinian West Bank population increased to three million spanning roughly 261 towns. On the Jewish side, it rose to 250,000. Progress and advancement skyrocketed in every field. Standards of living improved through the newly available, round-the-clock supply of electricity, improvements in hygiene, decreased child mortality, increased life expectancy through greater access to healthcare and immunizations, improvements in communication systems, all of which came—at a rate equal to or above—that of other countries in the Middle East.[66]

It was this type of enterprise the Jews had envisioned when they extended a hand to their new Arab neighbours in hopes of building a state as confreres, in what used to be the British Mandate. Flash back to

---

[65] Ibid, 180: "Letter of 23 May 1941: Robert Satloff, *Among the Righteous*, pages 85-6."

[66] George Gilder. *The Israel Test*, 49–51.

the British Mandate—Arab resistance through riots and strikes created a climate where the Balfour Declaration remained, at least for a time, just a piece of paper. To appease the Arabs, between 1922 and 1939 the Mandate issued several decrees known as White Papers in view to curb Jewish immigration and restrict Jews from buying Arab lands. Jewish settlements became vulnerable to harassment by marauding Arab bands. And, while the British Mandate was principally responsible for holding peace and security in the region, it kept a watchful eye to avoid jolting its penultimate goal to maintain strategic alliances within the oil-rich regions of the Middle East.

Meanwhile, beginning in 1920 Jewish settlers set up a defence force which aimed to protect the fledgling settlements that lay highly vulnerable to Arab attacks. It was named the *Haganah*. New defendable settlements required the construction of walls, watchtowers and barbed wire fences. Prefabricated building components were then assembled nocturnally at the nearest village and hauled by trucks within a twenty-four-hour timeframe, the whole in order to minimize the enemy's opportunity to mobilize and attack.[67]

By 1939, and at the outset of the Second World War, Jewish population in Palestine had surpassed 400,000.[68]

---

[67]   Abba Eban, *My People*, 386.

[68]   Ibid, 386.

17

WHAT'S IN A NAME?

WHAT CAN HISTORY DIVULGE about the Jewish sense of belonging to an ancient land held so dearly in prayer books, in wedding ceremonies, and in funerals throughout the ages? Why do Jews in the Western Hemisphere turn eastward toward Jerusalem in prayer for the deceased, and likewise Jews of the Orient westward during religious service?

According to the World Book Encyclopaedia, the *Land of Canaan* was inhabited by the Amorites, Canaanites, and other Semitic peoples who entered the area about 2000 B.C.E. The area came to be known by that name. It was at around the time between 1800 and 1500 B.C.E. that a Semitic people called the Hebrews or Israelites made the movement from Mesopotamia and settled in Canaan. Some Hebrews later went to Egypt and were led out by Moses several hundred years later during the 1200's B.C.E., making their return to the Land of Canaan. By 1000 B.C.E. the Land of Canaan was mostly held by the Twelve Tribes of Israel (Asher, Benjamin, Dan, Ephraim, Gad, Issachar, Judah, Manasseh, Naphtali, Reuben, Simeon and Zebulun).

As we have seen, the Hebrews whose religious practice centred around belief in one God, were neighboured by peoples who worshiped many gods. For about 200 years the Hebrews were in constant conflict with other peoples of Canaan and the neighbouring areas. Among their strongest enemies were the Philistines, who controlled the south western coast of Canaan—known as *Philistia*.[69]

Constant warfare with the surrounding neighbourhoods led the Hebrews to demand to be led by a king, and they chose Saul as their leader. His successor, David, unified the nation into what became, by

---

[69] *World Book, Inc.*, Volume 15, "Palestine," article by Michel Le Gall. (Chicago: Scott Fetzer, 1994), 103-4.

about 1000 B.C.E. the *Kingdom of Israel*. As we have seen in previous chapters, the kingdoms of Israel and Judah fell captive to conquering empires. As a result, the land subsequently changed hands many times after the expulsion of the Jews from Jerusalem, the city that King David built as his capital, later glorified by David's son, King Solomon, who built the first Temple for the worship of God. Israel continued as a united state until the death of Solomon around 922 B.C.E., after which the northern tribes split from the tribes to the south. Whereas the northern state continued under the name *Israel*, the southern state was called *Judah*, and kept its capital, Jerusalem. "The word *Jew*, which came to be used for all Hebrews, comes from the name *Judah*."[70]

However, there is more to the *name* than modern political correctness cares to divulge. Before establishing the derivative of the newly coined name that gained currency over the past 2000 years as *Palestine*, it may be helpful to cite the many hands through which Jerusalem was passed after its conquest by the Assyrians in 722 or 721 B.C.E.: the Babylonians in 587 or 586 B.C.E., who destroyed Solomon's Temple in Jerusalem; the Persian King Cyrus—who conquered them and allowed a group of Babylonian Jews to go back and rebuild and settle in Jerusalem—and whose Persian Empire ruled most of the Middle East, including Judah, from about 530 to 331 B.C.E.; Alexander the Great who conquered the Persian Empire and died in 323 B.C.E., leaving his empire to his generals; Seleucus, one of Alexander's generals, who founded the Seleucid dynasty that controlled much of the land by 200 B.C.E., allowing at first the practice of Judaism; the Jews who re-established an independent kingdom called *Judah* after revolting under the leadership of the Maccabeans, who drove the Seleucids out when Antiochus IV tried to prohibit the practice of the Jewish faith in the land.[71]

Roman troops invaded Judah in 63 B.C.E.; they called the area: *Judea*. Jesus Christ was born in Bethlehem early on during Roman rule. Jewish revolts in 66 and 132 C.E. resulted in the expulsion of the Jews from Jerusalem in 135 C.E., whereby the Romans coined the name *Palaestina*

---

[70] Ibid, 104.

[71] Ibid, 104.

for the area, referring to *Philistia*.[72] As previously mentioned, *Philistia* was home to one of the ancient enemies of the Jews, the idol worshiping Philistines who had disappeared from the historical stage more than 600 years earlier. After the Romans drove the Jews out of Palaestina, *Palestine* in English, most of the Jews fled their homeland, although some Jewish communities remained in Galilee in the northernmost part of the land. The Roman Empire governed Palestine until the 300's C.E., followed by the Byzantine Empire, in whose time Christianity spread to most parts of the land.

It seems apt to mention a sufficient amount of historical data surrounding the name change from Judah, or Judea, as the Romans originally called it, to the new nomenclature of Palestine.

First, it must be established that it was by order of the Emperor Hadrian. What kind of man *was* the one who ordered that Judea be renamed Palaestina, rekindling the memory of ancient wounds of times gone by when Israel's major challenge was to fend off the Philistines, whose giant warrior Goliath was crushed by a young lad by the name of David? It may be relevant to ask too where Hadrian hailed from while on a discussion about what's in a name.

In the famous eighteenth century English historian, Edward Gibbon's fourth of six volumes of *The Decline and Fall of the Roman Empire*, Hadrian appears to have been the first emperor to,—in a manner unprecedented and undisguised,—assume full legislative power, such that:

> ...this innovation, so agreeable to his active mind, was countenanced by the patience of the times and his long absence from the seat of government. The same policy was embraced by succeeding monarchs, and, according to the harsh metaphor of Tertullian, 'the gloomy and intricate forest of ancient laws was cleared away by the axe of royal mandates and *constitutions*.' During four centuries from Hadrian to Justinian, the public and private jurisprudence was moulded by the will of

---

72   Ibid, 104.

the sovereign, and few institutions, either human or divine, were permitted to stand on their former basis. The origin of Imperial legislation was concealed by the darkness of the ages and the terrors of armed despotism; and a double fiction was propagated by the servility, or perhaps the ignorance, of the civilians who basked in the sunshine of the Roman and Byzantine courts.... His [the emperor's] humble privilege was at length transformed into the prerogative of a tyrant; and the Latin expression of 'released from the laws' was supposed to exalt the emperor above *all* human restraints, and to leave his conscience and reason as the sacred measure of his conduct.[73]

Perhaps it is even further relevant in our discussion about names to outline the succession of ruling bodies that followed the Roman Empire to grab hegemony over *Palestine*. During the 600's C.E., Moslem Arab armies conquered the greater part of the Middle East, including *Palestine*. They were followed in the 1000's by the Seljuk Turks, who took control of Jerusalem in 1071, which was captured three decades later by the Crusaders in 1099, until the Moslem ruler, Saladin, attacked *Palestine* and took over in 1187. Then, in the mid-1200's, the Mamelukes of Egypt established an empire that eventually annexed *Palestine*. They, in turn, were followed by the Ottoman Empire, which defeated them in 1517. From that time, Jews emigrated from various parts of the Mediterranean and settled in Jerusalem and other parts of *Palestine*.[74]

In light of the fact that, toward the end of Ottoman rule, *Palestine* was a desolate stretch of desert land peopled sparsely mainly by Bedouins and shepherds, the question needs to be asked: where does the Arab claim to *Palestinian statehood* fit into the canvas painted by either ancient or recent history? Eli E. Herz makes the case that, "Most Arabs living west of the Jordan River in Israel, the West Bank (Judea and Samaria) and Gaza

---

[73] Edward Gibbon, *The Decline and Fall of the Roman Empire*, Volume 4, 430-31.

[74] *World Book, Inc.*, Volume 15, "Palestine," article by Michel Le Gall. (Chicago: Scott Fetzer, 1994), 104-5.

are newcomers who came from surrounding Arab lands after the turn of the 20th century because they were attracted to the relative economic prosperity brought about by the Zionist Movement and the British in the 1920s and 1930s."[75]

A further question that begs to be asked is whether the so-called *Palestinian* populace embraces a single dialect that distinguishes it from any other people. Is that dialect known by an accent that is distinctly *Palestinian?* The answer to this very basic question about national identity can be traced to the fact that Arabs, whose native names and dialects originate from countries stretching as far as Tunisia in North Africa, came at the behest of the Jewish arrivals in Palestine even before the twentieth century. They came looking for work since the arrival of Jews and a British presence meant the coming of new job opportunities. In the words of Tsafrir Ronen:

> … the way to Palestinian Hell was paved with the good intentions of Christian Zionists like Lord Balfour, the British foreign secretary. In the Balfour declaration, and by the decree of the Mandate, they decided, based on historic rights, to grant Eretz Yisrael to the Jewish people. Yet they called it Hadrian's Roman name, Palestine, which had originally had the precise intention of blotting it off the map.
>
> From that moment on, the way was prepared for the birth of the Palestinian fiction.
>
> The name Palestine, by which the British accidentally called the land, bore the seeds of destruction of the Palestinian bluff, as if the entire Land was the stolen property of the Palestinian people, an ancient, rooted people, thousands of years old. This was such an incredible but successful fabrication that large portions

---

[75] Eli E. Hertz, 31 March 2008. *Palestinians: 'Peoplehood' Based on a Big Lie.* [online] Available at: http://www.mythsandfacts.org/article_view. asp?articleID=53&order_id=2. [Accessed 10 July 2010].

of Israeli society fell into its snare. In the report presented in 1938 to the League of Nations, the British made it very clear: "The name 'Palestine' is not a country but a geographic region."[76]

While Jewish settlers in *Palestine* struggled to realize their dream of renewed nationhood in their ancient Holy Land, Germany's Adolf Hitler designed plans to uproot Europe's Jewish presence. It started with the formation of the Nazi Party. Hitler emerged on the political arena in 1920. A staunch Jew hater, he was catapulted to political prominence through fiery rhetoric and rallies that called for the elimination of Jews, whom he blamed for all the economic woes of his country. In 1924, an armed assault landed Hitler in prison after a failed attempt to topple the German Democratic Government.

Hitler's autobiography, *Mein Kampf*, whose 'racial ladder' has earlier been discussed in some detail, was written in prison as a political manifesto. It laid down the Nazi agenda for the Third Reich and defined the German people as Aryans, whom he considered a superior race born to rule all others, including Jews, Russians and the many different Slavic peoples he viewed as inferior races. In 1933, newly released from prison, Hitler rebuilt his party and became chancellor of Germany.

After securing governance by absolute power, Hitler propagandized hatred toward their gifted minority and institutionalized anti-Jewish laws to successively deprive the Jews of Germany of the most basic civic and human rights. Jews, regardless of their enormous contributions to science and German culture, and unfalteringly patriotic military service, were no longer considered citizens. Intermarriage with Aryans was forbidden, and a Christian institute was appointed to systematically obliterate any mention of Jewish influence in Christian folklore and traditions, even though Jesus himself along with his apostles was a Jew.

---

[76] Tsafrir Ronen, 26 May 2008. *Hadrian's Curse – The Invention Of Palestine.* [online] Available at: http://tzafrirronenen.blogspot.ca/2008/05/hadrians-curse-by-tsafrir-ronen.html. [Accessed 10 July 2010].

On the 9th and 10th of November of 1938, in a dismal event referred to as the *Kristallnacht*—Crystal Night—most German cities were ravaged by German troops, who raided Jewish synagogues, homes, and businesses, and ruthlessly smashed the windows of shops belonging to Jews, killing about one hundred Jews. About 20,000 souls were raped, looted or sent to concentration camps far from their cities. *Kristallnacht* was conducted in retaliation for the assassination of a German embassy officer in Paris by a young Jewish refugee named Herchel Grynszpan. By that time about 250,000 German Jews immigrated to whichever country gave them entry. Ironically, it was also a time when the Nazis themselves encouraged the Jews to leave Germany.

The Jewish Agency and the Jewish Distribution Committee worked hard from neutral neighbouring countries to rescue distressed Jews and offer them safe haven. Many Christians, particularly in France and the Netherlands, did their best to protect and take many into hiding.

In Palestine, in March 1939, a third decree known as the Malcolm McDonald White Paper bashed the hopes of European Jewry to seek refuge in the Promised Land, to prevent a Jewish majority in Palestine in the foreseeable future. At the close of that time frame, Jewish immigration would no longer be permitted without the acquiescence of the Arabs of Palestine. The White Paper also stated that the British government would withhold any obligation to facilitate any further immigration to develop the Jewish National Home regardless of the will of the Arab population.

Churchill voiced his mind to the House of Commons on the 23rd of May in 1939, corroborating similar statements above:

> So far from being persecuted, the Arabs have crowded into the country and multiplied till their population has increased more than even all world Jewry could lift up the Jewish population. Now we are being asked to decree that all this is to stop and all this is to come to an end. We are now asked to submit, and this is what rankles most with me, to an agitation which is fed with foreign

money and ceaselessly inflamed by Nazi and by Fascist propaganda.[77]

Churchill's account of the facts on the ground was accurate on both counts. Between 1922 and 1939 the number of Arabs, many of them illegals, that entered Palestine exceeded that of the Jews. As mentioned earlier, they hailed from countries as far off as Morocco, Algeria, Tunisia, Libya, Egypt, Yemen, Iraq, Iran and Syria, and their numbers also included those coming from Transjordan, Sudan and Saudi Arabia. All were drawn to Palestine by its opportunities for jobs and "its growing prosperity—opportunities and prosperity often created by the Jews there." Significantly, it is critical to note that the 1948 statistics included many of those Arab immigrants as being "'Palestinian'" Arab refugees.[78]

Further to the east, in Iraq, its government acquiesced to public pressure and closed its borders to Jewish refugees from Germany. It had become clear that "Hitler's malign influence had penetrated to the heart of a proud Muslim land in which Jews had long held an honoured place."[79]

The text and timing of the Malcolm McDonald White Paper was a blatant attempt to passively allow the entrapment of eight million of Europe's defenceless Jews under the mercy of one of history's cruellest tyrants.

---

[77]   Martin Gilbert, *In Ishmael's House*, as quoted from *Hansard*, Parliamentary Debates, House of Commons, 23 May 1939.

[78]   Gilbert, 175.

[79]   Ibid, 176.

18

WORLD WAR II AND BEYOND

WORLD WAR II ERUPTED when German troops invaded Poland on the 1ˢᵗ of September, 1939 and expanded the offensive into Denmark, Belgium and Holland. By mid 1940, Paris fell under the flag of the Third Reich. While much of the civilized world watched German atrocities and in many cases betrayed the names of Jewish citizens to the Nazi apparatus, as was the case under the Vichy government in France, the indifference or belligerence of communities in other parts of the world, such as those throughout Arab lands, inspired Hitler to calculate a plan for the total annihilation of Judaism from the face of the Earth. By 1941, the entire apparatus that was designed to enforce his infamous "Final Solution" had been put into place.

While, today, some twenty-first-century European countries acquiesce to the demands of their Moslem minorities to ban any mention of the Jewish Holocaust from scholastic literature, others are haunted by the question "Where was God when the Nazis systematically exterminated millions of Jews in death camps between 1941 and 1945?" Still others continue to express dismay in that Hitler's mission remains unaccomplished.

In May of 1940, while the march of the German army spread in every direction of the compass, Weizmann, in a letter addressed to Winston Churchill, pleaded that a military unit of 50,000 Palestinian Jews be allowed to stand by in the event of possible Germano-Arab invasion of Palestine. Later that year, the British government approved the enlistment of a limited number of Jewish soldiers in separate units within the British army. By September 1944 a Jewish brigade of 35,000 was deployed alongside the Eighth Army under General Montgomery, who forced a retreat of Rommel's troops in North Africa.[80]

---

[80] Abba Eban, *My People*, 420.

The Fascist armies had reached as far as El Alamein in Egypt, and Stalingrad in Russia. And, while the British Mandate kept the lock on Palestine and barred distressed European Jews from taking refuge in the ancient homeland of Judaism, the Arabs hailed the German advance, counting the hours until they could welcome Hitler as their new master. In the Arab countries, and even in Iran, as I remember, opportunists seized upon the idea to divide Jewish homes, properties, and businesses among themselves once the Jews were dealt with by the Nazis. As a gentlemen's agreement of sorts just before the war had played its final chord, it was commonly acknowledged and publicly apparent that Jewish property in Iran would be redistributed among the Moslems.

While the German army advanced as far as Stalingrad, the Allies sought to prevent Russia's neighbour to the south—Iran—from falling under the Reich's reach. On the Persian side, Reza Shah was weary of economic exploitation of his country by the British during the long reign of the Qajars. Their dynasty ended by military coup whereupon he gained accession to the throne. Reza Shah turned instead to the Germans for help to build the country's infrastructure. The shah had refused at the time to expel German nationals residing in Iran and denied the use of the railway to the Allied armies. According to 1940 British embassy reports from Teheran, there were no more than a thousand German citizens living in Iran, belonging to professions ranging from technicians to spies.

In August of 1941, instigated by Reza Shah's Declaration of Neutrality in World War II and his flat refusal to allow the Allied armies right of passage on Iranian soil, Britain and Russia invaded and occupied Iran by a massive air, land and naval assault. The shah received this news with disbelief and saw it as a personal humiliation and defeat. Unable to fathom how fifteen Iranian divisions had surrendered without much resistance, while some of his troops dispersed and went home, and still others were locked up in their barracks by the Allies, he formed a war cabinet to direct the defence. But resistance seemed glaringly more costly than surrender, and by mid-September of 1941, Reza Shah "dismissed [his prime minister] Mansur and appointed the loyal and respectable Forughi...."

Abbasqoli Golshah'iyan, minister of finance at the time, is known to have explicitly confirmed that: "...it was the cabinet that had asked Forughi to tell the shah to abdicate and that Forguhi, having said he personally believed that that was the wish of the Allies, saw the shah and told him so."[81]

Iran thus became a training ground for military personnel, and a supply chain for transport of arms to Russia for the war effort against the German enemy. Soon to be known to the Allies as the Persian Corridor, and because of her importance in the Allied victory, Iran was dubbed "The Bridge of Victory" by England's Winston Churchill. Iran safeguarded the oil supplies, and more importantly, offered the use of the trans-Iranian railways and motor roads, which supplied around 5 million tons of war material to the ailing Soviet army, along with another 2 million tons to the British forces stationed in the Middle East.[82]

When World War II ended in mid 1945, the free world rejoiced in the Allied victory over the Axis Powers. Hitler committed suicide in his bunker along with Goebbels, (Reich Minister of Propaganda in Nazi Germany from 1933 to 1945). Italy's Mussolini was executed, his body hung for public display, and Japan was dwarfed by the two atomic bombs dropped on Hiroshima and Nagasaki by the Americans. From that point forward, rebuilding began for all the nations ravaged by war, except for the Jewish people. The British government totally ignored the promise affirmed in the Balfour Declaration for the "establishment in Palestine of a national home for the Jewish people."

After the war, the British government continued to uphold the 1939 White Paper's ban on allowing some of the two million stranded European Jews to return to their homeland. At one point, President Truman suggested to British Prime Minister Attlee to allow 100,000 European

---

[81] Homa Katouzian. *The Persians*, 230, referring to Abbasgholi Golsha'iyan, *Yahddasht-ha-ye Abbasgholi-ye Golsha'iyan* in *Yaddasht-ha-ye Doctor Qasem Ghani*, ed. Cyrus Ghani, vol, 4, Zavvar, Tehran, 1978, 557.

[82] Ibid, 233.

Jews entry to Palestine. That proposal was aborted by foreign minister Bevin on the grounds that "driving Jews from Europe is not acceptable."[83]

British gunboats guarding Palestine's coastline spotting vessels that carried Jewish immigrants chased them off by force. As any kind of political solution seemed unattainable, the Zionist Movement turned into open conflict with the British Mandate. Among several sporadic acts of sabotage, in June 1946 the Haganah blew up eight bridges on Palestine's frontiers to disrupt communications with the neighbouring countries. In the following month of July, they blew up part of the King David Hotel, the seat of Jerusalem's civil and military administration.[84]

Sabotage, conflicts, curfews and arrests continued until the Mandate realized for all practical purposes that Jewish settlers were steeped in the hope and the will necessary to fight for a national homeland, no matter what the cost. The British Empire at that time, which held the banner of colonial prowess and maintained it with ever greater diplomacy through the purchase of power, land and personal favours from local chieftains and people of influence, had to contend with the Jews, who were no stooges on the battlefield, and who proved to be a tough bunch to be won over. The British in Palestine were confronted with dedicated people ready to fight to the end for their dignity and identity as a collective. By April of 1947, weary of constant attacks on its outposts, the British government left the question of Palestine's future destiny in the hands of the United Nations General Assembly. Meanwhile, all restrictions against Jewish inhabitants, including the strict immigration ban, remained intact.

In July 1947, the famous vessel renamed *Exodus 1947*, carrying over 4,500 souls, mostly Holocaust survivors, sailed from France in an attempt to disembark its weary passengers in the Holy Land, the only place on Earth willing to receive them. Before reaching the shores of Palestine, and well within international waters, a British navy convoy surrounded the ship and forced all of its passengers aboard a vessel that transferred them to a temporary camp on the island of Cyprus, a British colony at the time.

---

[83]   Abba Eban, *My People*, 432.

[84]   Ibid, 437.

Foreign minister Bevin suggested sending the passengers back to France, their point of departure. They moored the embattled ship *Exodus* in the port of Haifa and deported the refugees via three of their own ships the whole way back to France.

The three ships arrived at a port near Marseilles on the 2nd of August. The immigrants refused to disembark and conducted a twenty-four-hour hunger strike, demanding to be returned to Palestine, and the French refused to take them in. The immigrants remained in squalid conditions inside the ships for three weeks. Finally, the ships sailed to Hamburg, after which their weary passengers were taken to a British-occupied zone on German soil and forcefully evacuated from the ships, to be transferred to various camps in the German interior.

When the story of the gruelling ordeal of *Exodus 1947* was finally covered by the French media, it soon formed the crest of the wave that moved the conscience of the civilized world. The General Assembly of the United Nations, the body now in charge of the "Palestine Question," saw the plight of the passengers of the returned ship. Some of the committee members were present in Haifa and at other locations, witnessing the atrocities dealt toward the exhausted refugees. Abba Eban, Israel's future ambassador to the United Nations, who had worked for Weizmann in London earlier in his career, was one of them. He had been appointed as a liaison officer to the United Nations Special Committee on Palestine when he succeeded in attaining approval for the Resolution. He changed his name to the Hebrew *Abba*, meaning "Father," a name that was seldom used informally. Eban saw himself in the role of a father in relation to the birthing of the new nation of Israel. Abba Eban was extraordinarily renowned for his diplomatic and oratory skills.

"In April 1947, the Soviet Union, represented by its UN delegate, Andrei Gromyko, shocked the Arabs and exhilarated the Jews by supporting the idea of a Jewish State in a part of Palestine."[85]

On 29 November 1947, the United Nations General Assembly passed Resolution 181, with 33 against 13, and 11 abstentions. It was

---

[85]   Abba Eban, *Heritage: Civilization and the Jews*, 324.

a vote for the installation of a Jewish state in a partitioned Palestine, juxtaposed alongside an Arab state and economically linked to ensure extensive integration and accessibility.[86] This represented over two thirds majority favourable to the Partition of Palestine into Jewish and Arab segments. The United States, the Soviet Union, many European countries, and members of the British Commonwealth voted in favour of the Resolution, while Britain abstained; the Arab and Moslem countries unanimously voted against it.

For the Arab world, it was a religious question. An independent Jewish state in their midst was inconceivable; the proposition was received as an insult. Thenceforth, they lost no time in preparing to crush the newborn state at its conception. Meanwhile, the British government set the timetable for a termination of its Palestine Mandate. That date was 14 May 1947. Until then, hoards of arms were smuggled in from surrounding Arab countries to the Palestinian Arab sniper bands. They were allowed free passage, unfettered and unhindered by the Mandate Authorities.

Arab ambushes caused heavy casualties to Jewish convoys that carried food, supplies and other necessities to isolated settlements. Jewish resistance fighters faced two enemies head on, while their convoys were subject to searches by the British at each checkpoint. Haganah defenders came under arrest for arbitrary reasons; all the while, the fledgling country's borders were kept open to a growing Arab "brotherhood" of fighters from neighbouring countries that encircled it with the aim to aid their "brothers" against the partition.

Growing crises and hostilities prompted the United States and many members of the United Nations to second-guess the partition. Warren Austin, American ambassador to the UN, suggested temporary UN trusteeship in Palestine. That political development led the Arabs to put their massive invasion against the Jews on hold until the British Mandate expired. Meanwhile illegal Jewish immigration continued alongside arms that were mostly purchased and smuggled in from Poland and Czechoslovakia for the Jewish defence units.

---

[86]   Ibid, 356.

On 14 May 1948, the British high commissioner announced the end of the Mandate, boarding a cruiser with his staff and sailing away from Palestinian soil. At four o'clock in the afternoon of the same day, in the presence of 240 men, David Ben Gurion read the fledgling Jewish State's Proclamation of Independence at the Museum of Tel-Aviv. The following excerpt highlights details of that historic ceremony:

> *Eretz Israel* [the Land of Israel] *was the birthplace of the Jewish People. Here their spiritual, religious and political identity was shaped. Here they first attained to statehood, created cultural values of national and universal significance and gave to the world the eternal Book of Books.*

> *After being forcibly exiled from their land, the people kept faith with it throughout their Dispersion and never ceased to pray and hope for their return. …In recent decades they returned in their masses. Pioneers and defenders made desert bloom, revived the Hebrew language, built villages and towns, and created a thriving community … bringing the blessings of progress to all the country's inhabitants, and aspiring toward independent nationhood. …In the Second World War, the Jewish community of this country contributed its full share to the struggle of the freedom and peace loving nations against the forces of Nazi wickedness and, by the blood of its soldiers … gained the right to be reckoned among the peoples who founded the United Nations. …By the virtue of our natural and historic right and on the strength of the resolution of the United Nations General Assembly, hereby declare the establishment of a Jewish State in Eretz Israel, to be known as the State Of Israel…. The State of Israel will be open for Jewish immigration and for the gathering of the Exiles … it will be based on freedom, justice and peace envisaged by the prophets of Israel; it will ensure complete equality of social and political rights to all its inhabitants irrespective of religion, race or sex; it will guarantee freedom of religion, conscience, language, education and culture; it will safeguard the Holy Places of all religions; and it will be faithful to principles of the Charters of the United Nations. …We appeal to the United Nations*

> *to assist the Jewish people in the building-up of its State and*
> *to receive the State of Israel into the comity of nations. ...We*
> *extend our hand to all neighboring States and their peoples*
> *in an offer of peace and good neighborliness, and appeal to*
> *them to establish bonds of cooperation and mutual help with*
> *the sovereign Jewish people settled in its own land. The State*
> *of Israel is prepared to do its share in common effort for the*
> *advancement of the entire Middle East....*"[87]

The Declaration was signed by Ben Gurion and thirty-seven Jewish personalities, including Israel's future prime minister, Golda Mayerson (later Meir), on the Sabbath eve of 14 May 1948. The timeless benediction recited on the first night of every Chanukah was also invoked: "*Blessed art Thou, O Lord our God, King of the Universe, who hast kept us alive and preserved us and enabled us to see this day (season).*"

Hours later, the United States recognized the Jewish State and was promptly followed by the Soviet Union. But the moments of celebration were short lived. Hours after the Declaration of Independence, the newborn state was invaded by joint Egyptian, Lebanese, Syrian, Jordanian and Iraqi armies with an onslaught of tanks and bombers. Faced with the reality of defending itself against a formidable foe, it did whatever that was called for even as it was unmatched in both numbers and equipment.

Jerusalem was besieged by the well-trained Jordanian army. The only food and water available to the city's inhabitants were what could be transported by a single-engine training plane. As for the British Mandate, it deprived the Jewish people of the wherewithal to defend themselves after evacuating their troops, all the while keeping the doors open for the Arab armies to stockpile ammunition for a calculated assault. This was the opportunity the Arab world was counting on to wrap up Jewish presence in Palestine. But the Jewish defence, with a meagre resource base miraculously withstood the pressure from without, so much that, on 11 June 1948,

---

[87] David Ben Gurion, 14 May 1948. *Official Gazette*: Number 1; Tel Aviv, 5 Iyar 5708, Page 1. *Proclamation of Independence: The Declaration of the Establishment of the State of Israel*. [online] Available at: http://www.knesset.gov.il/docs/eng/megilat_eng.htm. [Accessed 10 May 2011].

the Arab armies, exhausted from the war effort, consented to a cease-fire intervened by Count Bernadotte, the United Nations mediator. To the Jews it was a sign that their God intended for Israel to be reborn.

"The Lord shall fight for you and ye shall hold your peace" (Exodus14:14).

Year after year, Israel remained coiled within a cycle of war and truce with her Arab neighbours, with no diplomatic end in sight, but she lost no time in building air and ground defence forces superior to those of all of her Arab neighbours combined. She armed herself with sophisticated warplanes and trained skilled pilots to rival the most advanced air force on Earth. Generals such as Yitzkhak Rabin, Moshe Dayan, Ariel Sharon, and scores of other valiant strategists led the Israeli army to victory against the enemy's surprise attacks.

From her inception, Israel offered citizenship to anyone of Hebrew faith arriving on her shores. Additionally, numerous other immigrants and refugees were absorbed, given papers and citizenship, health care, the right to vote, and access to education. They came from the four corners of the globe. The sad contrast of the narrative perpetuated onto the Arab Palestinians by their own brethren has left them vulnerable and without control over their destiny. Beginning at the time of Israel's rebirth in the Holy Land, the Arab states encouraged local Arabs to evacuate at its inception.

At this critical juncture in the region's history, something very sinister ensued, that the ayatollahs of Iran's Islamic Revolution also categorically failed to include in their anti-Israel orations on Friday prayers and other events of national scale. The Jews demonstrated the ability to defend themselves against the fire of those they had invited to join in nation building. Those Arabs who answered the call to leave their homes and join forces with the surrounding invading Arab armies, allowed themselves to be caught in circumstances that prevented their return! Where, indeed, a few hours earlier a fledgling new state that proclaimed independence among the comity of nations, extended a hand to Arab and Jew alike to build harmoniously a country of equal participants, a disinherited Palestinian people ended up instead marauding for decades without papers or statehood, living as perpetual pawns at the mercy of their Arab "brethren." Those nations, instead of helping them and issuing papers, preferred the animus of war, and remained fiercely patient in their special hatred for their tiny neighbour, stubbornly reluctant to recognize a right to sovereignty and their own flag.

Much work went underway to create an infrastructure with utmost expediency. Agriculture was industrialized to maximize the use of land— to develop new methods of water distribution, irrigation, desalination, forestation, and land reclamation in marshes through the planting of eucalyptus trees. The list grew onward. Of equal urgency was the need for health and welfare services, social security, social services, international trade and commerce, and scores of other national priorities, not the least of which were science, education, and the arts.

This process of self-actualization only increased Arab animosity toward Israel, until it burgeoned into ever more creative outlets, such as propaganda using the international media funded by oil money. Skirmishes and sporadic attacks on Israel became their modus operandi. Meanwhile, a new Goliath emerged from the Arab camp. His name was Gamal Abdel Nasser. Nasser became Egypt's president in 1956, the year the British along with the French and Israelis launched an attack on Egypt to liberate the Suez Canal, while the United States, acting under Soviet threat, pressured the three countries to withdraw.

Nasser was planning to unite all the Arab states under one banner. A military general and skilled orator, he needed a strong credential to enforce his plan to realize the Arab ideology's dream of wiping Israel off the political map. To that end, he befriended the Soviet Union and purchased more than 400 warplanes from the Russians on long-term credit. Nasser illegally expelled the UN emergency forces from the Sinai Peninsula. He amassed 1,000 tanks and 100,000 soldiers in the Sinai Desert and blocked the Strait of Tiran against Israeli marines. On other fronts, Syria and Jordan stood on their toes to invade Israel upon Nasser's command.

The year was 1967, and I remember the evenings we spent sitting on my parents' ground-level balcony of our two-storey house at the foot of the Alborz Mountains north of Teheran. It was hot in the summertime, and the sound of the crickets was the only background noise while my father played his usual card game of solitaire, alternately cajoling each of his grandchildren, in turn, onto his lap as he fed them chunks of fruit.

David Ben Gurion (1886 – 1973)
[Illustration by Sandra Koukou]

Abruptly one evening, the radio news anchor interrupted the blissful calm and began delivering the latest story about the escalating tension in Israel. As we all held our breath, with our ears poised in the direction of my father's small, leather-bound radio, it was becoming apparent that Nasser's armies and allies were busy preparing a sweeping and general battle. The news anchor's words affixed themselves onto many similar recollections, as we listened to him quote Nasser saying, "Today we prepare for battle, and by nightfall we will be having supper in Jerusalem."

While the Western powers maintained an attitude of non intervention, and the United Nations Security Council remained silent, on 5 June 1967 at 7:14 a.m., the Israeli air force took off for a pre-emptive attack on Egypt and destroyed about 300 Egyptian warplanes inside their own air base while Egyptian pilots were at breakfast. The Israeli Army, commanded by General Yitzchak Rabin, thrust into the Sinai desert and positioned itself on the east bank of the Suez Canal. On other fronts, Israeli forces reached the entire length of the River Jordan and captured the Golan Heights from the Syrians.

Jerusalem's Western Wall—Judaism's holiest site—and the whole of Jerusalem fell under Israeli control. General Moshe Dayan appeared six days later on our television screen standing by the Wall uttering the words: "We are here to stay."

General Dayan's statement was potent with significance on many levels relating to Jewish history, from ancient times when The Book was being written, down through the ages until the present.

> The Hebrew Bible mentions Jerusalem 669 times and Zion (Jerusalem) 154 times, which means that Jerusalem is mentioned in the Hebrew Bible 823 times in all. All synagogues around the world are built facing Jerusalem. For 2,000 years, since the destruction of the Second Temple in Jerusalem, Jews have prayed three times daily to return to the Land of Israel and to rebuild Jerusalem. Every year at the end of Yom Kippur services and at the end of the Passover Seder, Jewish congregations and families all around the world declare "Next Year in Jerusalem!"

> Finally, in 1967, our prayers were answered and Jerusalem
> was once again united under Jewish sovereignty.[88]

In the aftermath of the Six-Day War, and Nasser's utter defeat by the end of August 1967, the heads of eight Arab states gathered in Khartoum, Sudan to discuss future policy toward Israel. That conference concluded with three negatives: *(i)* no peace with Israel, *(ii)* no recognition of Israel, and *(iii)* no negotiation with Israel. The single positive outcome on the Arab side was a promise by the sheikhs of the Persian Gulf to help Nasser out of bankruptcy in exchange for ending the rhetoric about uniting the Arabs under one banner.

As it turned out, Abdel Nasser of Egypt died in September of 1970 and was succeeded by Anwar el-Sādāt, who hoped to win back the territory lost to Israel in 1967. The Egyptian leader el-Sādāt and his Syrian counterpart, the strongman Hafez Assad, chose Yom Kippur, the holiest day to Judaism, to make another surprise attack on Israel. On 6 October 1973, while most Israelis of all ranks were praying in their synagogues, the Egyptian army crossed the Suez Canal and pushed northward on the Sinai Peninsula. Simultaneously, Syrian troops made their thrust onto the Golan Heights and recaptured parts of what they had lost during the Six-Day War. Forty-eight hours after enemy attack, momentum was building on the Israeli side, and the tide turned toward Israel's advantage. The Syrians were pushed back and lost all of their gains and an additional 165 square miles at Golan.

In the Sinai, General Ariel Sharon led his troops through a corridor between the second and the third Egyptian armies, pushed southward, and took position at the Suez Canal. On 16 October 1973, Israeli troops crossed the canal, and on October 21st, Sharon encircled the Egyptian Third Army and held the entire western side of the Suez Canal, forty-two miles away from Cairo. About 70,000 Egyptian troops at Sinai were disconnected from the mainland with no food, water, and supplies. Israel made it clear to the Egyptians that further steps must be taken

---

[88]   Scott Kalmikoff, 05 April 2012. *Jerusalem is the capital of the State of Israel.* [online] Available at: http://www.silive.com/opinion/letters/index.ssf/2012/04/ jerusalem_is_the_capital_of_th.html. [Accessed 30 May 2012].

through direct negotiation. Egypt and Syria were reluctant to comply, and hampered the process with three *negatives* at Khartoum. They, instead, rushed their foreign ministers along with their counterparts from other Arab countries to the United States, and asked the US Secretary of State Henry Kissinger to create a miracle and force Israel to end the siege.

Kissinger's famous reply was that miracles normally took place in *their own* part of the world, a reference to Moses and the biblical Exodus.

The Yom Kippur War ended with the deaths of 2,700 Israeli, 3,500 Syrian, and 15,000 Egyptian soldiers. Kissinger eventually helped the Arabs negotiate a peace agreement with Israel.

Four years later, on 19 November 1977, Anwar el-Sādāt took a big step and went to Jerusalem to deliver a speech inside the Knesset, the Israeli parliament, and extended a hand in friendship to the Jewish State. His bold gesture opened the way to a newly forged peace agreement between Egypt and Israel at Camp David. In meetings held in the presence of the then American President Jimmy Carter, Anwar el-Sādāt and Israel's Prime Minister Menahem Begin concluded an agreement by which Israel handed the Sinai over to Egypt. The land for peace deal included an oil field that had been explored by Israeli scientists.

Immediately following the new developments, el-Sādāt advised the Palestinians to negotiate peace with Israel, accept their losses, and establish an independent state of their own. Their leader, Yasser Arafat, an Egyptian-born native, was unwilling to compromise. As a result, the Palestinians, who had never in the past enjoyed sovereignty, not less during Ottoman rule in the region, missed a golden opportunity for self-determination. Once again sidetracked by false leadership, they developed the techniques of suicide bombing that later culminated in the creation of an *intifada*. They launched rockets and purposefully targeted Israeli civilians, young and old, and carried out other terrorist activities, thereby diminishing their people's chances for self-determination. Their efforts failed to shake the make-believe enemy, Israel, into extinction.

El-Sādāt, a visionary who understood the merit in choosing peace over envy, paid the ultimate price for his courage to follow personal convictions and turn away from a centuries-old dogma of hatred toward Jews deeply engrained in the Moslem psyche. Sadly, a fanatic lieutenant in his own army assassinated Anwar el-Sādāt during an annual victory parade in Cairo.

Saddam Hussein, the Iraqi president (1937–2006), was another hopeful to lead the Arab world. His goal to attain the place of prominence formerly held by Egypt's Abdul Nasser led him to pick up where Nasser had left off by advocating the end of Israel in the Middle East. His ground and air power being no match to contend with Israel's military might, he decided to adopt nuclear power for his plan. France helped Saddam build an atomic reactor near Baghdad. At about the time Saddam's atomic plant was to be loaded with nuclear fuel, Israel, under Prime Minister Begin mobilized an operation to obliterate the project. On Sunday 7 June 1981, Eight F16A bombers and six F15A escorting fighters carrying additional fuel tanks the distance of 1,000 kilometres, left Etzion Airbase, flew over Jordan, passed over Saudi Arabia, and, unimpeded, reached the Iraqi atomic site. The bombers performed a surgical strike and totally destroyed the reactor, returning to their base without the need to refuel midway. On the political front, Israel was widely criticized for the attack, although the two countries were formally at war. Subsequent events proved that Israel's action had been a significant service to humanity.

Another Arab leader in the playing field of the Middle East was King Hussein of Jordan (1935–1999), a direct descendent of the Prophet Mohammad. He joined Egypt and Syria in the Six-Day War against Israel and lost the east of Jerusalem and Jordan's West Bank. Since 1970, King Hussein, a moderate monarch, began secret negotiations with Israel, and eventually developed a friendly relationship with Prime Minister Yitzchak Rabin, which led him in 1994 to sign a peace treaty between the two countries. That opportunity for peace wisely seized bore heavy significance as a rare pact between a distinguished descendent of Mohammad and the children of Israel, and promoted lasting peaceful and cordial relations between the two countries.

NEXT PAGE: Photographs of pages from a small leather-bound manuscript created by the author's father in Iraq, found in a box of memorabilia after the author's decease. These handwritten works in calligraphy continue to be followed by some members of the Iraqi Jewish community. The booklet was written in the Iraqi Hebrew alphabet (known as Hetzi Kulmous) and in the Iraqi Jewish language (Judeo-Arabic dialect).

TOP: A calligraphic depiction of a page of the Kabbalah by the Arie of Zaphat.[89] | **BOTTOM:** A page from the Passover Haggadah.[90]

MANY IRAQI JEWS USED TO HAVE HANDWRITTEN MANUSCRIPTS, mostly of the Pessach Haggadah. In 1948 the Iraqi police raided Jewish homes in search of Zionist related documents. Such a document, if found, would have caused problems to the Jewish family that owned it, Iraqi authorities being unfamiliar with this kind of hand writing. As a result many families decided to burn such manuscripts to avoid problems with the Iraqi authorities.[91]

---

[89] The left hand page depicts the first page of Kabbalah by the Arie of Zaphat. The right hand side is an explanation of this page of Kabbalah.

[90] The left side is the first page of the Passover Haggadah. The right side is an explanation of this page.

[91] Sami Sourani, 2014. Discussion on the historical significance of the above captioned, leather bound manuscript. [email correspondence] (Personal communication with the Editor, 17 June 2014).

Photographs of pages from a small leather-bound manuscript created by and bearing the seal of the author's father, Heskel Abraham *Koukou*, found by the author's daughter in a box of memorabilia after her father passed away in 2012. | The manuscript bears, among others, the Hebrew calendar date 5665, equivalent to 1904 in the solar calendar. | Heskel Abraham was most likely 21 years of age at the time he worked on this booklet.

PART IV

REFLECTIONS

19

THE LINK BETWEEN
ACTION AND DESTINY

MY FATHER WAS A BUSINESSMAN, AND HIS PASSION IN LIFE was to help the young acquire a modern education. In the 1930s, my family emigrated from Iraq and settled in Isfahan, a beautiful city in central Iran. I was only ten years old when we left our ancient home in Iraq. Isfahan at that time had a Jewish population of about 20,000 souls living mainly in the ghetto, led by one single religious leader who went by the name of Mullah Nissan. There was also a sort of overseer, a man named Agha Yehuda Gabbai, whom the people looked to as one to arbitrate in matters of civil dispute and to help resolve family disagreements. My father was concerned that the Jewish community in Isfahan needed a school to accommodate a large number of idling children. To that purpose, a parcel of land was secured by the Alliance Israelite Universelle of France, which drafted plans for the building of the school. Nonetheless, the project was aborted at the start of World War II.

It took no time for my father to set up a committee for the building of the school. He started by delegating Agha Yehuda Gabbai as president of the committee. My father then went about raising the funds on his own, gathering donations from anyone who cared to listen.

When I asked why he spent so much time and energy on that project, my father related a story of his own childhood, around 1904. His father enrolled him at the Alliance School in Baghdad, wanting him to benefit from a modern education, learn a foreign language, and at the same time learn about his faith. The following day his grandfather took him out of school and placed him in a *yeshiva*, a school for Talmudic study.

So, my father grew up to watch his friends engage in commerce with foreign countries, see their businesses flourish, unable himself to progress in the modern world, equipped as he was solely with a background in religious studies. As a result, he developed an obsession—and built a passion—to help others acquire the knowledge denied him, and the know-how to help them keep pace with modern developments in a fast-growing, industrialized world.

After that discussion, it suddenly dawned upon me that my grandfather's interference in my father's education back in Iraq was an act predestined to lead my father toward the fulfilment of his dream of building a school in Isfahan: *"There are many devices in a man's heart; nevertheless the council of the Lord, that shall stand"* *(Proverbs 19:21).*

In one of his fundraising activities, I accompanied my father to the Jewish ghetto. It was a typically hot midsummer afternoon. We had parked the car outside the ghetto limits and walked inside the premises. Our mission was to enter a certain old synagogue to collect a number of unused scrolls, bring them to a qualified scribe, and have them rehabilitated and rendered appropriate for people to dedicate to any synagogue of their choice. It was my father's strategy to generate funds for his brainchild, the special school project.

We were led, instead, to the house of the leader of that synagogue, who was also a member of the school building committee. A couple of other ranking members of the synagogue were present. They told us that the man in whose care were entrusted the master keys to any of the synagogue's facilities happened to be out of town and that no access was available before his return. In this way, they seemed intent to hold out and talk us out of our project, unwilling to relinquish their synagogue's treasure.

My father knew fully well that the entire Jewish population of Isfahan favoured building the new school. He knew that they were reluctant to lose this singular opportunity. So, he made his intention clear to remain in place until the key holder showed up. He said that he intended to walk out of the synagogue carrying the scrolls to the accompaniment of the sound of song and dance.

When King David delivered the Ark of the Covenant with the holy tablets to the Jerusalem, the City of David, *"David danced before the Lord with all his might, and David was girded with a linen ephod. So David and all the house of Israel brought up the Ark of the Lord with shouting, and with the sound of the trumpet"* (II Samuel 6:14–15).

As it happened, no more than a half hour later, we found ourselves standing inside the synagogue itself, collecting the scrolls, then preparing to depart. As we stepped outside the synagogue, we found our way along a narrow lane that meandered through the ghetto, coming across a band of musicians on their way to a nearby wedding celebration.

It was a brief segment of time before dark when the band took notice of the two of us, my father and I, our arms holding the scrolls in a tight embrace. No sooner had the troupe turned swiftly around to follow in our direction than the music had begun to play for us and continued the entire route to the car waiting on the edge of the ghetto's perimeter. My father's wish was fulfilled. I still recall the intensity of my realization at that very moment when I felt the divine presence, certain that He who had choreographed each scene, was leading us through each step to fulfil my father's dream.

The school that once existed only on a piece of paper was inaugurated a mere sixteen months thereafter—complete with furniture, books and a sports facility. It accommodated 1,200 boys and girls, regardless of religious background.

When my father originally left Iraq in the early 1930s, it was to establish a Chevrolet car and truck dealership. Life was good for the Jews in Iraq during the 1930s. Nevertheless, he seized a business opportunity and moved our family to Iran. Throughout the various stages in the growth of my father's business, many people were hired and fired, but one man, Abraham Youssian alone, remained with him until our departure to settle the whole family in the capital city of Teheran. The reason for that lasting bond was simple enough.

Abraham Youssian became my father's confidante. Mr. Youssian had a profound knowledge of The Book, and it was plain for everyone to see the genuine complicity between the two men. They both harboured a deep concern for others, which led them to a selfless desire to put themselves in the service of the community. As such, they both got involved in the minute details of the school's project and worked tirelessly toward its fruition. Before moving to Teheran, my father taught Mr. Youssian the ropes of his business and transferred the entire business to him, switching his role from employee to entrepreneur. A half century later, that bond of friendship has been playing a major role to shape my life here in the United States.

Evelyn and I were given political asylum. We settled in a rented apartment in a New York suburb. I was in my mid sixties and needed a new source of income to supplement my meagre savings, which were soon headed for depletion.

It happened that my brother-in-law, Albert Said Mehr, God bless his soul, left no stone unturned to find a solution to my dilemma. Albert got in touch with the son of an old friend of my father's. I was met with open arms the day I walked through the doors of their offices and started working immediately for an old Isfahani friend, who happened to be Abraham Youssian's son, Isaac. Miraculously, I was able to earn some vital revenue until the ripe old age of eighty-seven, thanks to none other than Isaac and his son, Eli. In a way, I was given carte blanche to work for a major industrial supplier that sold brake parts to all parts of the Americas as a family member in their midst. To my deep gratitude, I was made to feel no pressure whatsoever to retire until recently, when my changing health required it.

20

IN QUEST OF GOD

ALBERT EINSTEIN, PICTURED AS TIME MAGAZINE'S Person of the Century on the cover of its last edition before the ringing in of the New Year 2000,[92] once described man's search for God in the following way: "Everything in this being has a destiny—from the start to the end that is governed by a Power beyond our control. This destiny stands for the smallest creature to the greatest celestial body. Man, Plant, Celestial dust; they all dance to a tune whose Orchestrator is invisible."

Einstein is attributed to have said: "Science without religion is lame; religion without science is blind."[93] Through his theory of relativity which he first put forth when he was only 26, his theory of quanta, his paper on the theoretical basis for the photoelectric cell or the electric eye, and other ground breaking scientific contributions, he changed the foundations of physics and the way we look at concepts of time, space, mass, motion and gravitation. "Einstein developed his theory through deep philosophical thought and through complex mathematical reasoning."[94] Although he did not associate himself with any religion in an orthodox manner, he was deeply religious by nature, and never believed that the universe was governed by chance and chaos. "The universe to him was one of absolute law and order," and he firmly believed that there was a Being at work in the universe.[95]

---

[92] Time Magazine. 31 December 1999, Vol. 154, No. 27. *Person of the Century*. [online] Available at: http://content.time.com/time/magazine/0,9263,7601991231,00.html. [Accessed 20 August 2011].

[93] Attributed to Albert Einstein. *Albert Einstein Quotes*. [online] Available at: http:// thinkexist.com/quotes/albert_einstein/. [Accessed: 12 February 2012].

[94] *World Book, Inc.*, Volume 6, "Albert Einstein," article by Daniel J. Kevles. (Chicago: Scott Fetzer, 1994), 146.

[95] Ibid, 147.

Not all scientists believe in miracles; many avoid the question as to who is the creator of nature and its laws. Yet Einstein's spirit shows through with eloquence in the following statement, which has been attributed to him: "There are two ways to live: you can live as if nothing is a miracle; you can live as if everything is a miracle."[96]

During a telephone conversation in which my daughter, Sandra, shared some ideas about my writing with a friend, she cited some of Einstein's statements. After some reflection, her friend drew a comparison between the two figures of Moses and Einstein: "Where Moses first brought the *word* of God to the people, Einstein deciphered the *language* of God, interpreting it through the famous formula for the theory of relativity, $E=mc^2$."[97] Otherwise stated, Moses was God's messenger while Einstein was His interpreter. Both acted as intermediaries between the cosmic realm and their contemporaries, irreversibly effecting colossal shifts away from mankind's existing paradigms.

We have yet to discover the existence of life beyond Earth. We may or may not be alone in the Universe, but we are aware of the dance of the many billions of celestial bodies orchestrated and fully tuned into a system. We know this, since we can follow much of their activity with amazing precision using modern technology. So, it is humbling to consider how our very sustenance is guaranteed by our movement through the Solar System. Planet Earth's colossal mass suspended in empty space, spins every twenty-four hours around her core at a speed of 1,000 miles per hour, while she holds our vital atmosphere and the oceans inside a thin membrane, allowing no spill over. She does this while also diligently travelling a full circle around the sun at a mind-boggling speed of 670,650 miles per hour to complete one Solar Year.[98]

---

[96]   Attributed to Albert Einstein. *Albert Einstein Quotes*. [online] Available at: http://thinkexist.com/quotes/albert_einstein/. [Accessed: 12 February 2012].

[97]   Maurice Kaspy, 2012. Discussion on Einstein. [phone conversation] (Personal communication with the Editor, 26 March 2012).

[98]   *World Book, Inc.*, Volume 18, "Sun," article by Robert W. Noyes. (Chicago: Scott, 1994), 975.

We also know that the Earth spins on her axis at a slight tilt. Can we possibly take this fact for granted? This tilt is part of a design to vary Earth's exposure to the Sun's warmth, thus creating the Seasons. We may notice that shadows cast by objects constantly "relocate" themselves following a pattern particular to each day of the year. How miraculous that a tree's shadow relocates to the very same position after a full year's trek, many new leaves later and 365 days further down the line!

Pausing to reflect on the Sphinx's shadow in Egypt at say two o'clock in the afternoon on 6 June 2000, we realize that it corresponds exactly to its position on the afternoon of the same day in the year 1000 and at the same time of day! Some intention is clearly in place to keep it that way.

"And God said Let There Be Light: and there was Light" (Genesis 1:3).

As far as we can imagine, the Universe's galaxies and millions of other celestial bodies can do without light. However, we living beings cannot. This concept may help us realize that the Sun's purpose—its very raison d'être—is for mankind to see on the one hand, and to keep alive thanks to its heat and energy, on the other. Does this not place us then in a mighty significant position in the face of the Universe at large?

With our keen vision and tools, our curiosity leads us to another miracle: all the while that Earth circles around the Sun carefully keeping at a safe 91.4 to 94.5 million miles of distance—it remains far enough not to melt, and yet close enough not to freeze entirely. The biggest surprise for this author is that the Sun has given us such amazing light and soothing warmth from a distance of over 91 million miles for the 4.5 million years that Earth has been around.[99] The sun itself has been generously and unconditionally giving our planet sustenance for around 4,500 million years, all the while without the need to refuel!

Another marvel is that the Moon circles the Earth at an escape velocity of 1.5 miles every second, keeping us company wherever we may be.

---

[99] *World Book, Inc.*, Volume 6, "Earth," article by Sue Ellen Hirschfeld. (Chicago: Scott Fetzer, 1994), 17.

These precise movements are in themselves miracles that continue every second of our lives. How frightful to imagine an instance in which such gigantic celestial orbs within the myriads of galaxies may, for a split second, be left to their own devices! Perhaps this consideration can clue us into the magnitude of the miracle at work that manifests itself around us with perfect precision, so that we just ponder at the notion of … just who is in command?

These phenomena may truly remind one of God's response to Sarah, who laughs with dumbfounded disbelief at begetting a child in old age: *"Is anything too hard for the Lord?" (Genesis 18:14).*

At a social gathering, someone who learned about my intention to write a book on the subject of the Scripture, remarked that scientists' searches in the Sinai Desert found no trace of a tomb or any remains of the thousands of Israelites who wandered the desert for forty years, as written in the Bible; nothing was to be found!

I told him my book is based upon the premise that the Canonized Bible, irrespective of the controversies presented by modern scholars, is authentic. That said, Bible reading greatly benefits from group discussion to enable readers to enjoy a meaningful shared experience and a deeper exploration of its complexities.

And, if God is The Omnipotent, as depicted in The Book, one premise may be that HE purposefully eliminated any trace or evidence of human passage in the desert at Sinai:

A. To keep the sanctity of the area where HE addressed the nation at Mount Sinai, granted them the Torah and led them through, all the way to the Promised Land.

B. To measure the extent of our belief in HIM.

Albert Einstein (14 March 1879 – 18 April 1955)
When asked about his belief in miracles, he responded with the double
scenario, "There are two ways to live: you can live as if nothing is a
miracle; you can live as if everything is a miracle."[100]
[Illustration by Sandra Koukou]

[100]   Attributed to Albert Einstein. *Albert Einstein Quotes.* [online] Available at: http://
thinkexist.com/quotes/albert_einstein/. [Accessed: 12 February 2012].

21

SELF-HELP AND
PERSONAL DESTINY

WHAT IS OUR PLACE IN THE GRAND SCHEME OF THINGS? A common belief in Jewish religious circles holds forth that a messiah will appear, and a lasting peace will reign *only* when people become pious and follow the rules as written in the Bible.

I very often pause to think about this concept and somehow find it unthinkable that God adjusts His timetable according to the whims of mortals! I choose to believe that God Himself decides any such anticipated moment. The Book itself sheds light on the issue through the Prophet Jeremiah:

> But this shall be the covenant that I will make with the house of Israel ... I will put my law in their inward parts, and write it in their hearts; and will be their God, and they shall be my people. And they shall teach no more every man his neighbor, and every man his brother, saying, Know the Lord: for they shall all know me, from the least of them unto the greatest of them, saith the Lord: for I will forgive their iniquity, and I will remember their sin no more. (Jeremiah 31:33–34)

> When I say unto the wicked, thou shalt surely die; if he turn from his sin, and do that which is lawful and right; if the wicked restore the pledge, give again that he had, walk in the statutes of life, without committing iniquity; he shall surely live, he shall not die. None of his sins that he hath committed shall be mentioned unto him ... he shall surely live. (Ezekiel 33:14–16)

When God is so forgiving as to pardon the wicked who repent, He can be that much kinder to a person who unintentionally wrongs a neighbour, and repents toward a regrettable act. From this premise, we have reason to believe that each individual has a personal bank account of conscience within a system in which reward and punishment is, for better or worse, ultimately linked to a Higher Power.

> *Thus saith The Lord; Cursed be the man that trusteth in man, and maketh flesh his arm, and whose heart departeth from the Lord. For he shall be like the heath in the desert, and shall not see when good cometh; but shall inhabit the parched places in the wilderness, in a salt land and not inhabited. (Jeremiah 17:5-6)*

Jeremiah said that God summons us to trust in Him; he advises us not to place all our faith in other mortals. When we entrust our self-worth to others, when we worry about what others think instead of focusing on what God requires of us, we lose our true calling. Jeremiah's admonishment points to the fact that, in the absence of a mindset attuned to the higher power within, we resemble the heath that dwells in a salty land devoid of water. We become dry to the most fertile opportunities when they do miraculously show up.

> *Blessed is the man that trusteth in the Lord, and whose hope the Lord is, For he shall be as a tree planteth by the waters, and that spreadeth out her roots by the river, and shall not see when heat cometh, but her leaf shall be green; and shall not be careful in the year of draught, neither shall cease from yielding fruit. (Jeremiah 17:7–8)*

When we place our trust in the Lord, we look inward to measure what we alone can control—our personal worthiness—by the yardstick of the heart, instead of weighing our personal effectiveness on the scales of public opinion. God speaks to those who listen with all their heart and mind and soul. They truly live who can feel life from within, and their life becomes fertile as Jeremiah's metaphor of a "tree planteth by the waters."

Wherein lays glory?

> *Thus saith The Lord: Let not the wise man glorify in his wisdom, neither let the mighty man glorify in his might, let not the rich man glory in his riches: but let him that glorieth glory in this, that he understandeth and knoweth me, that I am the Lord which exercise loving kindness, judgment, and righteousness, in the Earth: for in these things I delight, saith the Lord. (Jeremiah 9:23–24)*

The Book's underlying principle is that the source of all blessing is the Almighty. We need not look any further, and He is not hard to find. If we go deep enough, we may find that His likeness has long ago taken residence in our hearts, as we stay alert to our natural capacity for *loving kindness, sound judgment,* and *righteousness,* and as we turn our *appreciation* toward Earth's perennial blessings. If this principle is beginning to sound like the Golden Rule, the story of Hillel Hazaken poignantly points in the same direction.

Hillel Hazaken was the greatest of the sages living during the time of the Second Temple. He was a simple woodcutter who came from Babylonia to Jerusalem to learn Torah from the Pharisee teachers of his time. Jewish tradition has lovingly preserved Hillel's teachings, one of which quotes the story of a heathen who approached the sage with a request:

> "'If you can teach me the whole Torah while I stand on one foot, you can make me a Jew.'"

To this proposition Rabbi Hillel replied:

> "'What is hateful to you do not do to your neighbor; this is the whole Torah; the rest is commentary. Go and study.'"[101]

"Thou shalt love your neighbor as thyself—I Am the Lord" (Leviticus 19:18).

---

[101]   Abba Eban. *Heritage: Civilization and the Jews,* 81–82.

The Ten Commandments ignite the spirit of the Golden Rule in that they invite us to love others as we love ourselves. Thus, the Ten Commandments are a mind jogger or memory card that one carries upon oneself in order to create a fruitful existence through honouring one's divine qualities. When the Ten Commandments are adopted as a personal handbook for a life of integrity, it follows that loving others begins with loving oneself enough to become an integral part of a bigger whole.

TEN COMMANDMENTS
(Exodus 20: 2–17)

1. *I am the Lord thy God, which have brought thee out of the land of Egypt, out of the house of bondage. Thou shalt have no other gods before me.*

2. *Thou shalt not make unto thee any graven image, or any likeness of any thing that is in heaven above, or that is in the earth beneath, or that is in the water under the earth. Thou shalt not bow down thyself to them, nor serve them: for I the Lord thy God am a jealous God, visiting the iniquity of the fathers upon the children unto the third and fourth generation of them that hate me; And shewing mercy unto thousands of them that love me, and keep my commandments.*

3. *Thou shalt not take the name of the Lord thy God in vain; for the Lord will not hold him guiltless that taketh his name in vain.*

4. *Remember the sabbath day, to keep it holy. Six days shalt thou labour, and do all thy work: But the seventh day is the sabbath of the Lord thy God: in it thou shalt not do any work, thou, nor thy son, nor thy daughter, thy manservant, nor thy maidservant, nor thy cattle, nor thy stranger that is within thy gates: For in six days the Lord made heaven and earth, the sea, and all that in them is, and rested the seventh day: wherefore the Lord blessed the sabbath day, and hallowed it.*

5. *Honour thy father and thy mother: that thy days may be long upon the land which the Lord thy God giveth thee.*

6. *Thou shalt not kill.*

7. *Thou shalt not commit adultery.*

8. *Thou shalt not steal.*

9. *Thou shalt not bear false witness against thy neighbour.*

10. *Thou shalt not covet thy neighbour's house, thou shalt not covet thy neighbour's wife, nor his manservant, nor his maidservant, nor his ox, nor his ass, nor any thing that is thy neighbour's.*[102]

As for loving oneself, God declares, "*Ye shall be Holy unto me, for I The Lord Am Holy*" (Leviticus 20:26).

"*Ye shall not make any cuttings in your flesh for the dead, nor print any marks upon you—I Am the Lord*" (Leviticus 19:28).

Since we are designed in His image, or with capacities and characteristics that mirror our higher power, there is no need to alter our physical aspects. The many miracles around us point to a specific intent for us to appreciate the way we are and how well we fit into the larger scheme of Creation. In this way, we are allowing nature's miracles to reveal themselves through us in ways that are harmonious to our intrinsic divinity. The practice of cutting the flesh for the dead recalls the Shiite ritual of causing physical injury to oneself during the *Day of Ashura*, the annual mourning for the martyrdom of the fallen imams. This practice is forbidden in Judaism as well as in Islam's Sunni denomination.

"*Ye shall therefore keep all my statutes, and all my judgments and do them…*" (Leviticus 20:22).

The Golden Rule extends beyond the realm of one's children and immediate family. Even as we watch our children succeed in life and feel that their joy is ours, we can extend this attitude beyond the family circle to include our fellow citizens of the world. We can share in their joy and

---

[102] One may note that the first five commandments relate to our relationship with the Creator, whereas the other half have to do with our relationships with one another. The commandment to honor parents appears in the first half of the twin tablets.

success. What gain lies in jealousy? What does one lose by welcoming a spirit of goodwill? After all, when the time arrives, rich and poor, able and unhealthy, we all leave worldly goods behind! In *Pirkei Abot*, a book of reflections on the ethics of the fathers, a truly legendary body of commentaries by the great sages, the question is put forth about who are the truly rich; we discover that true wealth comes hand in hand with happiness with one's lot. The implication is that wisdom is in doing our best to achieve our goals, and finding contentment in the fruit of our labour; for happiness is not what one wants, but being present to the mystery and wanting that which one has.

We sometimes feel like children without a clue as to how we managed to arrive in this world. Sometimes we desperately seek the Master Orchestrator, with precious little knowledge about the road ahead. Yet, through trial and error, children are able to figure out what pleases a parent. The brighter ones eventually catch onto their parents' concern for their welfare. If we can see our relationship with God along similar lines, we can diligently track the results of our actions. After some trial and error, we may find rewards from merely aligning our heart's desire with God's desire, by using the Golden Rule as a guide.

The Book is a compendium of human trial and error. It is also a point of reference for us, individually as separate beings nevertheless indelibly linked in our common humanity. We become aware of our own frailties and tendencies to err, especially when we see that some of the greatest leaders in biblical history display a whole spectrum of human frailty and error. The genius behind Judaism comes alive through a close look at towering figures in the Tanakh who become life size to us when we realize that they are just ordinary people like ourselves who face everyday challenges and must deal with them despite their own personal weaknesses. As we read about how they deal with the consequences of their sins, we can grasp a message that comes down to us through the ages. All we need to do is take the trouble to read between the lines. We can learn from their mistakes to adjust our ways of dealing with our own personal habits and mistakes by making simple changes and building character through setting an intent to learn from others. Life is too short to learn simply from one's own mistakes. The Scripture is much like a catalogue of human behaviour, a magnifying lens placed upon human virtue and vice. We deepen our understanding of ourselves by taking counsel from the many stories in The Book and find consolation in knowing how closely they are linked to the message of the prophets and sages.

As we advance down the aisles of a supermarket, we might choose a cart on which one of the wheels has lost its mobility. Similarly, it may be a character flaw that constantly hinders us from getting the positive results we desire in our lives. If we take the time to determine which wheel is the one that hinders the others from doing their job, we can realign its position, or change to another shopping cart altogether, since it no longer serves us. By examining a variety of situations and outcomes in The Book, we can apply our knowledge to better discern what God, our Father, desires for us as His children.

How do we go about putting our relationship with our Father at the forefront of our daily experience? In other words, how do we put our role as children of our one God into practice? To neglect the simple adjustments as we search down the many aisles of life is to deny ourselves the opportunity to discover, to heal, and to live a healthy and balanced life without stepping on the rights of others. Despite our many shortcomings, some of them genetic and others of our own making, we can work to remodel ourselves through personal choice and trust in the Master Orchestrator.

In ancient times, idols came in the shape of hand-crafted figurines, or one of the elements, such as the Sun, the Moon, or the rain gods. Today's idol worship clothes itself in runaway consumerism, greed, and the lust for power.

The Bible's many characters can serve as models to help us avoid the errors of the past. They offer a template for our own potentiality. Drawing from the prophets' admonishments, and from the conduct and achievements of the many biblical personalities, we may find them immortalized for the common good: our edification and that of future generations. The Book offers insight that points toward a manner of living aligned with social justice, or a set of principles and ideas that, when placed together, can serve as the building blocks of a just society.

22

THE POWER OF PRAYER

MY FATHER AND THE OLD TIMERS OF THE EARLY 1900s in Iraq shared their mutual concerns when hardship struck Baghdad in the form of drought. In those days, modern facilities were nonexistent. Sometimes the drought was so severe that our Moslem neighbours and coworkers had the habit of asking us Jews to pray for rain. When Jews recited the *Selihot*, a prayer in which there was a special supplication for rain, it oftentimes occurred that God granted our collective wishes!

"Call unto Me and I will answer thee and show thee great and mighty things which thou knowest not" (Jeremiah 33:3).

When we channel our spiritual energies through prayer, we come closer to God. When we communicate our thoughts to Him, we feel His presence in the stillness of our centeredness, and become better candidates to receive a positive response to our supplication.

The value of prayer lies in a state of peacefulness within ourselves, when we have set body and mind at ease. It is then that a sense of gratefulness overwhelms us at the humblest level, for the simple blessings of life: a bed to lie upon, food on the table, running water, and other basics that are, for billions of the world's living souls, only the stuff of dreams.

King David's farewell speech at old age runs along similar lines:

Wherefore David Blessed the Lord before all the congregation: and David said, Blessed be thou, Lord God of Israel our father, for ever and ever. Thine, O Lord, is the greatness, and the power, and the glory, and the victory, and the majesty: for all that is in the heaven and in the Earth is thine; thine is the kingdom, O Lord, and thou are exalted as head above all. Both riches and honor come of thee, and thou reignest over all; and

> *in thy hand is power and might; and in thy hand it is to make*
> *great, and to give strength unto all. (I Chronicles 29:10–12)*

These passages are heard in every synagogue during Morning Prayer services. Congregants recite them while standing as they listen in admiration to each word. In a house of prayer we are more inclined to feel the essence of His holiness and radiance—*Shekhina*; we allow ourselves to be touched by a sense of peace and serenity that readily infuses the soul in a place of worship.

Jews participate in Sabbath prayer to express gratitude for all that God has given in the past week and to ask Him to further His blessings. When life's challenges overwhelm the spirit, prayer strengthens the moral fibre and exposes the supplicant to God's mercy.

As a child, I accompanied my father to the synagogue on Sabbath days. I hardly understood the real purpose, but followed my father to please him. Amid prayers I stood when others did, and often fell to daydreaming. Sometimes someone patted me on the back from behind when I remained standing even as the congregation sank back into their seats.

My father and the rabbi's explanations of the rituals gradually oriented me toward a spiritual centeredness, and I developed an interest in the pattern that worshipers followed during a typical Babylonian Sabbath prayer service.

A Typical Babylonian Sabbath Prayer Service

1. A reading of passages from the *Tehilim*, the book of Psalms: each psalm is recited by individual congregants in random fashion; among them are Psalms 19, 90, 121, 122, 123, 136, 92, 145, 148, and 150.

2. A congregant recites David's blessing mentioned above from I Chronicles 29:10–13.

3. Taken from Chapter 14 of the Book of Exodus, verses 30–31, the Song of the Sea is recited melodically by a single congregant.

It was composed by Moses after the Red Sea parted for him to lead the Israelites through dry land.

4. Also recited is the *Nishmat Kol Hai.* Its literal meaning in Hebrew is HHH, "*the soul of all living beings.*" This beautiful piece of literature by an unknown author who praises God has been translated and incorporated in Sabbath prayer books worldwide.

5. Then there is the *Shema Israel (Hear O Israel, the Lord is Our God, The Lord is One)* from the Book of Deuteronomy, Chapter 6, verses 4–9, which continues in Deuteronomy 11:13–21.

6. The *Amidah* is a prayer during which all congregants stand in absolute silence and read silently from the prayer book. After a period of silent reading that lasts a few minutes, the *hazzan* (cantor) repeats the prayer out loud, and somewhere in the middle, the *kohanim*, direct descendants of Aaron, the high priests, face the congregants and bless them.

7. The Ark that holds the scrolls of the Torah is then opened up by a prominent member of the congregation, while the rabbi prays for peace, for the survival of soldiers in battle, and for the healing of the sick.

8. The cantor then recites a portion of Scripture from the Scroll, called a *Parasha.* The Five Books of Moses have been divided into fifty-two portions, one for each Sabbath of the year, starting from the first chapter of Genesis. They end with the last chapter of Deuteronomy.

9. Highlights of Jewish history come next and are recited by a single congregant. They evoke the fascinating connection between the *Parasha*, the Law that sets down a code of ethical behaviour on the one hand, and the *Haftara*, a notary-style testimony to all that was actually observed from written law. The *Haftara* pinpoints moments in history where those same ethical guidelines were either respected or went unheeded and ignored by the kings, priests, and ordinary folk.

10. Synagogues the world over adapt the same *Parasha* and *Haftara* portions to their respective prayer services on each particular Sabbath.

11. At this point, the rabbi conducts a discussion of the Torah portion of the week and expands on its relevance to current issues.

12. The *Mussaf* comes last as a brief *Amidah* as in number 6 above.

The selection of a text for prayer generally comes from the Torah, the Book of Psalms, the Book of the Prophets, Jewish history, and from prominent commentators. Prayer books are written with the text in Hebrew on the right hand page and a translation in the language of the land on the left hand page.

A study of 5,000 Israelis between the ages of sixty or older conducted over a seven-year period by Professor Howard Litwin of Israel University's Gerontological Data Center, showed a comparison of various factors influencing their longevity. The results of his research were published in the European Journal of Aging. "The data showed that the death rate was 75 percent higher among the group that did not attend synagogue than it was among the group that attended synagogue regularly."[103]

At Mount Sinai, God revealed His Ten Commandments to the people, who stood at its foot and listened in awe: "*Remember the Sabbath day to sanctify it. Six days shall you work and accomplish all your works; but the seventh day is Sabbath to The Lord thy God; in it thy shall not do any work*" (Exodus 20:8–10).

The above declaration is repeated in Exodus 23:12, Exodus 31:15, Exodus 35:2, and further on in the Five Books of Moses. It is a blessing from God who gives us the days of the week to build a livelihood and a day for reflection when we are invited to celebrate life's blessings. While the Orthodox school prescribes three prayers a day, one before sunrise

---

[103] Ofri Ilani, 21 August 2007. *Study: Going to synagogue leads to longevity.* [online] Available at: http://www.haaretz.com/print-edition/news/study-going-to-synagogue-leads-to-longevity-1.227864. [Accessed 10 April 2010].

(*Shahrit*), one before sunset (*Minha*) and one after sunset (*Arbit*), Jewish people are encouraged to keep a harmonious balance between earning a livelihood and practicing prayer, and to avoid doing one at the expense of the other. In fact, some rabbis are businessmen, simultaneously managing two careers, one religious and the other secular. Judaism further teaches people to give twenty per cent of their total wealth to charity.

THE KIPA CONTROVERSY

IN AN ENCOUNTER DURING WHICH I DESCRIBED MY WORK with a woman of the Jewish orthodox faith, her question to me was whether I wear a Kipa, the headgear of an orthodox Jew. I said I wear the Kipa at prayers in the synagogue, and on special occasions. She said I needn't bother about my work, since that fact disqualifies me altogether.

I replied that I am writing about The Book, and in it, the Turban is specified as the sole headgear for the "Kohen Gadol," the High Priest, and that it is considered somewhat of a crown, as he performs service in the inner chamber of the Holy Temple.

> *And they made the plate of the holy crown of pure gold, and wrote upon it a writing, like to the engravings of a signet, Holiness To The Lord. And they tied unto it a lace of blue, to fasten it on high upon the mitre; as the Lord commanded Moses. (Exodus 39:30-31)*

> *Thus shall Aaron come into the holy place; with a young bullock for a sin offering, and a ram for a burnt offering. He shall put on the holy linen coat, and he shall have the linen breeches upon his flesh, and shall be girded with a linen girdle, and with a linen mitre shall he be attired: these are holy garments.... (Leviticus 16:3-4)*

Rabbis and Jewish scholars, 'traditionally or conventionally,' wear the Kipa as part of their distinctive attire. According to the Scripture, no headwear is mentioned other than the one specified for the High Priest; therefore, a Jewish person can be in good shape with or without the Kipa.

23

THE BIG THREE:
INTERFAITH RELATIONS

"The miracle of monotheism is that unity up
there creates diversity down here."[104]

Rabbi Lord Jonathan Sacks
Chief Rabbi of the Commonwealth, Retired

I ONCE HAD A CONVERSATION WITH A MOSLEM WHO ASKED
my views about Islam. I answered that Islam is a reality, created by the
same God whom I worship. Therefore, I have great respect for it, and if
there is some truth in what they say about reincarnation, who knows—I
may return to this world as a Moslem! Then he stunned me by saying
one word: "*Impossible!*"

I tried to control my emotions; then I said, "I know about your belief
that anyone who is not a Moslem ends up straight in *Je'hannam*, or hell."

I continued, "First of all, I think when someone dies he leaves behind
all that can be incinerated from his remains. Moreover, the word *Je'hannam*
derives from *Gehinnom* in Hebrew. *Ge'* means valley, and *Hinnom* was
the name of the owner of a certain valley in south Jerusalem where
idol worshippers took their first-born child to be incinerated—a form
of sacrifice to their gods, in a ceremony called *Topheth*, or drumming.
The priest placed the child on the firewood as the drummers beat the
kettledrums loud enough to deafen the parents' hearing to the agonizing

104   Rabbi Lord Jonathan Sacks, Retired, 07 May 2010. *On the Dignity of Difference.*
[online] Available at: http://www.youtube.com/watch?v=wpuQHLisQns. [Accessed
11 June 2011].

screams of their child." For the interested reader, Scripture describes these rituals in II Kings 23:10, Jeremiah 7:31, Jeremiah 19:5–6, and beyond.

I continued to deliver my thoughts, saying, "Moslems usually start their letters and new projects with the beautiful phrase, 'In the Name of God, the Merciful and Compassionate.' How does a merciful and compassionate God create billions of non-Moslems, only to deliver them to *Je'hannam?*" I waited for an answer, but his silence was more eloquent than words.

Throughout world history, many religious leaders encouraged even the good to do evil in the name of religion. In the globalized world of today in the second millennium after Jesus, has the time finally arrived for religious leaders of all faiths to see that they have no choice but to find a way to coexist in peace?

The Spanish Inquisition initiated by Pope Gregory IX was named after the procedure instituted by Pope Innocent III (1198–1216) to track down and punish individuals accused of "heresy." Those who repented were subject to life in prison, and the obstinate were subject to torture and capital punishment, including burning at the stake.[105] Christianity has travelled a long path away from the Inquisition toward an era of coexistence with people of other faiths.

As Christians refer to non-believers in Christianity as "heretics," Moslems call non-believers in Islam *infidel,* an expression commonly used today by extremists. History thus repeats itself even cross-culturally, and the same phenomenon comes back centuries later, only under a different label.

On 16 April 2008, Pope Benedict XVI was the first ever to set foot in an American synagogue, and a third to ever enter a Jewish house of worship; he was invited for a private visit by Rabbi Arthur Schneier, Senior Rabbi of Park East Synagogue in New York. Said the Rev. James Massa, Executive Director of the Secretariat for Ecumenical and Interreligious Affairs for the United States Conference of Catholic

---

[105] *Encyclopaedia Judaica,* Volume 8, "Inquisition: The Early Institution," 1382.

Bishops: "Judaism is internal to Catholicism. It's different from any other kind of relationship with another religion."[106]

Islam has taken a twist down a different road in modern times. To illustrate this rift, one ponders the modern Ayatollah Ruhollah Khomeini's declaration before passing away, that his fight will continue until the flag of Islam shall be raised over the White House.

A newcomer to the religious arena was the Baha'i faith. Bahaism first appeared in Iran in the middle of the nineteenth century through Mirza Hossein Ali, a Shiite Moslem, who was later called Bahaullah. Bahaullah broke off from the mainstream and quickly found a substantial following. Bahaullah advocated that the Earth is but one country, mankind its citizens, and that what is most essential is the unity of all in a peaceful world devoid of violence.

The Baha'i teachings seem to offer an alternative to the centuries-old animosity between people of different branches even within the same religion. While 95 percent of Iraq's population is Moslem, distinguished by the three factions—Shiites, Sunnis, and Kurds—each worships the same God and the same prophet Mohammad; and shares the same book, the Holy Koran. When asked about their ultimate ideal, each one prefers that the other two be eliminated. Saddam Hossein, the once-strongman Sunni ruler of Iraq, eliminated thousands of Kurdish and Shiite citizens of Iraq using chemical weapons and other means; under his rule the elimination of groups other than his Sunni Arab minority was frequent. The very same problem dwells amongst numerous other populations across the globe.

Judaism has a different perspective on the issue of plurality: *"For all people will walk, everyone in the name of his god, and we will walk in the name of the Lord our God for ever and ever"* (Micah 4:5).

---

[106] Appeal of Conscience, 18 April 2008. *His Holiness Pope Benedict XVI makes historical and unprecedented first visit with Rabbi Arthur Schneier at Park East Synagogue.* [online] Available at: http://www.appealofconscience.org/news/article.cfm?id=100160. [Accessed 5 November 2011].

Pope Benedict XVI (born 1927) made a historic visit to a Synagogue
in New York on 16 April 2008, marking the first visit by a Pope to a
Synagogue in the United States. He visited the Cologne Synagogue
on 19 April 2005. Pope John Paul II, visited the Rome Synagogue on
13 April 1986.[107] [Illustration by Sandra Koukou]

---

107   Ibid.

Bahaism is outlawed in its birthplace, Iran; its places of worship in Persia have all been either closed or confiscated. Almost all Baha'i leaders, those whom the authorities were able to track down, have been executed at the Evin prison. I am saddened to recall that at least three Baha'i inmates at Evin, who were locked up in a neighbouring cell to mine, were called to the firing squad. Contrastingly, Bahaism's main shrine near Acre (pronounced *Acco*) in Israel holds the remains of Bahaullah, the founder of the faith. Its holiest place of worship is in Israel proper and is held under tight Israeli security. It receives millions of pilgrims and tourists year round.

While Judaism avoids proselytization, any individual who displays wholehearted desire to embrace the Jewish faith is seen as a qualified new believer. Sammy Davis, Jr. the famous black American actor and singer (1925–1990), converted to Judaism following a near fatal car crash. He developed an interest in Judaism after being visited in the hospital by a rabbi.[108]

The rabbi asked him: "Let me see, you are black, and you have lost one eye. Do you need another problem?"

"That's my business, Rabbi. Now, you do your job."[109]

My experience is that people are naturally drawn toward peaceful coexistence. They all want to offer a good education for their children and see them step into successful careers and pass good values on to the next generation. For all this to happen, society needs peaceful conditions in which citizens from all cultural spectrums can flourish harmoniously and reach their full potential. The problem arises when leaders—especially religious, fanatical leaders—bring the question of religion into matters of state. Life during the reign of the Pahlavi regime in Iran before the Islamic Revolution was not perfect, but at least there was peaceful coexistence

---

[108] Mark Levy. *Jews and All That Jazz: Al Jolson, Florenz Ziegfeld, Fanny Brice, Jerome Kern, Irving Berlin, George Gershwin, Artie Shaw and More.* [online] Available at: http://www.jewishfederations.org/page.aspx?id=957. [Accessed 16 November 2013].

[109] Source not found.

between people of different races and religions, and equally so between different language groups and ethnic backgrounds. We didn't question one another's beliefs; we accepted one another as we were and considered our multiplicity as a bonus. We understood that we each had something to offer that was unique and different. This diversity and unconditional acceptance added a special flavour to the mosaic that was Persian society. This was the legacy of the era before the fall of the Iranian monarchy.

My business partner was a secular Moslem. Our factory was a flourishing enterprise that created jobs and saved foreign currency required for imports of similar products. We engaged in business together for over twenty years. In good times and through adversity, we worked harmoniously as a team, with understanding and goodwill. That pleasant relationship endured even after the revolution robbed our business in the name of Allah.

What enabled Persians to coexist peacefully before the Revolution? Since the times of the ancient Persian Empire, the monarchy believed in freedom of religion. This, however, changed with the rise of Islam. Both Christians and Jews found themselves walking a tightrope under precarious conditions, not only in Arab lands, but also in Persia. When Reza Shah Pahlavi and his son, the late Mohammad Reza Pahlavi, were in power, they attempted to bring Persia back to the grandeur that was characteristic of the ancient Persian Empire. The Shahanshah—Persian emperor, also understood as King of Kings—often reiterated the principle that people need to be free to worship in any way that they see fit.

I remember a time toward the end of the shah's regime when unemployment was close to zero. As factory owners, my partner and I had trouble finding labour locally. So, we brought workers from India to keep operations running. The economic climate was booming, and unemployment was at a record low. Soon after Khomeini's arrival in Teheran in 1979, when reporters asked him what the revolution sought to change, his answer was, "Economics is of no significance here. We are here to advance the cause of Islam." When asked how religion can be reconciled with politics, the supreme leader's corrective was: "Islam *is* politics."

In *The Dignity of Difference: How to Avoid the Clash of Civilizations*, Rabbi Jonathan Sacks puts forth a compelling view on unity and difference:

> What we cannot do is place ourselves outside the particularities of language to arrive at a truth, a way of understanding and responding to the world that applies to everyone at all times. That is not the essence of humanity but an attempt to escape from humanity.[110]

Sacks, Retired Chief Rabbi of the United Hebrew Congregations of the Commonwealth from September 1991 to September 2013 and a member of the House of Lords since 2009, goes on to say:

> …God no more wants all faiths and cultures to be the same than a loving parent wants his or her children to be the same. That is the conceptual link between love, creation and difference. We serve God, author of diversity, by respecting diversity.[111]

It was this principle of diversity that Cyrus the Great, the benevolent Persian emperor, understood and espoused, curiously even as he was the sculptor of the world's first empire, back in the sixth century B.C.E. Rabbi Sacks encourages us to see this same respect for difference as it appears and reappears in the Tanakh, through various biblical figures, all of whom God accepts for what they are: "…Isaac *and* Ishmael, Jacob *and* Esau, Israel *and* the nations, choosing one for a particular destiny, to be sure, but blessing the others, each in their own way."[112]

---

[110]   Jonathan Sacks, *The Dignity of Difference: How to Avoid the Clash of Civilizations*, 54-55.

[111]   Ibid, 56.

[112]   Ibid, 56.

24

NATURE'S SILENT MESSAGES

ONE CAN APPLY INSIGHT GAINED FROM STUDY of the Scriptures to sharpen one's perception of nature's silent messages. They come in shapes and forms that are quite easy for the naked eye to pick out, if one looks closely enough. As long as one ponders the many signs in God's creation, it is hard to ignore the abundance of visual messages in certain foods, for example. Some are scientifically known to be beneficial to specific parts of the human body, and astonishingly, they resemble those same parts of the human organism. Clues you might say?

According to Scriptural text, God created plant life and made animals and fish—all this before humans entered the scene. Studies have shown that what He provided in that garden was intended to supply nourishment even before our arrival. Basic characteristics inherent in some fruits and vegetables are recognized by modern science as beneficial to our overall health and well-being.

For example, an avocado is visually akin to the shape and form of a human female womb and cervix. Avocadoes take exactly nine months to ripen from the time they blossom. As humans, we learned how to organize ourselves into agrarian societies much earlier than we cared to observe the clues so blatantly offered by nature herself, which Rabbi Lazer Brody has coined God's Pharmacy![113]

Rabbi Lazer Brody's Emuna Outreach Program creatively links characteristics of some of nature's gifts to humanity in a thought

---

[113] Rabbi Lazer Brody, 12 August 2008. *God's Pharmacy – the Original Chassidic Version.* [online] Available at: http://www.youtube.com/watch?v=H1K0FScTQa4\. [Accessed 10 November 2011].

provoking presentation that has attracted many awed viewers on the World Wide Web:[114]

> "The **TALMUD** and **MIDRASH** note that certain fruits and vegetables look like parts of the human body. There's a good reason for this, based on the deep wisdom of the Creator.

> "For example, a **Sliced Carrot** looks like the human eye with pupil, iris and radiating lines. Carrots are a rich source of Vitamin A, which greatly enhances blood flow to and function of the eyes.

> "A **Tomato** has four chambers and is red. The heart is red and has four chambers. The lycophen of tomatoes is conducive to a healthy heart and blood system.

> "**Grapes** hang in a cluster that has the shape of the heart. Each grape looks like a blood cell. Grapes play a profound role in cardiovascular and blood vitality.

> "A **Walnut** looks like a miniature brain, with left and right hemispheres, upper cerebrums and lower cerebellums. Even the crevices on the nut resemble the neo-cortex of the brain. Walnuts help develop neuron-transmitters for healthy brain function.

> "**Kidney Beans** actually heal and help maintain healthy kidney functioning. Notice how they look exactly like the human kidneys.

> "**Sweet Potatoes** look like the pancreas and actually balance the glycemic index of diabetics.

> "**Olives** assist the health and function of the ovaries.

---

114   Ibid, with special permission by Rabbi Lazer Brody to quote ideas and concepts cited in *God's Pharmacy*. See also http://lazerbrody.typepad.com/.

"**Grapefruits, Oranges** and other **Citrus Fruits** look just like the mammary glands of the female and actually assist the health of the breasts and the movement of lymph in and out of the breasts.

"**Onions** look like body cells. Today's research shows that onions help clear waste materials from all of the body cells. They even produce tears which wash the epithelial layers of the eyes.

"**Celery and Rhubarb** look just like bones and enhance bone strength. Bones are 23% sodium. If you don't have enough sodium in your diet the body pulls it from the bones, making them weak. These foods replenish skeletal needs.

"**Avocados and Pears** enhance function of the womb and cervix of the female and look just like these organs. Eating an avocado a week balances hormones, sheds unwanted birth weight and prevents cervical cancers.

"**Figs** are full of seeds and hang in twos when they grow. Figs increase the motility and count of male sperm and help overcome male sterility.

"The Talmud says that even the sinners of Israel are as full of good deeds as the seeds of a **Pomegranate**. There are exactly 613 commandments in the Torah and exactly 613 seeds in a pomegranate.

"Rebbe Nachman of Breslav teaches that plants grow by virtue of the rains. Rains fall by virtue of *emuna* (faith). Therefore, the greater our emuna, the greater shall be our supply of fruits and vegetables.

"How magnificent are your deeds, Hashem."[115]

---

[115] Ibid.

The dietary law that God sets down in the Book of Leviticus is that, among the animals that walk on all fours, we are only allowed to eat those beasts that have split hooves *and* chew their cuds. It is an "and" relationship, not an "or" relationship. Both conditions are required for God's law to be respected. The pig, for example, has split hooves, but it does not chew its cud. These symbols teach us to be selective, although taken in isolation it is easy to lose sight of their greater significance. The point we may miss is that God picks and chooses from the many varieties, because *He* created them. All this can only make us wonder at the vastness of Creation. *"These shall ye eat of all that are in the waters: whatsoever hath fins and scales … them shall ye eat. And all that have not fins and scales in the seas, and in the rivers … they shall be an abomination unto you"* (*Leviticus11:9–10*).

In this author's view, the animal kingdom and "God's Pharmacy" preceded the human species precisely to the extent that He intended to lay down the foundations of life. Through visual communication, God's Pharmacy seems to suggest a divine intent at work. Its message is ours to appreciate. It is also ours to find a way of acknowledging that we are part of a story of Creation that is yet unfolding.

In truth, we came into a system based on abundance, one that was pre-ordained to sustain our basic needs, and which eloquently delivers a Creator's desire for our very own well being. The question is now asked by many: do we care to organize ourselves into *sustainable* societies—both physically *and* spiritually—at this juncture in our evolutionary growth?

In my community of Iraqi Jews, food is a powerful connector. It brings families together and creates cohesion within the social fabric. Families gather around a festive meal to share in the ritual of food, especially since ingredients are fresh and recipes vary from simple to elaborate. Typically, there is a visible absence of excessively fatty or processed foods at our gatherings. Even today, true Iraqi Jewish tradition precludes these ingredients from appearing on the table dressed for a meal. For this reason, one delights in the mirth and jovial spirit characteristic of family and community gatherings, where ancient recipes survive the test of time and remain a powerfully unifying element. From this premise, it is fair to say that an appreciation for transmitted values that brings along with it a sense of kinship, serves as a bulwark against the ills of modern day angst and feelings of alienation.

25

COMMUNISM VERSUS RELIGION

"Camoni...Camocha" [Hebrew]: Like me ... like you.

KARL HEINRICH MARX (1818–1883), born in Tier on the river Moselle in Germany's Rhineland, authored the famous *Das Kapital,* thereby giving birth to Communism.[116] Communism made it a goal to close the gap between rich and poor; indeed, the goal of Communism was to eliminate poverty altogether. History has proven the opposite; Communism remained only a wish and not a reality.

God declared in The Book: *"For the poor shall never cease out of the land: therefore I command thee, saying, Thou shalt open thy hand wide unto thy brother, to thy poor, and to thy needy, in the land"* (*Deuteronomy 15:11*).

The free market system gives people incentives and avenues toward the creation of wealth, enabling them to "open their hands to the poor," a theme central to the Scriptures. Members of Communist societies look to government for what they are allowed to receive, with little chance to help others. The American philanthropist Walter Annenberg (1908–2002) who donated millions of dollars toward many causes is quoted as saying: "I have heard it said, that no good deed goes unpunished, but I don't intend to let that discourage me."[117]

---

[116] *Encyclopaedia Judaica*, Volume 11, "Marx, Karl Heinrich," 1071.

[117] Grace Glueck, 2002. *Walter Annenberg, 94, Dies; Philanthropist and Publisher.* [online] Available at: http://www.nytimes.com/2002/10/02/arts/walter-annenberg-94-dies-philanthropist-and-publisher.html?sec=&spon=?pagewanted=1&pagewanted=5. [Accessed 05 May 2011].

Helping the needy has its ups and downs. My father in his boyhood used to help his father collect dues from customers at the end of the week. Once on an errand walking through the *souk*, a roofed bazaar in Baghdad, he noticed a porter sitting in a corner crying. He approached him to ask the poor man if he needed help in any way. The man replied that he hadn't been called for work that day. He was hungry and had no money to buy food. My father told him to wait until he returned from an errand. True to his word, he showed up with a piece of bread and some dates, considered part of the daily diet in the Arab world. The gratified porter wolfed the stuff down as fast as his mouth was able to handle the big chunks, and then profusely thanked my father for his kind gesture.

When his fellow workmen noticed what had materialized, they scorned their fellow porter for accepting favours from a Jew, and got up to catch my father as he fled for safety. When my father first shared the story with us, all I cared to find out was, how he reacted when the men were set loose by their fury in pursuit of him! His bold reply was: nothing pleased him more in this entire adventure than to see the man downing the food with appetite and craving.

Communism eventually declined as a failed experiment, and the American President, Ronald Reagan, publicly advised Russian President Mikhail Gorbachev, to "tear down that wall."[118] In a matter of days, the Berlin wall, that iron curtain that cruelly separated East from West, came tumbling to the ground. President Reagan's speech at Berlin's Brandenburg Gate artfully addressed that historical breakthrough:

> In West Germany and here in Berlin, there took place an economic miracle, the Wirtschaftswunder. Adenauer, Erhard, Reuter, and other leaders understood the practical importance of liberty—that just as truth can flourish only when the journalist is given freedom of

---

[118] Ronald Reagan, 12 June 1987. *President Reagan's Address at the Brandenburg Gate.* [online] Available at: http://www.reaganfoundation.org/pdf/ Remarks_on_East_West_RElations_at_Brandenburg%20Gate_061287.pdf. [Accessed 30 May 2011].

speech, so prosperity can come about only when the farmer and businessman can enjoy economic freedom.[119]

Shortly after, the USSR itself deliberately announced its own divestment of Communism. Despite that one single gesture that made it seem as though Russia's Communism had never existed in the first place, it was mind boggling to consider the trillions of national funds that had gone into building Cold War arms instead of improving the lives of the Russian people.

The ideas in *Das Kapital* that once looked so promising to the deprived emerged as a total disappointment. On the other hand, many religious leaders have condemned the excesses of capitalism, often questioning its very foundations, where great disparities have encroached between rich and poor. But, while Communism assumes that wealth is out there to be shared, capitalism understands it differently. It knows that wealth does not grow on trees and that it needs to be somehow created through productivity. Capitalists create those opportunities that favour the production of capital.

Man has not yet found a practical formula to shorten the gap between the haves and the have-nots. But, in an era where much of political discussion revolves around issues concerning the environment, what can be simpler to implement than the economics handed to us by the Golden Rule as a banner for sustainable living: "…*thou shalt love thy neighbour as thyself: I am the Lord*" (*Leviticus 19:18*)?

---

[119] Ibid.

26

THE ROLE OF RELIGIOUS LEADERS

WHAT QUALITIES DO PEOPLE EXPECT from religious leaders? The answer to this question may vary from one culture to another, but most are likely to agree that religious leaders ideally should be individuals who strive to guide people down a pious path. They are God-fearing souls who care about the collective destiny. They encourage their congregations to be charitable and to conduct their daily affairs justly and peaceably. To be a religious leader in the true sense of the word requires faith, enormous dedication, and a deep sense of responsibility, a powerful conscience, courage, and all the more noble qualities that make their word worthy of a dedicated audience.

Religious leaders are a kind of link between God and the masses; their job is to remind their people about the Creator's intent for humanity. If this assumption can be held as a yardstick to measure their success, they are best helped in their role by exercising caution in choice of word and conduct.

God warns:

> Son of Man, I have made thee a watchman unto the house of Israel: therefore hear the word at my mouth, and give them warning from me. When I say to the wicked, Thou shalt surely die; and thou givest him not warning, nor speakest to warn the wicked from his wicked way, to save his life; the same wicked man shall die in his iniquity; but his blood will I require at thine hand. Yet if thou warn the wicked, and he turn not from his wickedness, nor from his wicked way, he shall die in his iniquity; but thou hast delivered thy soul. (Ezekiel 3:17–21)

In this passage from the Book of the Prophet Ezekiel, God has saddled the responsibility upon the religious leaders. Their job was to turn believers away from sin. Inasmuch as the wicked were warned, God promised to remain steadfast toward those leaders, even if the people they had admonished against evil continued in their corrupt ways, because "thou hast delivered thy soul."

> *Again, when a righteous man doth turn from his righteousness, and commit iniquity, and I lay a stumbling block before him, he shall die: because thou hast not given him warning, he shall die in his sin, and his righteousness which he hath done shall not be remembered; but his blood will I require at thine hand. Nevertheless, if thou warn the righteous man, that the righteous sin not, and he doth not sin, he shall surely live, because he is warned; also thou hast delivered thou soul. (Ezekiel 3:20–21)*

Conversely, God's promise holds true for the righteous. When a righteous man or woman turns to evil, God dissolves his good deeds. If a righteous person meets with a stumbling block that God places before him and the religious leader does *not* warn him about it, the leader is held accountable by God to answer for the blood of the good man whom the mentor has failed to turn back to the straight path.

After great success in establishing his kingdom, King Solomon began to amass great wealth for himself, the whole at the expense of his taxpayers. He then indulged excessively in carnal pleasures. At that point, the *Kohen Gadol*, high priest in the Temple of God, may have stepped in to warn the king against such excess and wrongdoing—yet he abstained from guiding his king down a wiser path! The situation went from bad to worse. In the absence of any intervention by the high priest, foreign women continued to seduce Solomon to worship their gods (I Kings, Chapter 11).

Perhaps the high priest did not second-guess the powerful King Solomon for fear of losing his job. By abstaining from correcting him, the high priest failed to set a solid example for Solomon's royal successors, and created a moral vacuum instead. The lack of a solid template of acceptable conduct went missing and eventually took the nation down a dangerous path.

> *Woe be unto the pastors that destroy and scatter the sheep of my pasture! … Therefore thus saith the Lord God of Israel against the pastors that feed my people; Ye have scattered my flock, and driven them away, and have not visited them: behold, I will visit upon you the evil of your doings, saith the Lord. (Jeremiah 23:1–2)*

Many trusted religious leaders in our time, clad as they are in holy garments, and entrusted to teach morality to the young, abuse them instead with shameful acts that instil lifelong psychological scars on their victims. Such acts solicit maximum penalty in The Book, the same document from which they draw the material they use in their sermons. Another phenomenon that shakes our conscience in modern times is the abuse of innocent children who are made to go forth with explosives tied around their waists to commit suicide and to kill innocent people in the name of God.

God may appear to hide His countenance:

> *Behold, the days come, saith the Lord God, that I will send a famine in the land, not a famine of bread, nor a thirst for water, but of hearing the words of the Lord. And they shall wander from sea to sea, and from the north even to the east, they shall run to and fro to seek the word of the Lord, and shall not find it. (Amos 8:11–12)*

In the absence of divine intervention, we need to remember the positive ideals gifted to us by our different faiths. It matters little where we practice our faith, whether we worship in a temple, a church, a mosque, a synagogue, or in an attic—as long as we build character and follow divine patterns in our lives. Whether we live by mottos such as "we the people" or any other that prescribes a recipe for social justice, most will agree that social cohesion is necessarily rooted in what the Scripture calls the Golden Rule. People the world over are beginning to see the need for all peoples to take action to be effective toward the collective good.

I often ponder the idea that, for any interfaith dialogue to be meaningful, religious leaders need to first generate understanding within their own denominations. They can hence form a congress similar to that of the United Nations, and set a goal for coexistence and mutual respect. Its charter can be drafted upon the idea that no one religious group may be allowed to impose its beliefs on any other. Rather, the members of this congress may find empowerment in seeking common grounds that foster coexistence. They can go even further—they can verily consider themselves enriched by their plurality.

God has given us everything we need, but we are depleting what we have been given as a birthright. When God entrusted humankind with the fruits of the Earth, He expected us to behave responsibly. If religious leaders can enter the vacuum and discuss common grounds and moral standards toward the environment, they can bring the world community along with them to view it as a possible cornerstone of interfaith dialogue. Our mere survival hinges upon our cooperation across all of our borders. In sensitizing their congregations about responsible behaviour, religious leaders will be effective in showing themselves creative and sincere, pointing—in unison—toward a more useful dialogue than any that has been taken to stage so far, including the monologue of corporate world government that only serves to blur our intrinsic plurality, the same diversity that God instilled in us and intended we enjoy, hold sacred.

Religious leaders through interfaith forums can share their successes *and* failures to make room for improvement, globally. To the extent to which they manage to spread the message that our Earth's resources *are* sufficient to sustain the servants of God, they need to sensitize us each to play our parts respectively. Indeed, if we can all recognize the importance of the part we play through mutual respect toward one another's ways and means not only to survive, but to thrive, we can open the doors of hope for trade alongside interfaith dialogue.

One religious leader who has done enormous service to the international community to foster interfaith dialogue is the Dalai Lama. When asked during a round table discussion by Leonardo Boff, a leading Brazilian theologian, what the best religion is, the Dalai Lama replied that he was not interested about a man's religion, or whether he was religious or not. What really mattered to him was a person's behaviour in front of peers, family, people at work, the community, and one's behaviour in front of the world.

He told Boff to remember that the Universe is the echo of one's actions and thoughts and that the law of action and reaction is not exclusive to physics. It pertains just as much toward human relations. According to the Dalai Lama, goodness brings on more goodness and evil brings more of the same. He pointed out our grandparents' wisdom and truthfulness when they admonished that one always receives what one desires for others. He described happiness as a matter of options instead of a matter of destiny. In the Dalai Lama's own words:

Take care of your thoughts because they become *words*.

Take care of your words because they become *actions*.

Take care of your actions because they will become *habits*.

Take care of your habits, because they will form your *character*.

Take care of your Character because it will form your *destiny*.

And, your destiny will be your *life* ... and ... there is no religion higher than the *truth*.[120]

This teaching is a cornerstone of the spiritual message of Persian prophet, Zoroaster, from whom the world was gifted with Zoroastrianism, the religion espoused in Persia prior to the rise of Islam. First grade classrooms throughout Iran before the Islamic Revolution of 1979, taught the alphabet in texts that carried the following key phrases from those ancient teachings, which children intuitively absorbed as they grew older...

---

[120] Sharon Saw, 06 May 2010. *A conversation between HH the Dalai Lama and Leonardo Boff* [online] Available at: http://sharonsaw.typepad.com/blog/2010/05/a-conversation-between-hh-the-dalai-lama-and-leonardo-boff.html. [Accessed 25 February 2012].

Think good *thoughts*.

Say good *words*.

Do good *deeds*.

Religious leaders wield enormous power to shape social norms and attitudes. When American soldiers arrived in Iraq in 2003, the locals initially rallied toward them with optimism as liberators from their dictator, Saddam. It didn't take long after the warm welcome on the streets as the long line of tanks passed through the streets of Baghdad—before the mullahs grabbed public opinion and turned it away during Friday prayer.

At the same time, some leaders of the West lived the fallacy that their style of political cohabitation was better for the people of Iraq than what geographical and historical research would reveal. Misinformation and superficial assumptions about otherness placed democracy against a rude encounter, and the beast of war awoke from its slumber. The American President George W. Bush and British Prime Minister Tony Blair thought it was necessary not only to route out the weapons of mass destruction which they believed the Iraqis had secretly stockpiled, but also to reshape a mixture of different cultures by the click of a button in remote control fashion. The theatre of war was likened to a home theatre, but the only channel that came on the screen was one depicting fiction rather than fact.

Meanwhile, the mullahs quickly managed to instil fear among the people, who swarmed into mosques during Friday prayers only to be reminded to do as they were told and ignore Western attitudes, which they warned were, by default, inherently corrupt.

Likewise, Westerners learned that, in the Middle East, democracy necessarily passes through a sieve—the mosque. Bush and Blair were obviously unaware of the fact that religious authorities of Koranic tradition have forever put out the message to the Universe that Islam and democracy are as unlikely to mix as oil and water.

Where the initial welcome by ordinary folk in the streets of Baghdad toward their American soldier liberators was one of cheering and jubilation, that mood was quickly mooted out by the mullahs in the mosques. It didn't take long before the headlines coming from Iraq were number counts of Sunni attacks on Shiites, and vice versa. The tragedy of the destruction of a holy Shiite mosque steeped in religious symbolism and possessing profound historical significance to that branch of Islam could not be ignored by anyone reading their morning paper. These events demonstrated how dramatically religious leadership can impact a people's destiny.

As long as we dwell on the role of religious leaders, the discussion extends to their broader role throughout history.

Christians believed that Jesus was the messiah whose arrival the Jews *were anticipating*, and invited them to join their faith. This change of faith required that Jews would relegate the words of their prophets to the dustbin of history. In so doing, they would be giving up their promise to follow and trust in the revelation that came with God's word delivered by the prophets. They would also be relegating Judaism to the pages of the archives in a library, meeting the fate of those empires whose torches have long been extinguished: the Greeks, the Persians, the Babylonians, the Egyptians, the Romans, the Phoenicians, and all the other empires that came and went with the tides of history.

On the other hand, Moslems consider Jews as infidels whose religion has been rendered obsolete by Islam, which they believe carries forth the ultimate will of God. As far as they are concerned, Jews and people of other faiths are subject to the sword in this world and to the fire in the next, unless they convert. Whereas millions of pagans in Europe and other continents were blessed and welcomed by the Christian faith, Islam punishes by death anyone who walks away and changes course.

Followers of the three major religions who constitute the majority of the Earth's inhabitants worship the very same God, and strive, each in his or her own way, to please Him and find favour in His eyes. With those basic ideals in mind, they can normalize relations among one another, as it is said *to love your neighbor as you love yourself*. And, as true believers in the omnipotence of God, none of the three schools with all their differences may have survived, as long as they have, without their Creator's consent. Another way of expressing this thought is that all faiths must have been supported by none other than their common God.

As for Judaism, God's message has been consistent through the words of the Prophets, and we are summoned to heed that revelation at this critical juncture in the human story. We seem to be called upon to finally grasp the secret of Creation. That secret beseeches us to find a formula to earn peace by celebrating our differences under the umbrella of respect for the very same God-given diversity that makes our world so interesting!

Mark Twain has much to say about the Jews in the following excerpt from Harper's Magazine in an article published in 1899:

> If the statistics are right, the Jews constitute but one percent of the human race. It suggests a nebulous, dim puff of stardust lost in the blaze of the Milky Way. Perhaps, the Jew ought hardly to be heard of, but he is heard of, has always been heard of. He is as prominent on the planet as any other people, and his commercial importance is extravagantly out of proportion to the smallness of his bulk. His contribution to the world's list of great names in Literature, Science, Art, Music, Finance, Medicine and Abstract learning are also way out of proportion to the weakness of his numbers. He has made a marvelous fight in this world in all ages, and has done it with his hand tied behind him. He could be vain to himself and accused for it. The Egyptians, the Babylonians, and the Persians rose, filled the planet with sound and splendor, then faded to dream-stuff and passed away; the Greek and the Roman followed, and made a vast noise, and they are gone; other people have sprung up and held their torch high for a time, but it burned out, and they sit in twilight now, or have vanished. The Jew saw them all, beat them all, and is now what he always was, exhibiting no decadence, no infirmities of age, no weakening of his parts, no slowing of his energies,

no dulling of his alert and aggressive mind. All things are
mortal, but the Jew; all other forces pass, but he remains.
What is the secret of his immortality?[121]

*Thus saith The Lord, which giveth the sun for a light by
day, and the ordinances of the Moon and the stars for a
light by night, which divideth the sea when the waves thereof
roar; The Lord of hosts is his name: if those ordinances
depart from before me, saith the Lord, then the seed of
Israel also shall cease from being a nation before me for ever.
(Jeremiah 31:35–36)*

We may never get to understand the bigger picture before God reveals
it Himself to mankind in some form, as He promised in The Book. As
inhabitants of our planet, we are best to leave our trivial differences
behind, and to help each other, knowing that we are all meant to take
our blessings along with our responsibilities of honouring the Earth's
plenitude of blessings.

The Book expresses through no ambiguous terms the role which the
Jew was destined to play on the historical stage:

*I The Lord have called thee in righteousness; and will hold
thine hand; and will keep thee, and give thee for a covenant
of the people, for a light of the gentile; to open the blind eyes,
to bring out the prisoners from the prisons, and them that sit
in darkness out of the prison house. I Am the Lord; that is
My Name; and My glory will I not give to another, neither
My praise to graven images. (Isaiah 42:6–8)*

Another example of a religious leader wielding influence to steer
people toward a certain kind of behaviour was demonstrated by Britain's
Retired Chief Rabbi Jonathan Sacks, who in 2009 declared a Green
Sabbath ahead of the climate talks that were to take place in an upcoming

---

[121] Mark Twain, 1899. *"Concerning the Jews"* from Harper's Magazine. [online]
Available at: http://www.simpletoremember.com/jewish/blog/mark-twain-and-the-jews/. [Accessed 10 November 2010].

United Nations summit in Denmark. The sixty-one-year-old rabbi asked British Jews to devote their conversations to the environment and pray for sustainability, saying, "There are some risks you just don't take ... and one is the risk of endangering the very viability of life on Earth."[122]

How can today's religious leaders in the Internet age within a global economy earn God's favour? To find answers to this question, let us imagine that religious leaders seize upon the idea to use their influence— and channel valuable spiritual energy—into building an effective global interfaith congress that they may wish to name the United Religions of the World (UROW). Let us, for an instant, imagine that the focus of this interfaith forum is directed upon the need to protect the environment, and that each religious leader demands that statesmen and stateswomen uphold the basic tenet that Mother Earth is willing to give her inhabitants an equal share of abundance, if only Mother Nature gets her just measure of protection. *"Nevertheless, if thou warn the righteous man, that the righteous sin not, and he doth not sin, he shall surely live, because he is warned; also thou hast delivered thou soul"* (Ezekiel 3:17–21).

"There are many devices in a man's heart; the counsel of the Lord, that shall stand" (Proverbs 19:21).

---

[122] The Associated Press, 04 December 2009. *U.K. chief rabbi declares 'green' Sabbath ahead of climate talks.* [online] Available at: http://www.haaretz.com/jewish-world/news/u-k-chief-rabbi-declares-green-sabbath-ahead-of-climate-talks-1.2771. [Accessed 13 February 2012].

EPILOGUE

WHERE WAS GOD IN THE FACE OF ALL THOSE CALAMITIES? It is a question often asked without delay. Let us start with the holocaust of the twentieth century and all others that befell humanity, and try to find an answer from the Scripture. Perhaps it is one and the same for all of them as well as for those who are disappointed that Hitler left behind an unfinished job when he committed suicide.

Once again, we refer to God's declaration as revealed through the words of the prophet Isaiah: *"Behold, the former things are come to pass, and new things do I declare, before they spring forth I tell you of them"* (Isaiah 42:9).

In light of this prophecy, we are asked to reflect upon a question that logically transpires: Can anything happen without His knowledge? Indeed, through Isaiah, God further declares: *"Remember the former things of old: for I Am God, and there is none else ... Declaring the end from the beginning, and from ancient times the things that are not yet done, saying, My counsel shall stand, and I will do all my pleasure"* (Isaiah 46:9–10).

This declaration invites us to further reflect upon the fact that human events occur the way He intends them to unfold. Indeed, God leaves no doubt as to what is working behind the scene, saying: *"I form the light, and create darkness; I make peace, and create evil; I the Lord do all these things"* (Isaiah 45:7).

It is difficult to perceive the underlying secret behind the Holocaust in its apocalyptic scale. All we are able to control are our own actions as best we can. *"The secret things belong unto the Lord our God; but those things which are revealed belong unto us and to our children forever, that we may do all the words of the law"* (Deuteronomy 29:29).

It was the plight of the Holocaust survivors that solicited worldwide outrage as they attempted to land as immigrants arriving by sea to

Palestine. For they were returned by the British via Cyprus across the Sea of Tarshish, a biblical name for the Mediterranean Sea, back to the port of Marseilles—and then back behind their all-too-familiar barbed wire fences in Germany. Worldwide outrage at the British actions was enough to set the stage for a United Nations resolution toward the establishment of a Jewish State. Hitler's aborted mission may thus have been the catalyst of a by-product totally contrary to, and unintended by, his unaccomplished project. Annihilating the Jews from the face of the Earth, whether they be in Europe, faraway Babylon or elsewhere, was his unfulfilled dream.

The Book of Lamentations may offer a clue to the underlying message in the biblical passages quoted immediately above through its description of Jerusalem's destruction in 587 B.C.E., when Jeremiah said: *"The Lord hath done that which He has devised; He hath fulfilled His word that He has commanded in the days of old: He hath thrown down, and hath not pitied"* (*Lamentations 2:17*).

A similar Holocaust befell the city of New York on 11 September 2001. The Prophet Amos had this to say about the destiny of man: that it is ultimately in the hand of God, and the best that mankind can do is good deeds to light up the world with peace: *"Shall there be evil in a city, and the Lord hath not done it?"* (*Amos 3:6*).

As I am writing today in 2012, sixty-four years have passed since the State of Israel appeared on the world map. This tiny country at the crossroads between East and West has continuously dominated the news headlines the world over and has remained the only one on Earth that many seek to eliminate, although Jewish roots in the Holy Land were evidenced throughout the pages of the canonized Scripture—and through archaeology no less.[123] The Arabs waged three major wars on Israel, who survived through multiple miracles as a result of those wars: *"Not by might, nor by power, but by my spirit, saith the Lord of hosts"* (*Zachariah 4:6*).

---

[123] Archaeology in Israel: List of Discoveries (2004 - Present). [online] Available at: https://www.jewishvirtuallibrary.org/jsource/Archaeology/archdiscovery2013.html. [Accessed 04 July 2014].

In spite of what Egypt and Jordan pledged as their three negatives at the Khartoum conference, they accepted America's mediation efforts to make peace with Israel, and Israel returned most of the territories captured at war in return for a mediocre peace. As for the Palestinians, Ariel Sharon, Israel's prime minister at the time, unilaterally evacuated all the Jewish settlements in the Gaza strip and gave the entire territory to the Palestinians as a peaceful gesture, for which his country was rewarded by a barrage of rockets aimed at its civilian population.

How does Israel's aspiration for peace fit alongside the Palestinians' bottom line that Islam is superior among faiths, a precept that seemingly underlies a yet bottomless rejection of a Jewish state in their midst? Does The Book offer a clear link between current reality and the word of the prophets?

> *Now in the first year of Cyrus king of Persia, that the word of the Lord by the mouth of Jeremiah might be fulfilled, The Lord stirred up the spirit of Cyrus king of Persia, that he made a proclamation throughout all the kingdom, and put it also in writing, saying, Thus saith Cyrus king of Persia, the Lord God of heaven hath given me all the kingdoms of the earth; and he hath charged me to build him a house in Jerusalem which is in Judah. Who is there among you of all his people? His God be with him, and let him go up to Jerusalem, which is in Judah, and build the House of the Lord.... (Ezekiel 1:1-3)*[124]

Iranians intuitively and historically are cognizant of the fact that their country has never had a conflict of interest with Israel in 2,500 years of history before the Islamic Revolution of Iran. We may pause to ponder for a moment on the outcome of a nuclear attack on Iran by a merciless Saddam Hussein of Iraq, had not Israel have eliminated the nuclear facility in Osirak back in 1981 prior to the Persian Gulf War which he pre-empted, a bloody conflict that lasted from September 1980 to August 1988 and was the 20th century's longest conventional

---

[124] The full story of The Temple's rebuilding in that era can be found in the Book of Ezra, followed by the Book of Nehemiah.

war after the Second Sino-Japanese War (1931 to 1940). Israel did not have any conflict of interest with Iran. Indeed, Iran would have been in great trouble if Israel did not eliminate the nuclear facilities of Saddam Hussein in neighboring Iraq.

Many centuries ago, in the days of ancient Egypt that was ruled by the Pharaohs, Persia dominated the Middle East. In those days, the great Persian kings were feared and respected by their neighboring countries. Those kings were famous in their benevolent support of minorities in their kingdom.

It was in the Middle East, including Persia, where the Jews lived for more than a thousand years before the coming of Islam. Monotheism is common to both Judaism and Islam. Jews worship one God and this is shown in the Ten Commandments, *"And God spoke all these words saying; I Am the Lord thy God, which have brought thee out of the land of Egypt... Thou shall have no other gods before me..." (Ex.20:1 and further).* Islam came to the Middle East, carrying the message of *Tow-heed,* the belief in one God. Both Jewish and Islamic monotheism came from one and the same source: Abraham, the father of monotheism, whose historical significance is inherent to Judaism as it is to Christianity and Islam.

Perhaps through all the analysis presented previously it may appear that the hand of destiny has an important role to play. Undoubtedly, the State of Israel is part and parcel of a plan charted by God, a symbol perhaps of His majestic authority to allow her to survive multiple wars and to flourish in an unfriendly environment. Perhaps one day, the leaders of countries in the Middle East may find much more gain in taking a course of peace rather than war. It would be a great miracle if leaders of Iran and other Middle Eastern countries could follow the path of Anwar el-Sādāt of Egypt and King Hussein of Jordan, who is a direct descendant of the Prophet Mohammad. They both initiated the process of peace with Israel.

Think good thoughts; speak good words; do good deeds: *"Pendar-e neek; goftar-e neek; kerdar-e neek."* That was when Zoroastrianism was the main faith base in the land, and the Pahlavi language was purely rooted in Persian. This mantra has remained encrusted through the centuries, an integral part of the Persian persona since the era of the world's first empire, that of the Persians. It still resonates through their vibrant spirit, wherever they may have taken refuge in their modern Diasporas. Preceding the Moslem conquest, the Arabic alphabet and Arabic root words had not yet been imposed on the Persian language. That triple pronged mantra has remained alive ever since, and despite the invasion of Persia by the Moslem hordes of Omar in the 7th century B.C.E.

Several historiographical narratives appear below in the words of the 17th century British historian, Edward Gibbon, in *The Decline and Fall of the Roman Empire*:

> 'Ye men of Cufa,' said Ali, who solicited their aid, 'you have been always conspicuous by your valour. You conquered the Persian king and scattered his forces, till you had taken possession of his inheritance.' This mighty conquest was achieved by the battles of Jalula and Nehavend. After the loss of the former, Yezdegerd fled from Holwan, and concealed his shame and despair in the mountains of Farsistan, from whence Cyrus had descended with his equal and valiant companions. The courage of the nation survived that of the monarch: among the hills to the south of Ecbatana or Hamadan one hundred and fifty thousand Persians made a third and final stand for their religion and country; and the decisive battle of Nehavend was styled by the Arabs the victory of victories.'[125] ...the standard of Mohammed was planted ... and a simple profession of faith established the distinction between a brother and a slave.[126] The end of Yezdegerd was not only unfortunate but obscure.[127]

[125] Edward Gibbon. *The Decline & Fall of the Roman Empire.* Volume 5 of 6, Chapter LI; *The Conquest of Persia, Syria, Egypt, Africa, and Spain, by the Arabs or Saracens – Empire of the Caliphs or Successors of Mohammed – State of the Christians, etc., under their Government,* 338-9.

[126] Ibid, 340.

[127] Ibid, 342.

Edward Gibbon describes the reaction of Byzantine Rome to the new religion of the Arabs by stating that the peace enjoyed after triumphing over the Persians by the Emperor Heraclius and the empire was once again disturbed by a new enemy whose religion had a power more strongly felt than it was clearly understood by the Christians of the East. The new invaders' "ruling passions" were a hatred of Christians, lust for spoil and an utter contempt for danger. Their religious confidence was not unshaken by the prospect of dying, nor was their calm resolution able to be ruffled by it. They entertained a frank and martial pleasantry of humour which the prospect of death was unable to suspend.[128]

> In the presence of both armies a venerable Greek advanced from the ranks with a liberal offer of peace; and the departure of the Saracens would have been purchased by a gift to each soldier of a turban, a robe, and a piece of gold; ten robes and a hundred pieces to their leader; one hundred robes and a thousand pieces to the caliph. A smile of indignation expressed the refusal of Chaled. 'Ye Christian dogs, you know your option; the Koran, the tribute, or the sword. We are a people whose delight is in war rather than in peace: and we despise your pitiful alms, since we shall be speedily masters of your wealth, your families, and your persons.' Notwithstanding this apparent disdain, he was deeply conscious of the public danger: those who had been in Persia, and had seen the armies of Chosroes, confessed that they never beheld a more formidable array. From the superiority of the enemy the artful Saracen derived a fresh incentive of courage.[129]

As a silent majority, modern day Iranians welcome the dream of peaceful relations, and crave a respite from the culture of hate that has characterized their government's relations with the West in recent decades. They dream of and aspire to enjoy once again the genuine regard

---

[128]   Ibid, 350-51.

[129]   Ibid, 351.

and respect of the world community for all that their country stands for, including rich history and a culture rooted in ancient and noble traditions.

> *"Many devices in a man's heart; the counsel of the Lord that shall stand."* (Prov.19:21)

WHERE DO WE GO FROM HERE?

SOME FALLACIES HAVE BEEN PROJECTED to make the world community believe that, only when peace is achieved between Israel and her Arab neighbours, can peace have a chance in the world. They neglect to consider that each region has its geography, its neighbours, its history and its disagreements. In the case of Israel and her Arab neighbours, it seems to be about religion, not geography nor history or a need for land on the part of the Arabs.

Asked by a *Jerusalem Post* reporter in an article published on 24 October 2007, whether Jews will ever be allowed to pray on the Temple Mount under Muslim control, Jerusalem's mufti Ikrema Sabri replied: "It is not the Temple Mount, you must say Al-Aksa. And no Jews have the right to pray at the mosque. It was always only a mosque—all 144 dunams, the entire area. No Jewish prayer. If the Jews want real peace, they must not do anything to try to pray on Al Aksa. Everyone knows that. Because Allah is fair, he would not agree to make Al Aksa if there were a temple there for others beforehand ... that wall is not part of the Jewish temple—it is just the western wall of the mosque."[130]

Similarly, prior to the Six-Day War, the Western Wall existed under Jordanian rule: it was desecrated, and Jews were denied access. The Western Wall is what remains of Jerusalem's Holy Temple of King Solomon, the holiest place in the Jewish narrative. The Al Aksa mosque was built upon the ruins of Solomon's Temple, which had been built, destroyed and rebuilt centuries earlier.

---

[130] Mike Seid, The Jerusalem Post, 24 October 2007. *Kotel was never part of Jewish temple.* [online] Available at: http://www.jpost.com/Israel/Article.aspx?id=79606. [Accessed 14 March 2012].

I recall a time in Iran where the now-thirty-plus-year-old clerical regime intended to destroy any trace of the ancient ruins of Persepolis, the seat of the first ruling dynasty of the Persian Empire, no doubt in view to build something more compatible with the present day reality of an Islamic regime. Persepolis is a world heritage site, where the remains of a grandiose palace bear testimony to a golden age in history, even after it was burned at the hands of Alexander's Macedonian generals. The people's opposition was a gut reaction, proving that the Persian psyche's penchant for thinking, saying and doing good deeds has remained faithful to its ancient roots. That move was successfully aborted due to the people's firm resolve, in the same way that it remained unflinching on the mullahs' call to discontinue the cherished Persian New Year celebrations of *Nowruz*, (literal "New Day"), which coincides with every first day of spring.

A SPIRITUAL BIG BANG?

THERE WAS A TIME WHEN GOD SHOWED HIS COUNTENANCE to man and offered signs as guidance. He talked to Cain, asking about his brother Abel's whereabouts. God's message to him was that Cain was responsible for his brother, a concept whose significance in a biblical context seems to imply the broader context of humanity [Editor's note: John Donne's poem *No Man Is An Island* can be seen in similar terms as the story of Cain and Abel with respect to responsibility of the one toward another: "No man is an island / Entire of itself… / Any man's death diminishes me, / Because I am involved in mankind, / And therefore never send to know for whom the bell tolls; / It tolls for thee."[131]]

God talked to Noah and commanded him to build the arc to protect the good of the Earth. God visited Abraham at his tent and promised to make of him the father of nations, after Abraham pleaded the case of others to be kept from harm. Then God confirmed His covenant to Isaac and his son, Jacob.

---

[131] John Donne, Submitted 03 January 2003, Edited 30 May 2013. *No Man Is An Island*. [online] Accessible at: http://www.poemhunter.com/poem/no-man-is-an-island/. [Accessed 05 January 2014].

God showed His presence to Moses almost daily, advising him on what actions to take. He listened to his questions and knew his fears. At one point, in the Sinai desert, "*The Lord said unto Moses, lo, I come unto thee in a thick cloud, that the people may hear when I speak with thee, and believe thee forever*" (*Exodus 19:9*). "*And Moses brought forth the people out of the camp to meet with God; and they stood at the nether part of the mount*" (*Exodus 19:17*).

There, at Mount Sinai, in the midst of fire, thunder, and thick clouds, God declared the Ten Commandments in the presence of all the people, who were terrified at the scene: "*And they said unto Moses, speak thou with us, and we will hear, but let not God speak with us lest we die*" (*Exodus 20:19*).[132]

God continued His direct talk with Joshua, who led the Israelites to the Promised Land. Thereafter, His messengers, the prophets, brought the word of God to the people and told of their visions and dreams.

In the previous chapters of this book, the reader may have gotten a glimpse of events in this world that followed a divinely charted path. Many events took place centuries after the prophecies of the biblical prophets, whose inspiration was summoned as a calling by the Creator Himself, enabling their admonishments to resound through the Jewish people unto the far corners of the Earth.

And finally, "*I will hide my face from them and see what their end shall be*" (*Deuteronomy 32:20*). God's hidden face in our time leaves the platform open to the religious leaders to help pave the way with truth to a life of peace and dignity for all mankind. We may recall a previously quoted passage:

> *Behold the days come, saith the Lord God, that I will send a famine in the land, not a famine of bread, nor a thirst for water, but of hearing the words of the Lord: And they shall wander from sea to sea, and from the north even to the east, they shall run to and fro to seek the word of the Lord, and shall not find it.* (*Amos 8:11–12*)

---

[132]   The reader may be inspired to read the full text as it appears in Chapter 20 of the Book of Exodus.

[Editor's note: Do we not, today, wander as Amos predicted above, surfing to and fro on the web, only to find authenticity diluted and much of God's word lost in translation? Are we not called upon by conscience and by a sense of decency to be troubled by what some have announced as an end to history? Furthermore, is any one mortal entitled to make such a sweeping determination on the head of humanity in any sense, large or small?]

What was the world for the Jews of biblical times but a miracle where God revealed His glory to a spiritually hungry and once enslaved nation at the foot of a mountain in the Sinai Desert? In the seeming absence of any sign or direct communication from God—in our hour of need—is it perhaps a spiritual *yes* that we are seeking from one another, a *big bang* of mutual acceptance and recognition at this juncture in the *history* of humankind? We have been given the tools. Until such time as God may renew channels of direct communication, can it be possible to trust in The Book to remind us that God's word is clearly unhidden from the critical eye, revealed, rather, in an intimate, life-size manner? Can we acknowledge that neither is His word far off, that it is very nigh unto us, in our mouths to express, and in our hearts to translate into action?

Are we able to carry home from reading anywhere in The Book that nil is qualified to trample on the Golden Rule by imposing theirs upon another's personal way of reaching toward a higher source? Can we recognize the vanity within the act of diluting—or adding to—an authentic word of divine proportions?

In a world where religious fanatics usurp the most basic rights from their people and threaten to export their dogma to other countries, still others in the civilized world find themselves at a loss to deal with the potential dangers on the horizon. They seem to have paved the way for a spiritual vacuum, the remainder of a steady and intentional move away from faith, the faith bequeathed to them by their generations past. They remain despondent, awestruck, and baffled at the intensity with which people from the East seem to hold fast to their faiths. This author's hope is to have inspired readers to gain their own perspectives about The Book, in a way that may encourage renewed journeys for newer and older travellers alike, and for those who yearn to discover or rediscover, each in their own way, a path paved by the wisdom of the written word.

According to the (retired) Chief Rabbi of the Commonwealth, Lord Jonathan Sacks, "Judaism has a structural plurality so perplexing and profound that though its two daughter monotheisms, Christianity and Islam, took much else from it, they did not adopt this: Judaism is a particularist monotheism." In the chapter entitled "The Dignity of Difference" from the book *Universalizing Particularity*, in which the editors compiled a number of his essays, Rabbi Sacks explains that, unlike the universalist monotheisms of Christianity and Islam, Judaism is a particularistic monotheism that "believes in one God but not in one religion, one culture, one truth. The God of Abraham is the God of all mankind, but the faith of Abraham is not the faith of all mankind."[133]

I cannot help but simultaneously hear the cacophony of prison voices ringing in my ears: "*Marg bar on se mofsedin, Carter o Sadat o Begin!*" Death to those three corrupt ones! This was only one of the mantras forced upon us prisoners, which we chanted in unison, marching in single file along the tall walls of the prison yard at Evin.

Those of us who originate from the Middle East are aware of certain ancient dogmas that have been all but written in stone regarding interfaith relations. Unequivocal zero tolerance of plurality in matters of faith leaves little room for dialogue or the yearning for peace of their moderate minds. Yet, in this new millennium, we seem poised and standing in wake of a spiritual big bang where the characters of the theatre of modern history remain mere mortals, actors on a stage as yet directed by the will of God. In the absence of a scenario where He reveals His glory through direct dialogue as in the time of Moses and the prophets, He seems to be evermore hovering over a yet evolving sequel to The Book!

Rabbi Sacks puts forth the notion that, just as God's desire is for all faiths and cultures to flourish in their diversity, a loving parent wouldn't want for his or her children to be the same. "That is the conceptual

---

[133]   Hava Tirosh-Samuelson and Aaron W. Hughes, ed. *Jonathan Sacks: Universalizing Particularity*, 45.

link between love, creation and differences. We serve God, author of diversity, by respecting diversity."[134] One can only be reminded of our own uniqueness as human beings.

What then can resemble the face of such a big bang? Searching for a hope inspiring source to heal the divide, I find myself, ruminating along a humble quest into the wisdom of the Hebrew Bible, where revelation resounds louder than the voices of Evin that still pound against my eardrum: *"Neither I shall hide my face any more from them: for I have poured out My Spirit upon the House of Israel, saith the Lord God"* (Ezekiel 39:29).

Many readers may be familiar with the famous inscription on the Isaiah Wall at the United Nations in New York, and still many are sensing the urgency of its message in the here and now:

> *And many people shall go and say, 'Come ye, and let us go up to the mountain of the Lord, to the house of the God of Jacob; and he will teach us of his ways, and we will walk in his paths: for out of Zion shall go forth the law, and the word of the Lord from Jerusalem. And He shall judge among the nations, and shall rebuke many people: and they shall beat their swords into plowshares, and their spears into pruning hooks: nation shall not lift up sword against nation, neither shall they learn war any more.* (Isaiah 2:3–4)

In a modern context, such a promise that gives hope for peace may seem elusive. Perhaps what is needed is divine intervention again, as in the times of Moses on Mount Sinai when God talked directly to the people, and where many souls simultaneously witnessed His presence. Alas, our politicians and religious leaders, and our economists and other masterminds seem locked in competition for an audience whose ears are already deafened by the cacophony. In a globalized world, too many specialists comment, too many corporations permit themselves to overstep long cherished local traditions, each creating a dent to weaken the foundations of the modern Tower of Babel. The din is heard, but seldom is it of solid content, or the audience one that is prone to analysis, like the critical thinker, or the

---

[134] Ibid, 48.

ruminator that chews its cud twice at least before digesting. We need to rebuild the staircase of respect for one another's otherness.

Perhaps, what is most needed is a sense of that which binds us despite our diversity. As Naïm Kattan, Order of Canada, puts in his Foreword in a text from the English translation of his novel *Adieu Babylone: mémoires d'un Juif d'Irak (Farewell to Babylon: Coming of Age in Jewish Baghdad)*, translated by Sheila Fischman, Order of Canada):

> I remind myself that peoples outlive their lands, even lands that are hostile. Some ungrateful people damage the legacy and the wealth of their land. I never forget that Abraham was born at Ur in Chaldea, not far from Baghdad. He is still the father of all the monotheistic religions, even if his message is handled roughly. His word endures, even when we do not hear it. That is his victory; it is also our hope.[135]

Concurrently, numerous are those around the planet who seek the spiritual in conversation. More and more people are following the wisdom of master spiritual healers and meditation practitioners such as Eckhart Tolle or Deepak Chopra, to name a few. Some change to a different faith than the one they acquired by inheritance to one that better resonates with the drummer beating within. A rapidly widening conversation of like-minded souls rises above the mainstream's cacophony, since there is a growing consensus, a spiritual big bang of sorts that clamours for a more sustainable path for humanity, both physically and spiritually. Here is the Prophet Micah's take on such an event: *"And they shall beat their swords into plowshares, and their spears into pruning hooks"* (Micah 4:3),—repeating with striking similarity that which was previously prophesied—in Isaiah 2:3–4, not too far above these lines.

In such a world as is ours in the twenty-first century of the Common Era, we as global citizens are uniquely positioned to attain the level of consciousness that allows for the lifting of *'spirits'* instead of weapons, for

---

[135] Naïm Kattan, Sheila Fischman, transl., *Farewell to Babylon: Coming of Age in Jewish Baghdad*, Foreword, 89.

an end to the debate about difference, for an age of curiosity where we seek one another's uniqueness—instead of one another's wealth. We can induce less mainstream and more presence of mind, so that our dialogue may resemble the prophet Micah's below, in which he further expands on Isaiah's positive message:

> *But they shall sit every man under his vine* [flag] *and under his fig tree* [belief]; *and none shall make them afraid: for the mouth of the Lord of hosts hath spoken it.* (Micah 4:4)

It is perhaps in this perspective that mankind can, indeed, enter a new era of *sustainable* history, a history at once ecological, humanistic and spiritual, a history where not only physical waste gets transformed into reusable composition, but where negative outlooks transform into kindness toward all sentient beings, since together we all represent essential elements of a larger whole. When we can see God's wholeness through differing perspectives on beauty, we may just be touching upon the penultimate purpose of all existence.

[Editor's note: Can our plurality be key to our own wholeness? Can it be perhaps in this way that we may witness a place at the epicentre of our being to embrace it as a source of spiritual wealth instead of a hindrance to our own vanity? Can we compete as gardeners, each in his or her own corner of Earth, instead of as plunderers of her resources? Can we author acts of loving kindness by allowing others the space to preserve their dignity and self-determination? Can this tried and tested toolkit that is The Book be once again rediscovered as a common denominator in the marketplace of ideas—and an anchor when the mind needs to recharge from its perpetual depletion— pitted as it is against the constant hum of automatic alerts and mobile devices we so heavily rely upon these days? Can we aspire to Cyrus' greatness by recognizing his message of acceptance which so clearly resonates in modern ears as it did for those over whom he ruled in distant times?]

Throughout my youth, and now approaching ninety, turning to one of the last twenty plus pages of The Book, I find that this monumental work

of the scribes delivers a bottomless message—not with a whimper—but
with a big bang:

*"For all people will walk every one in the name of his god, and we will
walk in the name of the Lord our God for ever and ever." (Micah 4:5)*

◆ ◆ ◆

TRIBUTE FROM A FELLOW
PRISON INMATE AT EVIN

Evin Prison, March 1980
The Accusation: Spying for Israel

I ARRIVED AT EVIN PRISON WITH MY EYES SHUT. It was at that moment it occurred to me that I had just spent ninety-two days in an isolated cell, measuring four feet by ten feet, which was used by the Savak for counter-terrorist activities; by its own protocol no one was to be held in such a space longer than a week. Wing number three in Evin Prison housed just over four hundred prisoners. Those prisoners were a mix of Mujahidin (Fadaian Khalgh), Communists, military generals from the reign of the Shah, ministers and parliament members, and of course, opium and heroin dealers and burglars who made a habit of armed robbery during the mayhem of post revolution.

Moukhsan Naderi was in charge of wing number three and managed it from the inside. He was arrested in Iran's central desert while importing roughly two tons of opium from Afghanistan. Naderi was a friend of mine during the Shah's days and he saw to it that I be spared any mistreatment. There were ten prisoners and two blankets per cell. We often ate our meals on the cell's cement floor. A week after my arrival at Evin, Avraham Beroukhim, then a twenty-five year old Jew, was sentenced to death. His crime was raising funds for Israel.

Around July of that year, some prisoners from wing number two were transferred to our wing; among them was Mr. Joseph Koukou. I had the pleasure of getting to know Mr. Koukou while providing photography services for the ad campaign of his factory, years before the revolution. We were reacquainted in Evin, and his presence unmistakably facilitated my stay there. Mr. Koukou, with whom I had many deep and spiritual conversations, was an intelligent, open minded and forward thinking man. Together with many imprisoned ministers and Parliament members, we spent much time with one another, making Evin's wrath somewhat tolerable, though ever so slightly.

242

Since inmates were not allowed to keep books other than the Holy Bible, many of our conversations had a biblical tone to them with possible outreach to modern society. From a spiritual point of view, all that time spent discussing the Bible with Mr. Koukou helped in some way to have saved my soul. It was very effective.

Many prisoners in Evin could not cope with the harsh conditions and eventually took their own lives. Inmates hanging themselves in the shower rooms were not a rare occurrence. Other inmates chose to hide their Jewish identity, an act of disdain in the eyes of Mr. Koukou. Nonetheless, if there was an opportunity to help someone, Mr. Koukou would always be the first to do so. One inmate by the name of Itzkhak Sanahi was known by everyone for his pride in Judaism. He was a factory owner whose various occupations included supplying the Imperial Iranian Air Force. Itzkhak Sanahi was sentenced to death in Evin.

My memories of Mr. Koukou are enough to fill a book. I will forever remember his bravery, loyalty, understanding and general knowledge. He was a true friend in what was the most difficult time of my life. His spiritual and mental support to me and many others during that horrible time will never be forgotten.

Dear Mr. Koukou, I will forever respect you and never forget you.

Firouz Farokhzad
New York, January 2014

BIBLIOGRAPHY

1906 Jewish Encyclopaedia, "The unedited full-text of the. Tarshish." [online] Available at: <http://www.jewishencyclopedia.com/articles/14254-tarshish>. [Accessed 20 August 2011].

Abdulezer, Morris, 19 February 2009. *"Baghdad hangings: remembering the horror,"* from a speech posted on *Point of No Return: Jewish Refugees from Arab Countries.* [online] Available at: http://jewishrefugees. blogspot.ca/2009/02/baghdad-hangings-remembering-horror-and. html. [Accessed 12 March 2011].

Abulafia, David. *The Great Sea: A Human History of the Mediterranean.* London: Allen Lane, an imprint of Penguin Books, 2011.

Appeal of Conscience, 18 April 2008. *His Holiness Pope Benedict XVI makes historical and unprecedented first visit with Rabbi Arthur Schneier at Park East Synagogue.* [online] Available at: http://www. appealofconscience.org/news/article.cfm?id=100160. [Accessed 5 November 2011].

Archaeology in Israel: List of Discoveries (2004 - Present). [online] Available at: https://www.jewishvirtuallibrary.org/jsource/Archaeology/ archdiscovery2013.html. [Accessed 04 July 2014].

Balfour, The Earl of. *Speeches on Zionism.* London: Arrowsmith, 1928.

Barber, Noel. *Lords of the Golden Horn: From Suleiman the Magnificent to Kamal Ataturk.* London: Macmillan London Ltd., 1973.

Ben Gurion, David, 14 May 1948. *Official Gazette:* Number 1; Tel Aviv, 5 Iyar 5708, Page 1. *Proclamation of Independence: The Declaration of the Establishment of the State of Israel.* [online] Available at: http://www, knesset.gov.il/docs/eng/megilat_eng.htm. [Accessed 10 May 2011].

Brody, Lazer, 12 August 2008. *God's Pharmacy – the original Chassidic version.* [online] Available at: http://www.youtube.com/ watch?v=H1K0FScTQa4\. [Accessed 10 November 2011].

Campbell, Thomas. *The Poetical Works of Thomas Campbell: Hallowed Ground, Stanza 6.* London: George Bell and Sons, York Street, Covent Garden, 1891.

Circle of Ancient Iranian Studies, The (CAIS),1999. *Cyrus the Great, the Father and Liberator.* [online] Available at: <http://www.cais-soas.com/CAIS/History/hakhamaneshian/Cyrus-the-great/ cyrus_the_great.htm>. [Accessed 10 September 2011].

Dalin, David G. and John F. Rothman. *Icon of Evil*. New York: Random House, 2008,

Diwaniyya Dayan Center Podcast: Middle East culture, history and politics, Submitted 16 April 2012. *The Al-Kuwaiti Brothers: Iraqi Jewish Musicians*. [online] Available at: http://www.diwaniyya. org/2012/04/story-of-iraqi-jewish-musicians-al.html. [Accessed 12 June 2012].

Donne, John, Submitted 03 January 2003, Edited 30 May 2013. *No Man Is An Island*. [online] Accessible at: http://www.poemhunter.com/ poem/no-man-is-an-island/. [Accessed 05 January 2014].

Eban, Abba. *Heritage: Civilization and the Jews*. New York: Summit Books, a Division of Simon & Schuster, Inc., 1984.

Eban, Abba. *My People*. New York: Behrman House Inc., Random House, 1968.

Edinger, Edward F. *Ego and Self: The Old Testament Prophets: From Isaiah to Malachi*. Toronto: Inner City Books, 2000.

Einstein, Albert (attributed to). *Albert Einstein Quotes*. [online] Available at: http://thinkexist.com/quotes/albert_einstein/. [Accessed 12 February 2012].

Encyclopaedia Judaica, Volume 8, "Inquisition: The Early Institution." Jerusalem: Keter Publishing House Jerusalem Ltd., Israel, 1972.

Encyclopaedia Judaica, Volume 11, "Marx, Karl Heinrich," Jerusalem: Keter Publishing House Jerusalem Ltd., Israel, 1972.

Encylopaedia Judaica, Volume 12, "Muhammad in Medina." Jerusalem: Keter Publishing House Jerusalem Ltd., Israel, 1972.

Encylopaedia Judaica, Volume 13, "Qurayza." Jerusalem: Keter Publishing House Jerusalem Ltd., Israel, 1972.

Ettefagh Synagogue, Summer 2009. Exterior Wall Inscription Honouring Donators. [online] Available at: http://www.7dorim.com/Tasavir/ kenisa_etefag.asp. [Accessed 01 July 2012].

Gibbon, Edward. *The Decline and Fall of the Roman Empire*: Volume 5, Chapter LI: *The Conquest of Persia, Syria, Egypt, Africa, and Spain, by the Arabs or Saracens – Empire of the Caliphs or Successors of Mohammed – State of the Christians, etc., under their Government*. Printed and bound in Germany: Alfred A. Knopf, a division of Random House, 1993 Inc., first included in Everyman's Library, 1910.

Gilbert, Martin. *In Ishmael's House: A History of Jews in Muslims Lands.* Toronto: McClelland & Stewart Ltd., 2010.

Gilder, George. *The Israel Test.* USA: Richard Vigilante Books, 2009.

Glueck, Grace, 02 October 2002. *Walter Annenberg, 94, Dies; Philanthropist and Publisher.* [online] Available at: http://www.nytimes.com/2002/10/02/arts/walter-annenberg-94-dies-philanthropist-and-publisher.html?sec=&spon=?pagewanted=1&pagewanted=5. [Accessed 05 May 2011].

Goodstein, Laurie, 4 April 2008. *Pope Adds Meetings With Jewish Leaders to U.S. Itinerary.* [online] Available at: < www.nytimes.com/2008/04/04/us/04pope.html >. [Accessed 05 November 2011].

Habas, Bracha. *The Gate Breakers.* New York: Herzl Press, 1963.

Hansard, Parliamentary Debates, House of Commons, 23 May 1939. [Quote by Churchill from Martin Gilbert's *In Ishmael's House: A History of Jews in Muslim Lands,* see bibliographical reference above].

Hertz, Eli E., 31 March 2008. *Palestinians: 'Peoplehood' Based on a Big Lie.* [online] Available at: http://www.mythsandfacts.org/article_view.asp?articleID=53&order_id=2. [Accessed 10 July 2010].

Hillel, Shlomo, *Operation Babylon.* Original Hebrew. Israel: Ednom Publishers, 1985; Translation New York: Doubleday division of Bantam Doubleday Dell Publishing Group, Inc., 1987.

Ilani, Ofri, 21 August 2007. *Study: Going to synagogue leads to longevity.* [online] Available at: http://www.haaretz.com/print-edition/news/study-going-to-synagogue-leads-to-longevity-1.227864. [Accessed 10 April 2010].

Irvine, J. Richard, 2009. *Community and Iranzamin Schools, Tehran, Iran.* [essay].

Kalmikoff, Scott, 05 April 2012. *Jerusalem is the capital of the State of Israel.* [online] Available at: http://www.silive.com/opinion/letters/index.ssf/2012/04/jerusalem_is_the_capital_of_th.html. [Accessed 30 May 2012].

Katouzian, Homa. *The Persians.* Great Britain: MPG Books Ltd., Bodmin, Cornwall, 2009, and Katouzian ref. to Abbasgholi Golsha'iyan, *Yahddasht-ha-ye Abbasgholi-ye Golsha'iyan* in *Yaddasht-ha-ye Doctor Qasem Ghani,* ed. Cyrus Ghani, vol, 4. Zavvar: Tehran, 1978.

Kattan, Naïm, Sheila Fischman, transl. *Farewell to Babylon: Coming of Age in Jewish Baghdad.* Vancouver: Raincoast Books, 2005.

Kaufman, Walter, ed. and transl. *The Portable Nietzsche*. New York: Penguin Group, 1976.

Keddie, Nikki R. *Modern Iran: Roots and Results of Revolution*. New Haven and London:Yale University Press, 2003.

Koukou, Heskel Abraham. Leatherbound Manuscript handwritten in Iraqi Hebrew alphabet calligraphy: Iraq, circa 1904 (5665 in the Hebrew calendar).

Koukou, Joseph. Handwritten Manuscripts I and IV of a set of 4 legal sized booklets: Tehran, circa 1982.

Levy, Mark. *Jews and All That Jazz: Al Jolson, Florenz Ziegfeld, Fanny Brice, Jerome Kern, Irving Berlin, George Gershwin, Artie Shaw and More*. [online] Available at: http://www.jewishfederations.org/page. aspx?id=957. [Accessed 16 November 2011].

Morad, Tamar, Dennis Shasha and Robert Shasha, Ed. *Palgrave Studies in Oral History, Iraq's Last Jews, Stories of Daily Life, Upheaval and Escape from Modern Babylon*. USA: Palgrave Macmillan, 2008.

Pinsk Stories. *Encyclopaedia of World Biography(c) on Chaim Weizmann*. [online] Available at: <http://www.eilatgordinlevitan.com/pinsk/ pinsk_pages/pinsk_stories_weizmann.html> [Accessed 12 October 2011].

Polonsky, Antony, *The Jews in Poland and Russia, Volume II*. Portland, Oregon: Oxford, The Litman Library of Jewish Civilization, 2010.

Reagan, Ronald, 12 June 1987. *President Reagan's Address at the Brandenburg Gate*. [online] Available at: http://www.reaganfoundation.org/ pdf/Remarks_on_East_West_RElations_at_Brandenburg%20 Gate_061287.pdf. [Accessed 30 May 2011].

Ronen, Tsafrir, 26 May 2008. *Hadrian's Curse – The Invention Of Palestine*. [online] Available at: http://tzafrirronenen.blogspot.ca/2008/05/ hadrians-curse-by-tsafrir-ronen.html. [Accessed 10 July 2010].

Sacks, Rabbi Jonathan, 07 May 2010. *On the Dignity of Difference*. [online] Available at: http://www.youtube.com/watch?v=wpuQHLisQns. [Accessed 11 June 2011].

Sacks, Rabbi Jonathan. *The Dignity of Difference: How to Avoid the Clash of Civilizations*. New York: Continuum Books, 2002.

Saw, Sharon, 06 May 2010. *A conversation between HH the Dalai Lama and Leonardo Boff*. [online] Available at: http://sharonsaw.typepad. com/blog/2010/05/a-conversation-between-hh-the-dalai-lama-and-leonardo-boff.html. [Accessed 25 February 2012].

Seid, Mike, The Jerusalem Post, 24 October 2007. *Kotel was never part of Jewish temple.* [online] Available at: http://www.jpost.com/ Israel/Article.aspx?id=79606. [Accessed 14 March 2012].

Stevens, David, 2011. *Some Amazing Facts About the King James Version.* [online] Available at: <http://biblicalinsights.net/?p=661/URL>. [Accessed 30 June 2011].

Telushkin, Rabbi Joseph. *Jewish Literacy: The Most Important Things to Know About the Jewish Religion, Its People, and Its History.* New York: William Morrow and Company, Inc., 1991.

The Associated Press, 04 December 2009. *U.K. chief rabbi declares 'green' Sabbath ahead of climate talks.* [online] Available at: http:// www.haaretz.com/jewish-world/news/u-k-chief-rabbi-declares-green-sabbath-ahead-of-climate-talks-1.2771. [Accessed 13 February 2012].

Time Magazine, December 31, 1999, Vol. 154, No. 27. *Person of the Century* [online] Available at: http://content.time.com/time/ magazine/0,9263,7601991231,00.html. [Accessed 20 August 2011].

Tirosh-Samuelson, Hava and Hughes, Aaron W., eds. *Jonathan Sacks: Universalizing Particularity.* London: Brill Academic Publishers, 2013.

Twain, Mark, 1899. "*Concerning the Jews*" from Harper's Magazine. [online] Available at: http://www.simpletoremember.com/jewish/ blog/mark-twain-and-the-jews/. [Accessed 10 November 2010].

Weisgal, Meyer Wolfe and Joel Carmichael, eds., *Chaim Weizmann: A Biography by Several Hands.* London: Weidenfeld & Nicolson, 1962.

Wilhelm, Richard, trans., *The I Ching or Book of Changes,* (Bollingen Series XIX). 3rd ed. Trans. into English by Cary F. Baynes. Princeton: Princeton University Press, 1967.

World Book, Inc., Volume 6. "*Albert Einstein,*" *article by Daniel J. Kevles.* Chicago: Scott Fetzer, 1994.

World Book, Inc., Volume 6. "*Earth,*" *article by Sue Ellen Hirschfeld.* Chicago: Scott Fetzer, 1994.

World Book, Inc., Volume 15, "*Palestine,*" *article by Michel Le Gall.* Chicago: Scott Fetzer, 1994.

World Book, Inc., Volume 18. "*Sun,*" *article by Robert W. Noyes.* Chicago: Scott Fetzer, 1994.

◆◆◆

ABOUT THE BOOK

IMPRISONED IN IRAN'S NOTORIOUS EVIN PRISON under Ayatollah Khomeini's rule directly following the 1979 revolution, Joseph Koukou survived his four years of imprisonment by translating and reciting to his cellmates the words of the Tanakh, the Hebrew Scriptures.

Born in Basra, Iraq, in 1924, Joseph Koukou and his family immigrated to Iran before the great escape of the mass of Iraqi Jews in the 1950s to start a new life after a history of 2,500 years in the land of Babylon. Proud of both his heritage and his newly adopted home of Iran he built a factory and raised his family, affording his children an English education at an American international school. Joseph Koukou's story ends with the flight from his captives brought about because of his youngest daughter, Sandra, then only twenty-four who stood bravely in front of the judicial court's top cleric under a blue sky, pleading with every fibre of her body to have her father released unharmed when almost all who entered those prison walls never left alive.

This book was written word for word by Joseph, although he did not survive long enough to see its completion. Sandra took it upon herself to fulfil her father's dream to completing this book. The fight against the clock to get his final thoughts on the content before he died provided the basis for Sandra's research and editing that went into the final draft.

The book is Joseph Koukou's interpretation of the Hebrew Bible and its relevance to our times. Through an unmistakeable love of his fellow human beings and what he referred to as "The Book," the author connects the dots between his Jewish roots and those of other faiths, seeking to inspire an appreciation of humankind's commonality and diversity alike.

Joseph Heskel Koukou (1924 - 2012)

ABOUT THE AUTHOR

JOSEPH HESKEL KOUKOU was born in 1924 in Basra, Iraq. At ten his family moved to Isfahan, Iran, where he learned Persian poetry and the art of calligraphy. Throughout his entire life, he would recite Persian poetry, an art form considered amongst the richest the world has seen.

Joseph Koukou married Evelyn David in Teheran and had three daughters and a son. An active member of Teheran's Iraqi Jewish community, he supervised financial aid for students to the Ettefagh School, which, along with an adjacent synagogue, was built by his father, Heskel Abraham Koukou, a man widely known for his dedication to the Iraqi Jewish Diaspora living in Iran. He had a successful manufacturing business in the auto parts field which was confiscated during Iran's 1979 revolution when he became a "guest" of Ayatollah Khomeini's revolutionary guard in Iran's notorious Evin Prison.

Faith was integral to Koukou during his time in Evin. While there he narrowly escaped execution at the hands of the Islamic Revolutionary Court, which had confiscated his factory in 1980 and seized the family assets all in the name of Allah. With the abrupt loss of a world he had striven to make and with the constant threat of death hanging over him, it was only his faith in God that sustained him and kept him alive. Upon his escape from Iran in 1986, Joseph made Great Neck, New York his home until he passed away in 2012.

The Hebrew letters 'kaf' and 'vav' form the family name, Koukou. Formerly Ghazal, the new name was decided upon by the author's grandfather, a textile merchant in Baghdad. The total numeric value of those letters adds up to twenty-six, which is identical to the numeric value attributed to the Hebrew word for God. Was the choice of name based on this understanding? Was this understanding Joseph Koukou's inheritance, a gift of faith that sustained his life?

INDEX

A

Aaron 71, 75, 76, 105, 199, 201, 237, 249
abaya 38, 47
Abe xxii, 10
Abiatar 82
Abraham x, xix, 12, 65, 66, 71, 94, 121, 124, 134, 135, 178, 183, 184, 230, 234, 237, 239, 248
Abulafia, David 98, 245
Abu Taleb 119
Achaemenids 54
Admiral Estéva 150
Adolf Hitler 115, 132, 149, 158
Adonijah 82
Agag 78
agriculture 109, 149, 170
Ahad Ha-Am 140
Ahijah the Shilonite 85
Alborz Mountains 6, 170
Alexander the Great 154
Allenby 145, 147
Alliance Israelite Universelle 181
Allied armies 115, 132, 147, 149, 162
al-Muthanna 150
Alouf, Rabbi Shimon H. xxi
altar 72, 94, 107
Amalek 78
Amalekites 78
Amir Feisal 145, 146
Annenberg, Walter 213, 247
Antiochus IV 154

Arabian Peninsula 119
Arab nationalism 146, 148
Aramaian 95
Arazi, Yehuda 100
archives 39, 41, 222
Ark of the Covenant 72, 183
Assad, Hafez 173
Austin, Warren 166
Ayatollah Khomeini xvi, 24, 29, 53, 149, 251

B

Baal 92, 94
Bababozorg 35, 37
Babylon 54, 99, 100, 104, 106, 111, 112, 114, 117, 132, 133, 228, 239, 247, 248, 251
Babylonian Jews 55, 114, 154
Baghdad ix, 23, 100, 113, 132, 133, 150, 175, 181, 197, 214, 221, 222, 239, 245, 247
Bahaism 18, 204, 206
Bahaullah 204, 206
Balfour Declaration 142, 145, 148, 152, 157, 163
Balfour, James 142
Balkans 151
Bani Sadr 40
Barber, Noel 31, 32, 245
Basra 9, 100, 150, 251
Bathsheba 81

Beheshti, Mohammad 39

Ben Gurion, David 138, 167, 168, 171, 245

Ben-Porat, Mordechai 99

Bethlehemite 78

Bible v, vi, vii, viii, ix, xvi, xvii, xviii, xix, 2, 3, 4, 54, 59, 68, 86, 90, 98, 113, 121, 123, 137, 172, 188, 190, 196, 238, 243, 251

big bang 234, 236, 238, 239

Bilu 137

biochemistry 140

Blair, Tony 221

blessing xi, 3, 68, 85, 86, 95, 96, 122, 131, 139, 167, 192, 197, 198, 200, 208, 224

Brandenburg Gate 214, 248

Bridge of Victory 163

British embassy 162

British Mandate 145, 152, 162, 164, 166, 168

bullock 20, 94, 201

Bush, George W. 134, 221

Byzantine 155, 156, 232

C

Caliph xix, 232

Camoni...Camocha 213

Campbell, Thomas 5, 9, 245

Canaan 153

Carthage 98

Chaldea 105, 239

Chaldeans 92, 112, 116

chariot 88, 149

chief rabbi of Teheran 16

Chopra, Deepak 239

Chosroes 232

Christianity 118, 155, 203, 230, 237

Christians 113, 118, 159, 203, 207, 222, 231, 232, 246

Chronicles 76, 82, 97, 98, 122, 198

Churchill, Winston 142, 150, 161, 163

Clostridium acetobutylicum 142

Cold War 215

commentators 90, 200

Communism 213, 214

Communist 17, 24, 51, 213, 242

Community School 33

Count Bernadotte 169

Cradle of Civilization 134

Crusades 149

Cufa 231

cuneiform 54

curse xi, 95, 122, 132, 134, 158, 248

Cynthia x, xxii, 42, 55

Cyprus 99, 100, 164, 228

Cyrus Cylinder 54

D

Dachau 100

Dalai Lama 219, 220, 248

Das Kapital 213, 215

David xviii, 18, 55, 71, 76, 79, 80, 82, 84, 86, 88, 98, 131, 138, 148, 153, 164, 167, 168, 171, 174, 183, 197, 198, 245, 246, 249

Davidic Dynasty 85

Davis Jr., Sammy 206

Dayan, Moshe 169, 172

Dead Sea 67

Declaration of Neutrality 162

Deuteronomy xx, 2, 74, 84, 92, 103, 118, 121, 199, 213, 227, 235

Diaspora 120, 122, 137, 231

Donne, John 234, 246
draught 93, 109, 191
drumming (X-ref to "Topheth") 202

E

Earth xix, 7, 24, 64, 67, 73, 75, 76, 80,
  92, 94, 96, 101, 102, 108, 112, 117,
  120, 122, 133, 161, 164, 169, 186,
  187, 192, 193, 197, 204, 219, 222,
  224, 228, 234, 235, 240, 249
Eban, Abba xix, 54, 137, 141, 144, 152,
  161, 164, 165, 192, 246
Ebensee 100
Ecbatana 231
Ecclesiastes 83, 87, 89, 90
Edomites 84
Edward Edinger 4
Egypt 52, 67, 71, 72, 78, 84, 88, 121, 149,
  153, 156, 160, 162, 170, 173, 175,
  187, 193, 229, 230, 246
Einstein, Albert xi, 1, 185, 186, 189, 246,
  249
El Alamein 162
Eliab 79
Elijah 71, 92, 94
Elijah the Tishbite 93
Eliphaz 20
Elisha 71, 92, 94
Emperor Heraclius 232
empires 113, 116, 154, 222
emuna 209, 211
energy 1, 4, 181, 187, 225
Eretz Yisrael 137, 157
Esau 68, 208
Evelyn ix, x, xxii, 29, 53, 55, 57, 127, 184
Evin xvi, 6, 16, 27, 29, 35, 39, 41, 44, 50,
  52, 206, 238, 242, 243

exile 71, 111, 113, 114, 116, 120, 131,
  167
Exodus ix, 13, 64, 71, 72, 99, 106, 113,
  114, 115, 133, 165, 174, 193, 198,
  200, 235
Exodus 1947 165
Ezekiel 71, 92, 105, 106, 108, 113, 116,
  124, 190, 216, 225, 229, 238
Ezra xi, 54, 112, 114, 133, 229

F

famine 93, 104, 218, 235
Farewell to Babylon 113, 239, 247
Farsistan 231
fatwa (X-ref to "mufti") 148, 149
Fertile Crescent 113, 134
Firouz Farokhzad 6, 243
Foroughi, Mohsen 17
Forughi 163
Freedom Square 132, 134
Friday prayers 38, 45, 169, 221
führer 150

G

Gabbai, Agha Yehuda 181
Gabès 151
Galilee 155
Gehinnom 202
Genesis 8, 63, 65, 66, 68, 70, 73, 85, 86,
  132, 135, 199
Ghods 29
Gibbon, Edward 155, 156, 231, 232, 246
globalized xvi, 203, 238
GNP 151
God's Pharmacy 209, 210, 212, 245
Goebbels 163

goftar-e neek 230

golden age 51, 234

golden rule 2, 110, 192, 193, 195, 215, 218, 236

Goliath 79, 155, 170

Golshah'iyan, Abbasqoli 163

Gorbachev, Mikhail 214

Greeks 54, 116, 117, 131, 222

Gromyko, Andrei 165

Grynszpan, Herchel 159

Guadalquivir 98

H

Habas, Bracha 100, 247

Hadrian 155, 158, 248

Haftara 199, 200

Haganah 152, 164, 166

Haggadah 177

Haifa 145, 165

Haj Amin al-Husseini 148

haji 21, 22

Hallowed Ground 5, 9, 245

Hamadan 231

hamas 101

Hamburg 40, 165

Hassan Al Bakr 132

headwear 72, 201

Hebrews 153, 154

Hebrew University 140, 147

Herzl, Theodor 138, 141

Hetzi Kulmous 177, 178

hexagram 4

hezbollah 40

Hillel 99, 100, 114, 192, 247

holocaust 100, 114, 117, 161, 164, 227, 228

Holy Land 64, 96, 102, 104, 109, 116, 118, 132, 145, 158, 164, 169, 228

horses 10, 84, 88, 149

Hossein, Saddam 132, 204

House of Lords 143, 208

I

idols 103, 196

Imam 19, 25, 194

inquisitions 114, 117

interfaith 202, 219, 225, 237

interfaith dialogue (nest under "interfaith") 218

interfaith relations (nest under "interfaith") 202

intifada 174

Iraqi Jewish Synagogue of Teheran 12

Isaac xxi, 68, 71, 94, 131, 184, 208, 234

Isaiah 4, 63, 71, 92, 96, 99, 101, 102, 105, 120, 122, 137, 224, 227, 238, 240, 246

Isaiah Wall 238

Isfahan 55, 126, 181, 182

Ishmael xix, 135, 150, 160, 208, 247

Islam 20, 120, 149, 194, 202, 203, 207, 220, 222, 229, 230, 237

Islamic Tribunal 24

Israel xix, 21, 25, 29, 52, 64, 69, 72, 75, 76, 78, 80, 82, 84, 86, 88, 92, 94, 96, 99, 100, 102, 105, 108, 112, 114, 116, 118, 120, 122, 132, 133, 136, 137, 139, 143, 151, 154, 156, 165, 167, 169, 170, 173, 175, 183, 190, 197, 199, 200, 206, 208, 211, 216, 218, 224, 228, 229, 233, 238, 242, 245, 246, 249

Ithamar 105

J

Jabotinsky, Vladimir 145

Jacob 68, 70, 85, 86, 105, 120, 131, 134, 135, 137, 208, 235, 238

Jaffa 98

Jebusites 80

Jeremiah 71, 92, 102, 104, 112, 115, 119, 122, 136, 190, 191, 197, 203, 218, 224, 228

Jerusalem xi, 18, 21, 54, 71, 80, 84, 88, 92, 97, 101, 103, 104, 106, 111, 112, 116, 119, 131, 133, 139, 144, 147, 148, 153, 154, 156, 164, 168, 172, 175, 183, 192, 202, 228, 233, 238, 246, 249

Jerusalem Post 233, 249

Jesse 78

Jesus xix, 118, 154, 158, 203, 222

Jezebel 92

Job 11, 19, 20, 22, 26, 30, 56, 114, 151, 157, 160, 196, 206, 207, 216, 227

Jonah 98

Judah 55, 78, 81, 85, 86, 103, 111, 112, 132, 153, 154, 229

Judaism 4, 20, 71, 81, 96, 118, 154, 161, 162, 172, 173, 194, 195, 201, 204, 206, 222, 230, 237, 243

K

Kabbalah xix, 177

Kaiser Wilhelm II (X-ref to "Wilhelm II, Kaiser") 139

Kakh-é-dadgostari 39, 43

Karachi 57, 58

Kara Djehennem 32

Kattan, Naïm 239

Kayhan 41

Kedar 88

kerdar-e neek 230

Ketubim xvii

Khadija 119

Khartoum 173, 229

Khomeini (X-ref to "Ayatollah Khomeini") x

kingdom 64, 77, 82, 84, 86, 92, 98, 101, 102, 111, 112, 154, 197, 212, 217, 229, 230

Kingdom of Israel 77, 92, 154

King Hussein 175, 230

King James Version xvi, xviii, 249

Kings 39, 69, 71, 73, 76, 82, 84, 86, 88, 93, 94, 96, 101, 108, 122, 199, 203, 207, 217, 230

King Saul 76, 78, 82

Kipa 201

Kish 77

Kissinger, Henry 174

kohanim 105, 108, 199

Kohen 105, 107, 201, 217

kohen gadol 107, 201, 217

Kohen Gadol 107, 201, 217

Korah 75, 76

Koran xix, 19, 21, 23, 25, 204, 232

Koukou, Heskel Abraham 12, 124, 248

Kristallnacht 159

Kurd 204

L

Lamentations 104, 228

landlocked 99

Lebanon 88, 97, 101

Leon Pinsker 137

Levites 108

Lloyd George 142, 143

longevity 200, 247

Lords of the Golden Horn (X-ref to "Noel Barber") 32

M

Maccabeans 154

Maccabees 117, 131

Macedonian 234

Malachi 4, 63, 95, 246

manuscripts 60, 128, 177, 248

Marseilles 165, 228

Marx, Karl 213, 246

Mashad 19

Maureen x, xxii, 10, 42, 53, 56

McDonald, Malcolm 159, 160

Medes 54

Mediterranean 97, 98, 100, 109, 156, 228, 245

Mehrabad Airport 55

Mein Kampf 150, 158

Mesopotamia 114, 153

Micah 206, 240

Midian 71

Midrash 210

Milan 100

Moab 84

Mohammad 17, 21, 29, 30, 32, 38, 39, 40, 43, 48, 51, 119, 120, 146, 175, 204, 207, 230

monotheism 119, 202, 230, 237

Montgomery 161

Mooallem, Gladys ix

Moses xvii, xviii, xx, 2, 67, 71, 72, 75, 76, 92, 102, 104, 121, 122, 145, 153, 174, 186, 199, 201, 235, 237

moshavim (X-ref to "kibbutzim") 145

mount Carmel 93

Mount of Olives 84

mufti 148, 233

mujahed 29, 30, 38, 41, 51

mullocracy 27

N

Naaman 95

Nanati 37

Nasser, Gamal Abdel 170

Nation of Israel 64, 73, 87, 89, 165

Nazi 115, 150, 158, 159, 160, 162

Nebi'im xvii

Nebuchadnezzar 54, 104, 113

Nebuzaradan 104

Nehavend 231

Nietzsche 3, 7, 248

Nishmat Kol Hai 199

Nissan, Mullah 181

North Africa 150, 157, 161

Numbers, Book of 76

O

Odessa 137

Old Testament 4, 246

Omar Abd al-Azziz xix

Operation Babylon 99, 247

Operation Ezra and Nehemia 115

Orthodox 185, 201

Osirak 229

Ottoman 32, 114, 116, 118, 131, 136, 139, 148, 156, 174

P

Pahlavi 206, 230
Pakistan 56
Palaestina 155
Palestina 118
Palestine 31, 100, 118, 136, 137, 139, 140, 145, 147, 148, 152, 154, 156, 158, 160, 162, 164, 166, 168, 228, 248
Palestine Question 165
parasha 5, 76, 199, 200
partition 166
partner 24, 29, 41, 44, 50, 58, 207
party of God (X-ref to "hezbollah") 40
pasdar 45, 50, 53, 55
Paul 118, 205
pendar-e neek 230
Persepolis 234
Persians 6, 46, 54, 116, 163, 207, 222, 231, 232, 247
Pharaoh 72, 84, 88
Philistia 153, 155
Philistines 78, 80, 153, 155
Phoenicians 98, 222
Pietro 100
Pirkei Abot 195
plot 63, 71, 76, 91, 96
pogroms 114, 117, 136, 137
Pope Benedict XVI 203, 205, 245
Pope Gregory IX 203
Pope Innocent III 203
potter 103
prayer xxi, 5, 11, 16, 22, 31, 38, 40, 41, 45, 58, 84, 119, 120, 153, 169, 173, 197, 198, 200, 221, 233
Presbyterian mission 33, 44
princes 108

Promised Land 67, 73, 77, 99, 113, 116, 123, 159, 188, 235
propaganda 150, 160, 163, 170
prophecy xvi, 4, 74, 96, 101, 104, 109, 110, 122, 227
Prophet Ali 26
Prophet Nathan 84
proselytization 206

Q

qiblah 119
Qom 30, 33, 40, 41, 45, 48
quantum physics 1
Queen of Sheba 88

R

Rabbi Lazer Brody 209, 210
Rabbi Shimon Bar Yochai xix
Rabin, Yitzchak 172, 175
Rabin, Yitzkhak 169
racial ladder 150, 158
rain 93, 94, 196, 197, 211
Reagan, Ronald 214, 248
Rebbe Nachman of Breslav 211
Rebecca 68
refugees 57, 111, 133, 160, 165, 169, 245
religious leaders xvi, 97, 103, 111, 149, 203, 215, 216, 218, 221, 222, 225, 235, 238
Revolutionary Guard 33, 40, 46, 53
Reza Shah 17, 162, 207
Roman Empire 131, 155, 156, 231, 246
Romans 54, 116, 118, 155, 222
Rommel 149, 161
Russia 114, 137, 162, 215, 248

S

Sabbath xxi, 9, 76, 168, 193, 198, 200, 225, 249

Sabri, Ikrema 233

Sacks, Rabbi Jonathan 208, 224, 248

Sādāt, Anwar el- 52, 173, 174, 175, 230

Sahat El Tahrir (X-ref to "Freedom Square") 132

Said Mehr, Albert 184

Samaria 92, 156

same-sex 66

Samuel 76, 78, 80, 82, 84, 183

Sandra iii, ix, x, xxii, 8, 11, 28, 46, 53, 56, 141, 144, 171, 186, 205, 251

Sarah (X-ref to "Abraham") 65, 66, 188

Saul (X-ref to "King Saul") 76, 77, 78, 79, 82, 118, 153

Savak 16, 242

Scriptures, Hebrew iii, viii, xvi, xviii, 2, 7, 71, 86, 95, 118, 123, 251

Second Temple 113, 172, 192

Second World War 115, 132, 152

Seleucid 116, 154

Seleucus (X-ref to "Seleucid") 154

Selihot 197

Sereni, Ada 100

shah 16, 22, 24, 26, 40, 115, 162, 207, 242

Sharia 19

Sharon, Ariel 169, 173, 229

Shaytaneh-Bozorg 42

Shekhina 198

Shema Israel 199

Sheshbazzar 55

Shiite 19, 194, 204, 222

Shiloh 85, 86

Shilonite 85, 86

Shir ha Shirim (X-ref to "Song of Songs") 86

Shlomo Hillel 99, 114

Shofar Magazine xxi

showers 17

Sidonian 92

Sinai Desert 75, 172, 188, 235, 236

Sinai Peninsula 170, 173

Sino-Japanese War 230

Six-Day War 21, 133, 173, 175, 233

smuggler 56

Sodom and Gomorrah 67

solitaire 37, 170

Solomon 27, 71, 81, 82, 84, 86, 88, 90, 97, 106, 112, 154, 217, 233

Song of Songs 83, 86, 88, 90

Sourani, Sami viii, 177

Spain 97, 98, 114, 231, 246

Spanish Inquisition 203

Suez Canal 140, 170, 173

Sultan Mahmud 32

Sunni 194, 204, 222

Supreme Moslem Council 148

Syria 53, 140, 146, 160, 170, 174, 175, 231, 246

T

taghouti (X-ref to "Westernizer") 29

Talmud 113, 210

Tanakh vi, xvi, xviii, 7, 86, 91, 109, 110, 118, 136, 138, 195, 208, 251

Tarshish 97, 98, 228, 245

Tartessos (X-ref to "Tarshish") 98

Tate Gallery xvii

Technion University 145

Teheran xvi, 6, 12, 16, 30, 33, 39, 40, 42, 44, 50, 51, 52, 55, 124, 133, 162, 170, 183, 184, 207

Temple 18, 54, 71, 72, 84, 89, 97, 105, 106, 108, 111, 112, 118, 154, 172, 192, 201, 217, 218, 229, 233, 249
Temple Mount 233
Ten Commandments xviii, 64, 72, 193, 200, 230, 235
Tertullian 155
The Source 136, 192
Thummim, (X-ref to "Urim") 72
Time Magazine 51, 185, 249
Tiran, Strait of 170
Tolle, Eckhart 239
Topheth 202
Torah xvii, xix, xx, 5, 20, 76, 118, 188, 192, 199, 200, 211
Tsar Alexander III 137
Tunisia 150, 157, 160
Turkish rule 148
Twain, Mark 223, 224, 249
Twelve Tribes of Israel 77, 80, 85, 153
Tyre 97

U

Uganda 139, 142
ulama 40
United Nations 57, 115, 165, 167, 172, 219, 225, 238
Ur 72, 134, 239
Uriah the Hittite (X-ref to "Bathsheba") 80
Urim 73

V

vanity of vanities 87
verdicts 24
Vichy 150, 161

W

water 11, 17, 37, 65, 81, 94, 102, 108, 149, 164, 168, 170, 173, 191, 193, 197, 212, 218, 222, 235
Weizmann, Chaim 140, 144, 248
Westernizer 29
Western Wall 172, 233
White Papers 152
Wilhelm II, Kaiser 139
windows 97, 159
World War I 118, 139, 142

Y

Yahweh 54, 131
yam gadol 97
Yehovah 93
Yeshiva xx, 181
Yezdegerd 231
YHWH 66, 73
Yom Kippur War 174
Youssian, Abraham 183, 184

Z

Zachariah 228
Zahedan 56
Zedekia 111
Zionist 6, 29, 137, 139, 140, 142, 143, 145, 147, 149, 157, 164, 177
Zohar xx
Zoroastrianism 220, 230

CPSIA information can be obtained at www.ICGtesting.com
Printed in the USA
BVOW08s0256130515

400020BV00001B/3/P